Gardening Under the Arch

Dedication
To all who garden in spite of Jack Frost and Johnny Chinook.

Gardening Under the Arch

Homespun hints and money-saving tips from the rigorous high country of Alberta's Chinook Zone

Millarville Horticultural Club

Victoria • Calgary • Vancouver

TouchWood Editions
#108 – 17665 66A Avenue
Surrey, BC V3S 2A7
www.touchwoodeditions.com

Library and Archives Canada Cataloguing in Publication
Gardening under the arch : homespun hints and money saving tips from the rigorous high country of Alberta's chinook zone / Millarville Horticultural Club. -- Rev. and updated
Includes index.
ISBN 1-894898-43-5
1. Gardening--Alberta. I. Millarville Horticultural Club
SB453.3.C2G373 2006   635'.097123   C2005-907824-3

Edited by Corina Skavberg, Joe Wilderson, and SKB
Book design by One Below
Cover design by One Below
Cover photo by Anne Vale
All interior photos and line drawings provided by members of the
   Millarville Horticultural Club.
Printed in China
06 07 08 09 10 11/10 9 8 7 6 5 4 3 2 1

TouchWood Editions acknowledges the financial support for its publishing program from the Government of Canada through the Book Publishing Industry Development Program (BPIDP), Canada Council for the Arts, and the British Columbia Arts Council.

Acknowledgements

This book has been the cooperative effort of many people: the Book Committee, the authors, the typists, and the photographers.

The typists spent many hours transcribing the authors' work, some typed, some handwritten, into computer files. This involved lots of Latin and horticultural nomenclature terminology. We had two of these valuable people. Alexandra Vermunt did some of the early articles. We gave her the ones with long Latin lists since she was familiar with all that stuff, but in the middle of the book she moved away from the district. Paula Kroeker carried on alone right to the end. Their help was invaluable. Paula kept us straight on spelling, grammar, and punctuation so all our apostrophes should be in the right places. How these two, Paula and Alexandra, fit all this into their busy school-mom working lives is a marvel. We owe them big-time.

The regular Book Committee members met faithfully every week (except for a summer break) for two years: planning, writing, editing, and proofreading until we had the finished product put together.

Anne Vale, Chair
Arlene Jelfs, Secretary
Deb Francis
Sandy Gregg
Paula Kroeker
Theresa Patterson
Irene Smith
David Teskey
Ida Wegelin

We had a lot of fun doing it, got to know each other better, and are still good friends.

We would also like to thank Theresa Patterson and Mary Poffen-roth, who single-handedly sold all 27,500 copies of the 1980 version of the book through five printings. This involved storing the new books in their basements, finding a market, delivering books to bookstores, collecting the money and keeping track of it, not to mention filling hundreds of mail orders. They really should have a medal.

We are indebted to Vale's Greenhouse Ltd. for the extensive use of their photocopier and paper to make multiple copies for the editing of the material.

The authors, all local gardeners, many born in the area, shared their expertise and submitted their work to the harrowing experience of being edited. Their reward is seeing their articles in print and knowing that their contributions went into the fabric of the book we are all so proud of.

Anne Vale spearheaded the Book Committee. She was incredibly efficient and organized, and cracked the whip to keep the writers moving and the meetings on time. Her vast knowledge about all things pertaining to plants was extremely helpful, but it was her sense of humour that made the weekly meetings so much fun as we sipped our tea and pored over the articles. Anne kept everything running smoothly—the book couldn't have happened without her.

We hope this new version of the book will be as successful as the old. Most of the original articles are still in this new book, updated, plus a lot of completely new chapters, giving the 2006 edition an entirely fresh look

Note—For Alberta Agriculture horticultural publications contact:
Phone: 1-800-292-5697
Website: www.agric.gov.ab.ca/publications
Email: publications.office@gov.ab.ca
For Agriculture and Agri-Food Canada publications:
Phone: 1-866-452-5558

Table of Contents

Foreword to the 1982 Original Edition

When first we embarked on this project there were just two of us with a goal in mind but a rather muddy vision of how best to achieve it. To start the project rolling, questionnaires dealing with general gardening matters were given to all the members of our club. Upon their return it quickly became clear to us that an editing committee would be required to review all the material submitted.

With great relief we found that those members we approached to sit on this committee were more than willing to help, and indeed this attitude of willingness to help has been the reason behind the accomplishments of the Millarville Horticultural Club.

With the formation of this group of men and women of all ages and interests, the project slowly began to taxi down the runway. Meeting initially at each other's homes, we began to discover how best to tackle our project and work effectively as a unit. Soon the project was in full flight with weekly meetings at which we had a delightful time developing the book's concept and content, all the while adding to our knowledge of gardening and of each other. It has been a happy experience.

Our aim has been to provide a book which we hope will be useful to all gardeners, whether they have been gardening for years or are just starting out. We share with you a love of gardening and all the special moments it brings: From the first sunny day in spring when you start to dig your beds, to that cold winter's day when you enjoy a fresh baked pie made from the fruit you have grown. We share too your pride in the sea of colour you have created with your flower beds; we watch with you all the beautiful birds flitting from shrub to vegetable patch; and we understand your tinge of sorrow as the autumn frost ends it all for another year.

That our book is now completed means our project is finished. That it is of help to you means it has been a success.

Sandy Gregg
Millarville Horticultural Club

Foreword to the New Edition

Here it is, twenty-four years later, and our little book has been going strong ever since I sat at my farmhouse table and wrote the above foreword all those years ago.

So many people in the Millarville Horticultural Club have put in countless hours of their time over the past two dozen years performing the many tasks involved in getting our book into your hands. In 2004, after five printings and a huge commitment of time, the club members decided that they would not undertake another printing of *Gardening Under the Arch*. It was a difficult decision, as our book still had lots of life in it, but it had to be.

Little did we know that as this decision was being made, a gentleman walked into a bookstore to look for something to read before getting on a flight from Calgary. Spotting a copy of *Gardening Under the Arch*, he bought it. Shortly thereafter he called the Millarville Horticultural Club to ask if we would consider turning over the book's publication to TouchWood Editions, part of the Heritage Group. We were asked if we would update and expand the book. The club said yes.

Just as we had done from 1980 to 1982, we started meeting weekly to review submissions for this new version of our book. Three of us from the original committee were joined by a group of enthusiastic individuals equally dedicated to extending the life of this wonderful publication. It is wonderful for the information it imparts, for the financial assistance it has provided to so many local students and projects, and because it is the work of a community of gardeners who have devoted hours of their time to share what they have learned with you. Truly it is a work of heart.

From all of us to all of you, welcome to *Gardening Under the Arch*.

Sandy Gregg
Millarville Horticultural Club

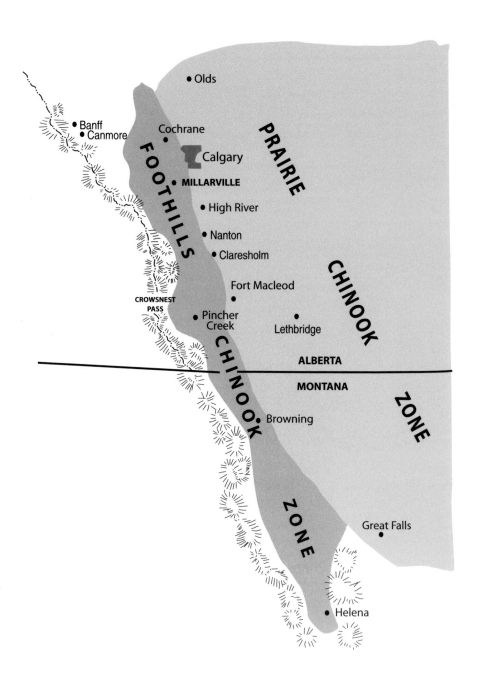

• Olds

• Banff
• Canmore

• Cochrane

FOOTHILLS

PRAIRIE

Calgary

MILLARVILLE

• High River

• Nanton

• Claresholm

Fort Macleod

CROWSNEST PASS

• Pincher Creek

Lethbridge

CHINOOK

CHINOOK

ALBERTA

MONTANA

Browning

ZONE

ZONE

Great Falls

Helena

1

Weather

The Chinook Zone
by Theresa Patterson

To live in the Chinook Zone of southern Alberta and Montana is both a privilege and a challenge to those who love gardening. The snow-capped Rocky Mountains with a clear blue sky framed by dark clouds forming a distinctive arch are truly a sight to behold. Fronting the mountains are range upon range of purple and blue foothills with their lovely mixtures of evergreens, aspens, native shrubs, and wildflowers. The prairies spread out to the east with their waving crops of grains and grasses.

This whole region is often subject to periods of warm, dry air, usually accompanied by strong winds, both in winter and summer. A mass of moist, warm air builds over the Japan Current in the Pacific Ocean. As it moves eastward over the land this air mass rises sharply to clear the barricades of the coastal mountains. The temperature drops abruptly at these altitudes and the moisture falls as rain or snow. Once across the Rockies the now drier mass descends swiftly over the eastern slopes, gaining power and warmth as it rushes out of the mountains to the foothills. When we see the familiar arch of cloud over a strip of blue sky in the west reaching from horizon to horizon and showing the curve of the earth above the outline of the mountains, we know we are in for a chinook, or "snow eater," as the First Nations people call it.

A chinook arch over the Alberta foothills.

Temperatures rise so fast that you can see the mercury jump anywhere from ten to thirty degrees in half an hour. The snow is whipped up in a whirling cloud, and driven by the fierce winds disappears incredibly fast, leaving vulnerable plants without their insulating blanket of snow. The chinook can last anywhere from a few hours to two or three days. In some winters one chinook follows another, giving us a mild, dry winter, or we may get prolonged periods of cold weather when we all wonder when the next break is coming.

The challenge for gardeners lies in these sudden, unexpected changes of temperature in winter when trees, especially seem, to get confused about just what season it really is. Prolonged warm spells after the leaves have fallen and there is little or no snow cover can cause the sap to start to flow and buds to break when dormancy should be the rule. Lilacs have been known to bloom in the fall and apple trees to blossom. How confusing can that be?

Experienced gardeners have learned some ways to compensate for Mother Nature's tricks. We look for hardy varieties of trees, shrubs, perennials, grasses, and bulbs that have proven to be successful in the area. To counter the ups and downs of temperature and humidity we find ways to keep the ground frozen around the roots with various mulches that do not readily thaw out in a warm spell. Piling snow around trees and bushes at the dripline helps to keep the ground cold. Perennials also appreciate a blanket of snow.

When putting in new plantings we look for areas where snow tends to pile up and stay put. Also, we look for microclimates in our gardens. These are places where there is protection from drying winds, such as buildings, fences, or established plantings. A cozy corner, shall we say.

A good watering in the fall before the ground freezes ensures that the roots of plants will not dry out. During winter warm spells we check to see if the ground around plants is moist, and water if necessary.

The damage from chinooks is caused by several factors. If the ground warms up, the sap in trees can start to flow. When the temperature drops suddenly the sap freezes, causing cells to burst, resulting in cracks and splits in the trunks of trees leaving access to diseases. A protective screen around trunks of young trees can help to prevent damage.

A chinook wind can be strong enough to cause breakage of immature trees. Staking young trees can be helpful. Snow fences break the wind and catch the snow as well.

Many seed and plant catalogues provide a map of hardiness zones from 1 to 10, 1 and 2 being the hardiest, down to 9 and 10 the least hardy. These zones are based on the lowest average winter temperatures and are a useful guideline but not a strict rule. The Chinook Zone is basically Zone 3, which means plants should be able to withstand temperatures down to −30°C. Other factors which the maps do not show include altitude, exposure to winds, and number of frost-free days, which determine the length of the growing season, and this can vary greatly from year to year.

The challenges are great but the rewards are even greater when you successfully beautify your property with some of the many plants available to us. Do not be afraid to stretch the limits of the zone designations, as Zone 5 plants may do just fine. Providing some shelter from wind and adequate cover in the winter prevents frequent thawing and freezing of the roots and damage from drying winds.

The Chinook
by Arthur Patterson

Down through the foothills of Alberta
Out across the prairies wide,
A Chinook wind is blowing
From out the Great Divide.

When it's coming we're not certain,
No one seems to know,
But we're happy when we feel it,
As it melts the winter snow.

Or in the heat of summer,
Say the middle of July,
You may see an arch a-forming
Over in the western sky.

Then a cool breeze starts a-blowing
And you take another look,
And find it is the makings
Of a dandy cool Chinook.

Or in the dead of winter,
When we're in a deep, deep freeze,
Oh, it's great to feel the heating
From a warm Chinooking breeze.

But watch that wily wind in winter
And sometimes in the fall.
It may start the buds a-budding
When they shouldna bud at all.

The thermometer goes to eighty
Then plummets ten below,
And gives a chill and a winter kill
To everything here below.

Oh, Chinook winds are blowing and the snow is fast a-going
From the foothills of Alberta
Out across the Prairies wide
A Chinook wind is blowing
From out the Great Divide.

When it's coming we're not certain,
No one seems to know,
But we're happy when we feel it
As it melts the winter snow.

The Art of Gardening Under the Chinook Arch: Planning Your Garden With the Help of Local Wisdom

To garden in Chinook Country you must be both an optimist and a philosopher! First consider what makes gardening in the shadow of the Rockies so different from other regions:

- Chinooks bring abrupt weather changes.
- Altitude: Downtown Calgary is 1000 m (3400 ft) and the foothills up to 1500–1800 m (5000–6000 ft) above sea level.
- Unpredictable snow cover.
- Short growing season, anywhere from 40 to 90 frost-free days if you are lucky! Sometimes our plants are freeze-dried on the hoof.
- Dry air and periodic drought.
- Temperature variation all year long. (If you don't like it, wait five minutes.)
- Hailstorms and fierce winds.
- Searing heat in midsummer and winter lows of −40° at times.
- Even on hot summer days the nights can be very cool.

- Soil and water pH are high (8.0 on average).
- Wildlife: Deer, moose, elk, bears, porcupine, gophers, moles, and skunks are frequent visitors, and now raccoons have appeared in southern Alberta. Also, in acreage and ranching country we contend with miscellaneous escaped livestock ranging from emus, alpacas, and sheep to horses, cattle, and even a buffalo.

What makes us think we can grow anything at all here? Captain Palliser was sent by the British government to survey southern Alberta in 1857. He sent back a report that the shortgrass prairie was not fit for human habitation, was semi-desert, and could never be expected to be inhabited by settlers.

This is where optimism comes in. Our region is known as "Next Year Country." Captain Palliser admitted that there were good areas where trees and crops could grow. In spite of all these appalling conditions, which would make the heart of any gardener quail, you only have to look at what nature can do to understand how to find solutions.

July hail devastates a perennial garden.

Rudbeckias are unharmed by a little snow in   *Icicles adorn a Nanking cherry,*
the summer.   *September 2000.*

The carpets of wildflowers of amazing brilliance in spring and summer, the way nature allows trees to flourish on the sheltered side of the hills and in gullies where snow collects, are our inspiration. Many factors mitigate the harsh conditions:

- Long hours of daylight in summer: 4 a.m. to 11 p.m. at the summer solstice and even longer the further north you go.
- Fewer bugs and slugs survive the winter.
- Lots of sunshine all year long. The high altitude means the light is very intense, and plants grow quickly.
- Clean air; no pollution or acid rain.
- Brilliance of colour in the flowers.
- Wooden structures last much longer (although composting takes longer, there being only three months when things will rot).

*Wildflowers in profusion
after wet summer.*

We all agree that groundhog predictions do not work for us, but the local wisdom that decrees that ninety days after a fog comes rain, is fairly dependable. Rain is also on the way when wind is from the east or when dust blows upwards from the ground. Rain is often very localized and depends on which cloud you happen to be under. At other times a three-day rain of biblical proportions causes rivers to turn to raging torrents. Hail can be so destructive that in a matter of minutes it will strip every leaf off the trees and level crops and gardens to resemble chopped spinach. This is where the philosopher in us is useful. Oh, well, next year will be better.

Gardening starts in late spring and is very intense with the rush to get everything cleaned up and planted by late May or early June so that it will have time to bloom before the first frost. Even then, tender annuals may be at risk. Sometimes we are in doubt as to whether we are experiencing the first frost or the last frost! Frost may also come with a full moon in August.

Then there is the September rush to beat freeze-up: vegetables harvested, gardens put to bed, mulch applied, and so on. Winter comes as a respite for your aching back and a change of focus to social events, hobbies, and catching up on reading the gardening magazines that have accumulated in the busy months.

All these problems can be solved one way or another, and all these difficulties tend to make us more resourceful. We learn to notice where things like to grow, how to provide shade and shelter, and to make use of low-lying spots that have more moisture. Remember: Cold air slides downhill. Valley bottoms will be cooler than hilltops. South- and west-facing slopes in the wild will support only low-growing, drought-resistant plants, whereas taller trees and shrubs and shade-loving plants flourish on the sheltered side of the hills. Our prevailing winds are from the southwest. Storms usually come in from the north or northwest.

Shelter can be provided by walls, fences, or buildings. Early settlers wisely built in valleys out of the wind and near water, saying "You can't eat the view." These days the view is often all-important. Deeper wells can be drilled, but exposure to wind is far more severe on a hilltop

Fair weather in the foothills.

with a wonderful view. Providing shelter must come before planting. A berm of soil will help, with planting of drought-resistant shrubs such as buffaloberry, sea buckthorn, or wolf willow on the leeward side.

The secret of success is to grow the right plant in the right place. The judicious choice of suitable plant material is everything! Work with nature, not against it. Go for a hike and study where plants like to grow. Group your plantings where it is easy to get water to them. Even the most drought-resistant of plants need water until they become established. Soaker hoses work well without wasting valuable water. Use mulch to stop evaporation around tree plantings. Plant perennials closely so they prop each other up and shade their own roots. Shade can also be provided in other ways. Every house has at least two shady sides. Lath shelters or arbours can be contrived to shade seating areas. Mountain ash and Amur cherry like the company of other trees to shade their trunks from sunscald. All this wise gardening is called "xeriscaping." Xeri is the Greek word for "dry," not "nothing."

Styles of gardening vary according to taste from formal, very organized, to cottage style or a plant collector's zoo. There are no rules, only guidelines. Your garden is yours to do what makes you happy.

Considerations include season of bloom, preferences not only from the plant's point of view but your own likes and dislikes, soil conditions, height, and colour scheme, but above all, put each plant where it prefers to grow. Happy plants do better.

Start with a scale plan. The services and hard landscaping come first. This means preparing the ground, sloping drainage away from the house, installing pathways, fences, structures such as decks, and so on. Then you can get on with the fun part of planting. If you have moved to a house with an existing garden, wait a year to see what you have before making radical changes. Don't take on too much at once.

A well-planned perennial garden provides constantly changing colour all summer.

Consider what time you have available, your own physical capabilities, and budget constraints. Work with what you have.

As any gardener will tell you, a stage of complete perfection is seldom achieved. Your hosts at any garden you visit will always wish you could have been there yesterday or a week from now to see a pet planting at its peak.

Betty Nelson's Weather Diary

Betty Nelson, a lifetime Millarville gardener, kept a weather diary, of which an excerpt is shown here. It gives a good illustration of the extremely variable frost-free dates over eleven years.

1970	Planted veg. garden first week May	Good year, corn ready Aug. 12	Fall frost Sept. 9
1971	Planted veg. garden first week May	Hard frost July 3	Hard frost Sept. 14
1972	Planted veg. garden first week May	Cold spring & summer	Hard frost Sept. 20
1973	Planted veg. garden first week May	Hot May. Frost June 10	Hard frost Sept. 15
1974	Planted veg. garden first week May	Wet May, hot June	Hard frost Sept. 1
1975	Planted veg. garden second week May	Dry, late spring. Hail July 3	Hard frost Sept. 3
1976	Planted veg. garden second week April	First half April hot & dry. Frost June 5, 13	Hard frost Sept. 8
1977	Planted veg. garden third week April	Dry, hot April. Snow mid-May	Hard frost Sept. 27
1978	Planted veg. garden first week May	Light frost June 6	Hard frost Sept. 15
1979	Planted veg. garden second week May	Late, cold spring. Frost 1st week June	Hard frost Sept. 29
1980	Planted veg. garden third week April	Early spring, leaves out April 27	Hard frost Sept. 25

Helpful Hints

* Heat storage: Stone walls, big rocks, concrete sidewalks, or basement walls all store heat from the sun and protect tender plants at night.
* Collect rain water in barrels, horse troughs, cisterns, or whatever you have handy. Lids keep out mosquitoes and prevent birds and kittens from drowning. A tap at the base makes filling watering cans easy.
* To stop leaks in your wooden rain barrel, put in some horse bran or porridge oats. Save all the rainwater you can. It's good for your house-plants.
* When planting under an overhang or broad eaves, install soaker hoses in spots the rain never reaches.
* Water at daybreak on frosty mornings to save plants.
* To beat frost, sow seeds early and cover with newspaper on cold nights in late May or June. It is much easier to cover small plants in spring than big plants in late August, e.g., corn, beans, zinnias, potatoes.

2

Gardening Management

Soils
by Anne Vale

The quality of your soil determines to a large extent the range of plants that will be happy in your garden. If you learn to recognize the type of soil you possess, you can work enormous improvements with the addition of amending substances.

The soils in the foothills vary widely in texture and acidity. Roughly speaking, the further west you go the more acidic the soil becomes. As the land begins to flatten out to the east and open up into farming country it becomes more alkaline.

Soil should be like a sponge, absorbent with good drainage pores large enough to permit the penetration of air. It should feel springy when walked upon and not pack down too badly after a heavy rain. It should smell clean and fresh and not sour or musty. If it cakes and cracks when the weather is hot and dry, or turns to a sticky bog when wet, you have not added enough humus. The word "humus" means virtually any decayed organic matter. If it is not already decayed when you add it to the soil, the bacteria that normally feed the plant roots will be diverted to decay the fresh manure, sawdust, leaves, straw, or whatever you have used as an additive, and will not be available to your plants.

An old rotted hay or straw stack bottom is an excellent source of

humus with which to improve the texture of your soil. If you are lucky
enough to have leaves to rake, these will help a lot if they are dug into
the ground. An old gardener's saying is, "Always pay the soil back for
what you take out of it." The return of organic matter to the soil is the
best way of doing this.

The term pH is used to describe the acidity or alkalinity of the
soil. It is measured on a scale of 1–14. Most plants are happiest near the
neutral zone between 6.0 and 8.0.

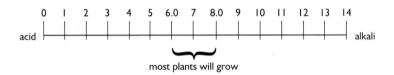

A good household test is to put a teaspoon of the soil to be tested
in a clean saucer and pour on a few drops of vinegar. Vinegar, being an
acid, will not react with another acid material, but when coming into
contact with alkali it will fizz and bubble. If your soil erupts like Mt.
St. Helen's, you have a very alkaline condition. If there is no reaction at
all, it is acidic. With practice it is possible to tell the degree of pH fairly
accurately. If the pH of your soil is way out of line it will tie up the nutrients in the soil and make them unavailable to the plant.

Having determined the pH of the soil, next consider the texture,
which is equally important:

- *Clay Loam*—Parts of the region have heavy clay soil, which is very
  hard to work with unless conditions are perfect. Such soil can be
  improved by the addition of coarse builder's sand to break it up a
  little and promote drainage. Do not use fine grained sand, such as
  play sand, which will do more harm than good. The sand available
  here is usually very alkaline, so remember to watch out for this and
  correct it with the addition of peat moss or sulphur. Generous applications every year will also help to break up the clay.

Helping Grandpa.
Robert Webb with
grandson Justin Delver.

- *Sandy Loam*—The light, shallow, sandy soil found along the river valleys has perfect drainage and is easy to work, but will dry out very quickly and leach out all its food value into the underlying gravel if a layer of humus is not dug in every year. Alberta soils in general are very short of humus, and it is hard to overdo the application of organic matter.
- *Loam*—Many of our local gardeners are lucky enough to have good, deep, rich, black loam, but even these lucky people will find their soil easier to work if they make generous applications of humus.

If you wish to obtain a more scientific measurement of the pH of your soil, buy a soil testing kit, or send a sample away to a soil-testing laboratory for analysis. Soil that is too acidic is seldom a problem in this area, but if encountered it may be corrected by the addition of some lime. A half-and-half mixture of dolomite lime and calcium carbonate (the agricultural kind) applied at the rate of one kilogram per eighteen square metres (one pound per hundred square feet) should help. If, on the other hand, your soil is too alkaline, you may add sulphur at a maximum rate of one kilogram per eighteen square metres (one pound per hundred square feet). Both these chemicals are long lasting and will not need to be done again for several years. Apply only in fall when plants are dormant. Peat moss will also add acidity to the soil but has several disadvantages when added in sufficient quantities to alter the pH. It is very expensive and hard to moisten with cold water. If added dry it tends to repel water rather than attract it and it contains no nutrients at all. Humus in the form of compost, well-rotted manure, or leaves is a better alternative. Manure and compost should be well rotted beforehand. It should be black and crumbly with no odour and almost back to the state of soil again. Leaves may be added when raked in fall but are better composted first.

All of the above organic matter can be added to the soil in fall. It can either be dug in or laid on top. The worms will take it down deep, for you. A layer 5–10 cm (2–4 in) is sufficient. If it is too deep the plants will suffocate. When buying topsoil it is important to ensure that it has not been sprayed with any herbicide within the last ten years or so. Most chemicals persist in the soil over a long period and will be harmful to growth. If you can obtain a sample of the soil before you buy it and try to grow seedlings in it, that is the best test. Tomato seedlings are quick to show herbicide contamination. They will develop distorted leaves if any herbicide is present.

Helpful Hints

For anything that loves acid, such as larch trees, put rhubarb leaves and stalks around the base of the plants.

Fertilizer
by Betty Nelson

Besides soil, water, air, and sunlight, plants need nutrients or plant food to grow and produce well. Some of these nutrients are already in the soil, depending on how well it has been farmed and taken care of. If the soil has been used a lot without having had anything put back, it will be lacking in plant food and so will only produce weak, sickly plants.

Flowers. Potash—for growth, superior blooms, and disease resistance.

The main plant food elements are:

1. *Nitrogen* (N)—builds plant protein, which encourages leaf and stem growth and gives rich green colour and rapid growth. It is good for leaf crops and lawns. Too much will burn and kill plants.
2. *Phosphorus* (P)—builds plant sugar, which helps to develop roots and flowers. Good for young plants when transplanting. Also good for root crops.
3. *Potassium* (K) (Potash)—for growth—increases vigour of plants; helps disease resistance; and promotes better flowers, seeds, and fruit.

Gardeners should always replace these nutrients or plant foods by one of the following:

1. Adding and working into the soil well-rotted manure—cow, horse, sheep, or chicken. Cow manure is the safest, followed by horse manure. Chicken and sheep manure are much stronger in nitrogen and can burn and kill plants if too much is used. One advantage of sheep manure is that it is weed free; the rest will usually produce a good crop of weeds. Using manure tea will get away from the weed problem. This is

Leaves. Nitrogen—for plant protein, rich green leaves.

made by soaking well-rotted manure in water and using the water for plants. Place a shovelful of manure in a burlap sack and suspend in a bucket or barrel that is set to catch the heat of the sun. This will keep particles from clogging your watering can. Or, after a rain collect water from puddles in your corrals. Manure tea will not add any humus to the soil.

2. Adding compost and working into the soil.

3. Adding and working into the soil: grass clippings, straw, leaves, etc. There is no danger of burning plants with this, but the soil will probably need some fertilizer containing nitrogen and phosphorus, as the rotting process uses up some of these elements. However, it will greatly improve the texture of the soil by adding humus to make it loose and healthy.

4. Adding bone meal is very good for bulbs. It contains a lot of phosphorous. Bone meal is slow-acting but long-lasting.

5. Adding commercial chemical fertilizers, which all display a formula consisting of three groups of numbers. The first number is the percentage of nitrogen (symbol N). The second number is the percentage of phosphorus (symbol P). The third number is the percentage of potassium (symbol K).

Roots. Phosphate—for plant sugar to develop roots and flowers.

Example:

- 11–48–0. This fertilizer would contain 11% nitrogen, 48% phosphorus, and no potassium; therefore it would be a good fertilizer for root crops.
- 16–20–0. This fertilizer would contain 16% nitrogen, 20% phosphorus, and no potassium and would be a good formula for most gardens.
- 20–20–20. This fertilizer would contain 20% nitrogen, 20% phosphorus, and 20% potassium and would be a good fertilizer for flowering plants.

Apply commercial fertilizer as directed on the container but be on the safe side and use a little less than called for, as too much can burn and even kill your plants.

Broadcast fertilizer lightly before spring tilling and seeding. Later on, if necessary, add a little more along both sides of the row and work into the soil, or around individual plants. If plants get about 5 cm (2 in) high and have enough moisture but look pale and unhealthy, and are not growing, they will probably benefit from the addition of fertilizer. Also, most garden plants benefit from a light application of fertilizer just before they bloom or produce vegetables or fruit.

Legume crops such as peas and beans produce their own nitrogen; therefore they don't need a fertilizer with a high percentage of nitrogen.

Wood ashes contain lime which, when worked into the garden, reacts to release the nitrogen in the soil, making it available to your plants. They are also a good source of potassium. Wood ashes are said to discourage insect pests.

Some gardeners recommend the use of green manure, which is a cover crop, usually oats, barley, or rye. It is left to grow only to 15 or 20 cm (6 or 8 in), then turned into the soil. In mild climates the cover crop can be planted as vegetables that are removed from the garden. However, with our short foothills growing season, it is best to plant only where you are summerfallowing a portion of the garden.

Helpful Hints

Add a handful of Epsom salts early each season for acid-loving plants. Spruce trees also benefit from this treatment, where soil is alkaline.

COMPOST

Compost is an excellent soil conditioner—the water-holding capacity of sandy loam is improved greatly by the addition of compost, and heavy clay is made more porous by mixing with compost. Compost provides nutrients to plants over a long period of time in a form that is readily available to them. It also provides trace elements that are not available in commercial fertilizers.

Basically, compost is made by the decomposition of organic matter. This can be garden wastes, grass clippings, sawdust, kitchen wastes, and so forth. These are usually built up on a pile with alternate layers of soil. Water and oxygen are essential for decomposition; thus the pile should be regularly turned to supply oxygen to all parts of the pile. It should be moistened when required. To speed up the decomposition process, a compost pile can be covered with black plastic to retain heat and moisture. When compost is ready it smells rather fresh and earthy, and is dark in colour and humusy in texture. It usually takes about six to eight weeks in the summer to form, but to create compost here in this length of time, the use of a commercial rotting agent is often required. Winter's cold temperatures completely halt development of compost. Rotting is limited to the warmest months, but because Alberta is so dry, things often don't rot without assistance during most summers. A good idea is to have three compost piles: one that is being added to, one that is being turned, and one that is ready for use.

Helpful Hints

* To speed up composting, add a handful of red wriggler worms (available at fishing stores). Red wrigglers eat the compost, and neat worm castings are left. In winter the wrigglers can survive and multiply if they can burrow into the ground.

* Any yarrow, native or cultivated, is a great compost accelerator. Yarrow is also edible.

PEST CONTROL
Herbicides, Insecticides, and Fungicides

Indiscriminate use and over-use of any of these can be very dangerous. They can destroy good plant life, beneficial insects, and bird life, as well as poison children and pets. They can pollute our water and environment for years to come.

Caution
When using chemicals of any sort wear protective clothing including rubber gloves, rubber boots, face mask, etc. Read the label carefully and be sure you get the dilution right. Dispose of unused chemicals at a toxic round-up in your municipality.

Herbicides check and stop growth of undesirable plants. Insecticides are used to kill insect pests. Fungicides help prevent and control plant diseases. These are all chemicals; their use can be a blessing or a curse. You may say, "Why use them?" There are certain circumstances when one of these chemicals has to be used to control a very bad weed, insect, or plant disease, which if not controlled, will take over your property and spread to your neighbour's. These undesirables have to be brought under control quickly before they gain momentum. Careful and knowledgeable use of one of these chemicals can be very advantageous. For example, some of the really bad weeds, such as toad flax and quack grass, have to be controlled with an herbicide. Nothing else will stop them from taking over your property and spreading into your neighbour's. Some insect pests and plant diseases, if not checked when they start, can also spread rapidly and destroy your garden and again spread to your neighbour's gardens.

With the use of the right product as soon as you see a problem start you can wipe it out, but if left unchecked it will spread and require a lot more treatment to bring under control. So the answer is to keep a close watch on your yard for bad or unusual persistent weeds; heavy insect damage; or sick, wilting, and dying plants.

METRIC CONVERSION TABLE

Metric	Teaspoon	Table-spoon	Ounce	Cup	Fluid Measure	Weight
5 ml	1					
10 ml	2					
15 ml	3	1	½			
30 ml		2	1		$1/8$	
60 ml		4	2	¼		
75 ml		5	2½		$1/3$	
90 ml		6	3		$3/8$	
120 ml		8	4	½		
150 ml		10	5		$2/3$	
180 ml		12	6	¾		
210 ml		14	7		$7/8$	
250 ml		16	8	1	½ pt.	
280 ml		18	9		1⅛	
360 ml		24	12	1½	¾ pt.	
500 ml			16	2	1 pt.	1 lb.
750 ml			24	3	1½ pt.	1½ lbs.
1000 ml			32	4	1 qt.	2 lbs.
2000 ml			64	8	2 qts.	4 lbs.
4000 ml			128	16	1 gal.	8 lbs.

Converting Volume:

litres x 0.95 = quarts
pints x 0.57 = litres
quarts x 1.1 = litres
gallons x 4.5 = litres

Converting Weight:

kilograms x 2.2 = pounds
grams x 0.035 = ounces
pounds x 0.45 = kilograms
ounces x 28 = grams

CONTROL OF GARDEN PESTS

Identify your enemy before using the big guns. Very often if a plant looks sick it immediately gets sprayed with everything at hand. This will often make the plant sicker, and you, too. A good, strong stream of cold water will do more good than anything. Even if you see holes on the leaves make sure your pest is still present and not hatched and gone. Very often the problem is a cultural one and not an insect at all.

Our members have used the following ideas to assist them in control of garden pests:

Ants
- plant mint by your house, especially near the doors, to keep ants out
- pour boiling water over nests
- put up nest boxes for flickers, as they love to eat ants

Aphids
- to repel, plant nasturtiums, marigolds, petunias, garlic, and chives throughout your vegetable garden, and nasturtiums and petunias under your fruit trees
- to repel, plant chives with your rose bushes
- ladybugs, green lacewing flies, and wasps all eat aphids

Cabbage Butterflies
- wasps eat eggs of cabbage butterflies
- catch with a butterfly net and destroy
- to repel, plant dill, rosemary, thyme, sage, lavender, or mint with crops bothered by cabbage butterflies
- also repelled by marigolds
- use an electric bug zapper
- encourage birds to nest in or near your garden

Cabbage Worms (larvae of adult cabbage butterfly)

- place a heaping tablespoon of wood ashes mixed with earth around the stem of plants bothered by cabbage worms

Colorado Potato Beetle

- plant green beans beside potatoes to keep beetles off
- plant horseradish, either end of your potato patch, but bear in mind it spreads rapidly
- hand-pick and destroy

Cutworms

- to repel, scatter dampened wood ashes around plants
- bantam hens and bluebirds love them
- remove both ends of a tin can, place around plants and push down in the soil about 5 cm (2 in) to protect from cutworms

Deer

- fence your garden
- keep a large dog that lives outdoors (but don't let your dog run at large, or you will have some very unhappy neighbours. If your dog bothers your neighbours' cattle you will probably lose him. It is also against the law for dogs to chase wildlife.)
- 5 cm (2 in) chicken wire mesh laid over perennial beds in winter will stop deer from pawing off winter cover. The same wire laid alongside your raspberry rows in summer will stop deer from eating the canes.
- commercial animal repellents
- motion-activated water jets work well

Flea Beetles

- steep catnip in water, strain, and spray on plants
- rotenone dust

Jerrid Driedger needs cages to protect this garden from herds of marauding deer.

Mice, Pocket Gophers (a.k.a. Moles), Raccoons, Skunks, and Richardson's Ground Squirrels (Gophers)

- keep a good cat or dog
- place mothballs in gopher holes that are close to your garden
- plant mint around garden to repel mice
- use a box trap for pocket gophers
- use Victor #0 or #1 traps for gophers
- reputed to be repelled by garlic

Mosquitoes

- Kingbirds, flycatchers, and swallows eat mosquitoes in huge quantities. Encourage these birds by providing water and nest boxes. Dragonflies and wasps also feed on mosquitoes.

Rabbits

- plant dusty miller around garden to repel rabbits
- plant garlic, onions, and marigolds

Root Maggots

- to repel, scatter dampened wood ashes around plants
- spread crushed eggshells over soil surface around plants

Slugs

- pans of beer or saucers filled with vinegar and sugar set level with your soil attract and trap slugs
- place a board in your garden which slugs will hide under during the day. Overturn each day and destroy the slugs that have collected under it.
- soak used grapefruit halves in methyl hydrate, turn over, and place a little stick under one side so slugs can crawl under them. Lift in the morning and remove victims.
- remove all decaying debris or any ground cover, as well as bottom leaves of cabbages and lettuce.

Spider Mites

- wash off with a strong stream of cold water
- sulphur lime dormant spray

Rotenone or Deritox are reasonably safe insecticides. They should still be used sparingly and with caution, as they can upset the natural balance. They help control cabbage worms, Colorado potato beetle, red turnip beetles, flea beetles, and aphids. Insecticidal soap is very effective in controlling mealy bugs, aphids, scale, and caterpillars of all sorts, and will not hurt ladybugs. Diatomaceous earth works well against soft-bodied insects.

To control egg-laying insect pests, till your soil right after harvest to expose eggs to wind and sun, which will destroy them. Also, some insects like to lay their eggs on the hard autumn ground—tilling the soil will prevent this.

Practise mid-season feeding with organic fertilizers such as manure tea. Remember that healthy plants in a healthy soil usually will not attract pests.

There are various pesticides available to rid your garden of pests; however, improper use of these can cause residues to stay on vegetables grown for human consumption. As well, poisons are non-selective, so although they may kill harmful insects, they will also kill helpful insects such as ladybugs, which eat forty to fifty aphids and mites a day. Furthermore, due to the great risk to children, household pets, birds, and the environment in general, use of these products has become a matter of grave concern.

Is it not better to practise crop rotation, soil improvement, companion planting, and other harmless methods of protection? These methods do not always achieve complete success, but neither do the tremendous number of pesticides available on the market today. It has been proven that the more you use them, the more you have to use them, which is expensive and time-consuming. On the other hand, by using methods such as companion planting, you have nasturtiums and marigolds adding happy touches of colour to your vegetable garden, and you live with the knowledge that you are doing your small part to ensure a healthy environment for future generations.

Helpful Hints

* Ants dislike coffee grounds, so put coffee grounds where ants are bothersome.
* Sprinkling sharp sand around slug-susceptible plants will deter the slugs.
* A club member has observed that by using landscape fabric and a wood chip mulch around the base of her silver birch, the tree has been free of birch-leaf miners ever since.
* Put wood ashes on delphiniums in early spring to prevent infestations of aphids.
* Keep a pair of bantams and family in your garden. They will consume quantities of slugs and insects.

Weed Control
by Jerrid Driedger

Weeds are aggressive, invasive plant species and are difficult to manage. They may displace or significantly alter native plant communities and may cause economic hardship to private and public land. Weeds should not be tolerated among cultivated plants; they sap valuable moisture and nourishment from the soil at the expense of the plants we try to encourage.

Legislation in Alberta through the Alberta Weed Control Act classifies weeds as restricted, noxious, or nuisance plant species. Each class of weeds is treated differently. Restricted weeds are found in very few areas of Alberta, usually with low populations at any one location. They spread quickly and are designated "restricted" to prevent their establishment. If found, immediate destruction is required. Noxious weeds are already established in many regions of the province. They pose a large threat to native and valuable plant species; therefore the law requires eradication. Nuisance weeds are common to most parts of the province. These weeds are regularly seen in lawns and gardens and throughout rural and urban areas. Elimination is recommended, but not required. It is important to keep these problem weeds from being introduced or from spreading if they are already present.

Landowners and gardeners should be most concerned about noxious weeds, as they are invasive and difficult to eradicate. There are twenty-three types of noxious weeds in Alberta. The following is a list of the fourteen most common to the foothills area:

Bladder Campion	Ox-eye Daisy
Canada Thistle	Perennial Sow Thistle
Cleavers	Russian Knapweed
Common Tansy	Scentless Chamomile
Field Scabious	Tall Buttercup
Hoary Cress	Toadflax
Leafy Spurge	White Cockle

It is the responsibility of the rural landowner—farm or acreage—to remove noxious weeds. The Agricultural Fieldman is available to visit the site and inform you of the choices of eradication. If the infestation is not properly controlled, then the rural landowner may be issued a weed notice from the Municipal District Office, stating that you must properly deal with the infestation or the MD will do it at the owner's expense.

In rural settings there are several methods that can be used to eradicate weeds. For the proper chemical application to be used, information can be obtained from UFA or Agricore. Environmental considerations must be taken into account prior to any chemical use. Mowing is an effective method against weeds that spread only by seed, usually annuals. Mowing the plants several times during their growing season increases the amount of stress on them to the point of death or low reproduction. Cultivation is most effective against weeds that spread only by seed, usually annuals.

The bylaws regarding weeds in urban areas are different from those in a rural one. In an urban area you are required to take certain steps to remove noxious weeds from your yard. First dig out the weed, including as many roots as possible. Place the weed into a plastic bag and call the town office or the horticultural hotline so that the weed can be incinerated. Do not garbage or compost the weed, as it will spread the roots and seeds. Help to educate people about noxious weeds by spreading your knowledge and teaching others about how to identify and eliminate these invasive plants.

Numerous strategies are effective to keep your garden free of nuisance weeds. Hoeing regularly in your vegetable garden prevents annual weeds from becoming established. Common perennials including quack grass and dandelion must be dug out, as they spread by root. Dandelions also self-seed prolifically. Use organic mulch between the rows such as grass clippings, wood shavings, or straw. In the fall rototill the mulch into the soil. Denser planting of ground covers or perennials leaves less space for weeds, thus making mulch unnecessary. For tree and shrub beds, pin down heavy-duty black landscape fabric. Cover it with a mulch of 2 cm (¾ in) washed gravel, bark chips, or wood 10–15 cm (4–6 in) deep. This will reduce the labour of weeding. Whenever using landscape fabric, cut a large "X" in the fabric to allow the plant to expand and flourish.

When planting a new lawn, cultivating your soil to remove weeds before planting is well worthwhile. If purchasing soil be aware of the source. Screened soil contains fewer weeds. Some annual weeds quickly move in and stabilize disturbed soil and prevent erosion. Annual weeds serve as a temporary, but valuable service in shading seedling grass in a newly seeded lawn and will disappear once mowing has commenced and the lawn fills in. A healthy lawn will make it more difficult for weeds to grow. Keep the lawn thick with proper watering, fertilizing, and cutting. Higher mowing in lawns results in deeper roots and more vigorous grass, which is better able to compete with lawn weeds.

With modern technology at hand, digging is not a popular activity and we are tempted to try a less physically demanding and less time-consuming approach. Before considering chemical use be sure that you have done whatever you can to eradicate the weeds first in an environmentally friendly manner. Chemicals are not recommended for annuals. Proper knowledge about types of weed killers, application, and risks involved must be obtained from a professional prior to use.

Weeding the old-fashioned way gives the perfect excuse to get out in the garden and appreciate its development throughout the growing season. Just remember never to compost any weeds or you will find yourself visiting the garden to weed more often than you may enjoy.

Helpful Hints

❊ To get rid of moss on the roof, spray with zinc sulphate.

❊ To keep grass from growing between bricks in a walk, sprinkle the spaces with salt or pour salted boiling water on the grass or weeds.

DEER-RESISTANT PLANTS

Deer are browsers, snacking on whatever they fancy as they pass through your yard. They prefer new shoots on healthy, well-watered plants. In general they will try anything, but they do tend to avoid thorny, hairy, or aromatic foliage. In a harsh winter deer will eat any plant to survive. Local populations of deer seem to develop a taste for plants which in other areas are left unscathed. The following list of deer-resistant plants was compiled from several sources, mainly from a survey of our club members:

Trees
Chokecherry
Manitoba Maple
Spruce

Shrubs
Barberry   Lilac
Buffaloberry   Potentilla
Caragana   Sea Buckthorn
Cotoneaster   Spirea
Elder   Wolf Willow
Honeysuckle

Vines   *Vegetables and Herbs*
Clematis   Comfrey
Hops   Potatoes
Virginia Creeper   Rhubarb
                             Sage

Deer taking a break from their yard lunch.

Perennials

Anemone	Lady's Mantle
Anthemis	Lamb's Ears
Artemesia	Lamiastrum
Bleeding Heart	Liatris
Daylily	Lily of the Valley
Delphinium	Lupins
Echinops	Monarda
Euphorbia	Monkshood
Forget-me-not	Nepeta
Foxglove	Oriental Poppies
Gaillardia	Peony
Gas Plant	Pulmonaria
Helenium	Shasta Daisy
Hepatica	Snow-in-Summer
Hollyhock	Snow-on-the-Mountain
Iris	

Annuals

Calendula	Marigold
Dusty Miller	Nicotiana
English Daisy	Petunia
Foxglove	Rudbeckia
Larkspur	Snapdragon
Lobelia	

Encounters With Wildlife
by Joleen Francis

When encountering wildlife, every situation is different, and for the most part your reaction will determine the outcome. Animals will attack usually because they are sick or in a defence mode.

- *Black Bears*—Back away slowly and keep your eyes on the bear (not direct eye contact). Remember, bears rarely attack humans. Try to make a lot of noise when working outside (whistling and singing). If you are attacked roll yourself up into a ball, protecting your vital organs, and stay in this position until the bear leaves. If the bear is attacking you at night or it is a predatory attack, fight back.

- *Cougar*—If a cougar is stalking you, try to get away but do not run. The cougar will take size into consideration (small children are easy prey). Fight back if you are attacked.

Dump it and they will come.

- *Foxes, coyotes, raccoons, and skunks*—Do not get cuddly with or habituate these animals, as some carry rabies and will make your home their home.

- *Ungulates (elk, moose, deer, and caribou)*—Let them be and walk away. Do not attempt to get closer to the animal or harass it. Be wary during the fall rut when animals will be combative. If it is sick or injured call the Fish and Wildlife office in the Alberta government.

If you are attacked make yourself as large and threatening as possible. Pick up a garden tool or stick, and pick up small children off the ground. Keeping a clean yard and getting rid of the food source will eliminate most animals.

Contact your local Fish and Wildlife office to find out more information. Always report any encounters with aggressive or injured animals to Fish and Wildlife.

Deer stretches to reach a backyard winter snack.

Companion Planting
by Ida Wegelin

A fascinating project for gardeners to experiment with is companion planting. It has been observed that there are some plants which when planted close to each other stimulate the growth of the neighbouring plants while other plants planted in close proximity tend to retard growth. It has been noted that some plants attract harmful insects away from your desired crop, while the scent of other plants is so repulsive to harmful insects that the insects will find a more pleasant habitat elsewhere.

The following table will give you a starting place for experimenting in this field.

Subject	Friendly Herbs and Vegetables	Friendly Flowers	Foes
asparagus	annual herbs, dill	aster family, cosmos	onion family
beans	savory, tarragon, basil, dill, potatoes, beets	salvia, snapdragons, tansy, marigolds	garlic, onions, peppers, sunflowers, gladioli
beets	most vegetables, onions, lettuce	-	pole beans
broccoli	parsley, dill, sage	aster family, alyssum	pole beans, tomatoes, strawberries
Brussels sprouts	fennel, dill	alyssum, asters, zinnia	pole beans, tomatoes, strawberries
cabbage	dill, carrots, onions, celery, hyssop	asters, calendula, Queen Anne's lace, chrysanthemum	pole beans, tomatoes, strawberries
carrots	onions, caraway, chives, coriander	calendula, chamomile	dill
cauliflower	dill, celery	zinnias	pole beans, tomatoes, strawberries
celery	cabbage, beans	cosmos, snapdragons	parsnips
corn	beans, peas, potatoes, squash, cucumbers, lettuce, parsley	nasturtiums, sunflowers	tomatoes

Subject	Friendly Herbs and Vegetables	Friendly Flowers	Foes
cucumbers	radishes, corn, beans, cauliflower, cabbage	nasturtiums, marigolds	potatoes, sage
garlic	carrots, onions, beets	most plants	beans, peas
leeks	most plants	most plants	beans, peas
melons	radishes	nasturtiums, marigolds	-
onions	most vegetables, beets, carrots	roses, petunias	beans, peas
peas	most vegetables, beans, carrots, turnips	edge the bed with low-growing flowers— marigolds, alyssum, calendula, pinks; edge raised beds with wave petunias	onion family, gladioli
peppers	coriander, fennel, basil, onions, spinach, tomatoes, carrots	marigolds, cosmos, gazania	fennel, kohlrabi, beans
potatoes	beans, parsley, corn, coriander	marigolds	pumpkin, tomatoes, apples, raspberries
pumpkin/squash	corn, radishes	nasturtiums, tansy, sunflowers, buck-wheat	-
radishes	cabbage, kohlrabi, beans, beets, carrots, lettuce	-	hyssop
spinach	radishes, cauliflower, pole beans, peas	-	-
summer squash	radishes, beans, corn	-	-
Swiss chard	most plants	most plants	-
tomatoes	basil, dill, peppers, garlic, eggplant, onion, parsley, carrots	marigolds, nasturtiums	corn, dill, potatoes, cabbage family
turnips	most vegetables	-	-

3

Woody Plants

Trees and Shrubs
by Anne Vale

HARDY VARIETIES

The chinooks are a limiting factor in growing many varieties otherwise hardy on the prairies. Trees and shrubs with a low dormancy rate can be triggered into growth by spells of warm weather out of season, only to be zapped when the temperature falls back to winter levels. Dryness of soil and air is another obstacle to the success of many varieties. Don't be discouraged. There are many different choices of shapes, sizes, and textures to try. Further on in this chapter a list of suggested trees and shrubs for varied locations is given.

SITING

Fences, buildings, shelterbelts, natural contours, or berms; all can create microclimates where you may have success with an otherwise borderline hardy shrub. A grouping of shrubs together can collect a good insulating snowdrift. Low-lying spots collect rainwater and snowmelt to help those trees that prefer more moisture. Save the high spots and thin sandy soil for those plants that are drought-resistant. This is explained more fully in the Landscaping and Xeriscaping chapter.

This woven willow fence provides instant shelter or shade where needed.

TIME OF PLANTING

I prefer to plant as early in the spring as possible. I do not recommend fall planting in this area, although some members have had success with this method. In the spring the plant has everything going for it, but in fall it is doubtful whether the plant will have time to become established before an Alberta winter sets in.

METHODS OF PLANTING

Trees to be dug up and transplanted must be moved in a dormant condition before they get leaves. Never leave the roots drying in the air while you dig the new hole. If it has to be dug before its permanent site is ready, put it in a large pot or garbage bag with some soil and keep it well watered until you can plant it.

When planting trees and shrubs that have already leafed out, it is important not to disturb the roots. Trees are purchased from garden

A fieldstone wall shelters this exposed garden from chinook winds.

centres in many kinds of containers. The biodegradable pots, such as compressed peat, tar paper, or wooden baskets, may be planted intact except for slashing the sides and peeling back the rim. If you leave the rim of the pot sticking out it will act as a wick and draw the moisture out of the soil. More permanent containers must, of course, be removed but take care not to disturb the root ball. If the plant has leaves already it needs the fine root hairs to replace the moisture lost by transpiration into the air from the leaf surface. Smaller trees planted by hand should have a hole dug at least twice as deep and twice as wide as the size of the root ball. The bigger the hole, the better your chance of success.

Taller trees should be staked for a few years until established. Plant deep enough so that the graft is below the surface of the soil or at the same depth as in the nursery. A rim of soil around the edge of the hole will retain water until it has had a chance to soak in. The tree should be kept deeply and thoroughly watered throughout its first few years until it has a good root system. Lawn sprinkling is not sufficient to water deeply planted trees. This will only encourage shallow roots waiting near the surface for the next handout.

Larger trees planted with a tree mover should have a bigger hole than the tree plug dug first and partly filled with a mud slurry before the tree goes in so that the roots have somewhere to go. All cracks around the edge should also be filled with the slurry. Larger trees should always be guy-wired with at least three wires to prevent the tree from blowing over. Thread the wire through pieces of old garden hose to prevent chafing of the tree. Leave the wires in place for at least three years.

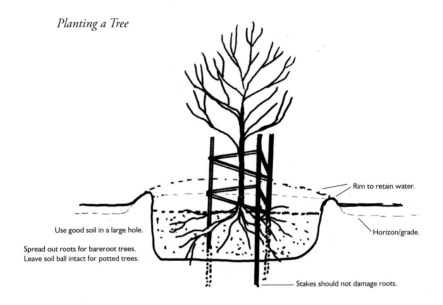

Planting a Tree

Rim to retain water.

Use good soil in a large hole.

Horizon/grade.

Spread out roots for bareroot trees.
Leave soil ball intact for potted trees.

Stakes should not damage roots.

FERTILIZER

The time to fertilize your trees and shrubs is in the spring of their second and subsequent years. Use a fertilizer high in phosphorus (10–52–10, for example) to stimulate root growth. Once you have a good root system the top half will follow naturally and not be forced into lush growth before the roots are well enough established to provide sufficient nourishment. I do not recommend fertilizer at planting time with either chemicals or manure. It is easy to be heavy handed with the fertilizer in the attempt to get a good start, and burn the tiny roots that are trying to form. If you feel you must do something, try an old trick and put a small shovelful of oats or barley in the bottom of the hole. These will ferment, and the heat from this process will encourage roots to form. With fertilizer always err on the short side. It is easy to add more but hard to correct an over-application. Trying to force fast growth with fertilizer is tempting in our short growing season but this leads to more winterkill of over-fertilized trees.

Once again I would like to emphasize that you should fertilize only in the spring. April and May are best. June is too late. The tree must have time to slow its growth and ripen its new wood before onset of winter.

WINTER CARE

After leaves have fallen but before freeze-up, water your young trees and shrubs deeply and thoroughly. This will ensure that they freeze deep down and that they do not dehydrate over the winter. Also, on a warm day in late fall use an anti-desiccant spray on your young evergreens to protect them from drying winds in winter. If you want to mulch them, wait until after freeze-up. A mulch that prevents the ground from freezing is an open invitation to mice to move in and take up residence for the winter. They particularly like a nibble of fresh bark and will kill many valuable plants. A rodent repellent may be painted on the bottom of the trunk.

PRUNING

This district is no different to any other for following the rules for good pruning. The basic objects of pruning are (a) to achieve a natural shape, (b) to maintain the health and vigour of the plant, and (c) to keep it to a manageable size. Cuts should be made cleanly and as close to the trunk or limb as possible so as not to make an amputated-looking stub.

Pruning

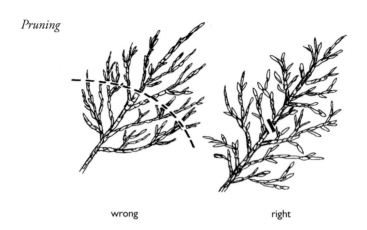

wrong   right

You should remove any dead or diseased wood and also any branches that cross over or rub on each other before they get too big. Try to avoid making the whole tree look as if it has had a bad haircut by carefully selecting which branch to remove or shorten without spoiling the shape of the tree. No wound dressing is necessary or recommended. The tree will heal itself naturally.

Not all trees like to be pruned at the same time of year. This is fortunate, as it spreads the workload out over slack times of year.

WHEN TO PRUNE

- *Flowering shrubs*—Should be pruned immediately after flowering to give them time to make buds for next year. If you prune them in spring you will remove all the blossoms.
- *Deciduous trees*—May be done at any time in winter when they are dormant, with the exception of birch, which should be pruned in June or July.
- *Pine*—Mugho pine should have their candles (extended buds) snapped in half in early June to keep them dwarfed and bushy. Taller species with long needles do not need much pruning and are best left alone.

- *Spruce*—Rarely need pruning. If absolutely necessary prune in July.
- *Junipers*—Prune in July when annual growth is complete. Use great care to make each cut from underneath each branch to leave a natural leader as the diagram opposite shows.
- *Roses*—See section on roses.

RECOMMENDED TREES AND SHRUBS

The cutoff height to separate trees from shrubs is 5 m (16 ft). Only the ultra hardy for the Chinook Zone are listed. Areas with a longer growing season and less extreme conditions have a wider choice of material. Also omitted from the list are plants with bad habits, such as those subject to frequent dieback, those which attract insect pests, or those which are not commonly available.

SHRUBS

- *Amelanchier alnifolia*—Saskatoon. Up to 2–3 m (6–10 ft) depending on conditions
  Tall native shrub with edible fruit and blazing red fall colour. Very prone to fire blight.
- *Berberis thunbergii*—Barberry. 0.5–1 m (1.5–3 ft)
  Newly reintroduced now that Agriculture Canada allows its use again, barberry is thorny with pendulous yellow flowers in spring followed by red berries. Red or pink-leafed forms are available. Full sun.
- *Caragana arborescens*—Caragana. 4 m (13 ft)
  This one sheltered many a homestead and can still be spotted marking the sites of old farmsteads out on the bald prairie.
- *Caragana lorbergii*—Fernleaf Caragana. (This is grafted.) 5 m (16 ft)
  Suckers that do not have ferny leaves should be pruned off. The variety 'Walker' is usually grafted on a standard stem at about 1.5 m (5 ft) and weeps down from the graft. Again, all shoots from the stem that are showing broader leaves should be ruthlessly pruned off as soon as they appear.

- *Caragana pygmaea*—Pygmy Caragana. 0.8 m (2.5 ft)
  Dense bushy shrub which makes an impenetrable hedge that never needs trimming. Typical yellow flowers.
- *Cornus sericea*—Red Osier Dogwood. 2–3 m (6–10 ft)
  This native of our river valleys is a shrub for all seasons. The white flowers are followed by white berries in late summer. The leaves turn red in fall and the stems remain red all year. Grows in any soil. Sun or shade.
- *Cotoneaster integrimus*—European Cotoneaster. 1.5 m (5 ft)
  Very hardy, attractive shrub with red berries from midsummer. Any soil. Sun or part shade.
- *Cotoneaster lucidus*—Hedge Cotoneaster. 2 m (6 ft)
  Can be trimmed to whatever height you require. Black fruit attracts the birds. Leaves turn fiery red in fall.
- *Crataegus cerronis*—Hawthorn. 4–5 m (13–16 ft)
  Very thorny, tall shrub with white flowers and reddish-brown berries loved by birds.
- *Eleagnus commutata*—Wolf Willow. 2 m + (6 ft +)
  Native shrub, silver leaves, fragrant yellow flowers followed by silver berries. Full sun.
- *Hippophae rhamnoides*—Sea Buckthorn. 4 m (13 ft)
  Tall, thorny, grey-leafed shrub. Females are covered with bright orange berries for most of the winter. Full sun.
- *Juniperus horizontalis*—Creeping Juniper. 10 cm (4 in)
  Many cultivated varieties are available. Flat-growing and very tolerant of drought and sun.
- *Juniperus sabina*—Savin Juniper. 0.5–1 m (1.5–3 ft)
  Many cultivated varieties available. A valuable foundation shrub. Full sun to part shade.
- *Juniperus scopulorum*—Rocky Mountain Juniper. 5 m (16 ft)
  Native to the southern part of Alberta, down into the United States. This one will take full scorching sun without burning but does tend to outgrow a tight space. Many cultivars available.

Sea Buckthorn berries.

- *Lonicera tatarica*—Honeysuckle. 2–3 m (6–10 ft)
  Tough, drought-resistant shrubs with sweet-smelling flowers in early summer. 'Arnold Red' is a recommended variety. Makes an informal tall hedge or fine tall specimen shrub. Needs well-drained soil and full sun.

- *Lonicera caerulea edulis*—Sweetberry Honeysuckle. 1.5 m (5 ft)
  Useful and beautiful medium-height bush, with pale yellow flowers and blue berries. A tough one from Siberia.
- *Philadelphus lewisii*—Mock orange 'Waterton.' 1.5 m (5 ft)
  'Waterton' is by far the hardiest variety. Highly scented with white flowers in early July. Full sun or part shade.
- *Picea glauca*—Spruce (see also Tree section). 0.5–1 m (1.5–3 ft)
  Several semi-dwarf cultivars are available for use as a shrub. Globe Blue Spruce is one of the best.
- *Pinus mugo*—Mugho Pine. 1–4 m (3–13 ft)
  This pine can be pruned to stay compact. (See pruning section.) Good foundation shrub. Full sun.
- *Potentilla fruticosa*—Shrubby cinquefoil 0.5–1.5 m (1.5–5 ft)
  Small, neat, drought-resistent shrub. Flowers usually shades of yellow or orange. Pink and white varieties also available. Water well until established.
- *Prunus tomentosa*—Nanking Cherry. 2 m (6 ft)
  Early pale pink blossom, followed by edible fruit that makes good jelly. Very hardy and reliable. Full sun.
- *Prunus triloba multiplex*—Double-flowering Plum. 2 m (6 ft)
  No plums! This one is sterile but covered with masses of deep pink double blossoms in spring. Full sun.
- *Ribes alpinum*—Alpine Currant. 1 m (3 ft)
  A valuable small, shade-tolerant shrub. Stays compact in part shade or full sun.
- *Ribes odoratum*—Missouri Currant. 1.5 m (5 ft)
  Highly fragrant yellow flowers. Black edible fruit makes good pies. Sun or part shade.
- Roses have their own section.
- *Sambucus racemosa*—Red Elder. 4 m (13 ft)
  Tall, fast-growing shelterbelt or individual shrub. Red berries follow white flowers. The cut leaf form 'Red Man' is available. Sun or part shade.
- *Sambucus racemosa*—'Sutherland' Golden Elder. 2–3 m (6–10 ft)

Double-flowering Plum (Prunus triloba multiplex).

A hardy, yellow-leaved variety which does not die back each winter. Must be in full sun for best yellow colour.
- *Shepherdia argentea*—Buffaloberry. 4 m (13 ft)
  Silver leaves. Female plants have red berries. Native to the eastern part of Alberta. Full sun.
- *Spirea x bumalda*—Dwarf Spirea 'Anthony Waterer.' 0.8 m (2.5 ft)
  Flat clusters of reddish-pink flowers in early summer. A good addition to perennial beds. Full sun or part shade.
- *Spirea x bumalda*—Spirea 'Goldflame.' 0.8 m (2.5 ft)
  Bright yellow leaves all summer. Small, pink flower clusters. Also good mixed with perennials.
- *Spirea trichocarpa*—Korean Spirea. 1.6 m (5 ft)
  Arching sprays of white flowers in early summer. Extremely hardy and reliable. Full sun.

Dwarf Korean Spirea (Spirea trilobata).

- *Spirea trilobata*—Dwarf Korean Spirea. 1 m (3 ft)
  Compact mounded shrub covered in clusters of small, white flowers in early summer. Very hardy compact shrub. Full sun.
- *Syringa meyeri*—Dwarf Korean Lilac. 1.5 m (5 ft)
  Covered in fragrant purple blooms in early summer, this lilac does not sucker and holds its dense shape very well. Full sun.
- *Syringa villosa*—Late Lilac. 3–4 m (10–13 ft)
  The villosa lilac makes a wonderful drought-resistent shelterbelt. A cultivated variety known as Preston lilac has bigger blooms and brighter colours.
- *Syringa vulgaris*—Common Lilac. 1.5 m (5 ft)
  The French lilac is grafted onto this one, so fancy varieties will sucker. Common lilac is purple or white, with a wonderful perfume. Full sun. It will not bloom in the shade.
- *Viburnum lantana*—Wayfaring Tree. 3 m (5 ft)
  Leathery wrinkled leaves. White flowers, black berries, and good fall colour in areas with a longer growing season. Full sun or part shade.
- *Viburnum trilobum*—Highbush Cranberry. 3 m (5 ft)
  Native to Alberta. Showy white flowers and edible red fruit. Good fall colour. Full sun or part shade.

TREES

- *Acer ginnala*—Amur Maple. 5 m (16 ft)
  Dainty, small, shrubby tree with glowing fall colour.
- *Betula pendula* 'Gracilis'—Cutleaf Weeping Birch. 6–15 m (20–49 ft)
  Graceful, silver-trunked tree. Needs a lot of water. Leaves turn golden in fall.
- *Fraxinus nigra*—Black Ash 'Fallgold.' 10 m (33 ft)
  A narrow, pyramidal, uniform, seedless ash that holds its leaves longer than other ashes. Ash is the last of the trees to leaf out and the first to drop its leaves in fall, but very hardy and long-lived. Full sun.
- *Larix laracina*—Tamarack. 15–20 m (49–66 ft)
  Native to Alberta in the high alpine regions. The larches are conifers

that turn gold and lose their needles in fall. New needles are a
wonderful soft green. Full sun.

- *Larix sibirica*—Siberian Larch. 15–20 m (49–66 ft)
  Pyramidal shape with tips of the branches curving upward.
- *Malus*—Apples. 5 m + (16 ft +)
  A big family of apples and crabapples. Buy locally for hardy variet-
  ies. Crabapples with pink blossoms produce small, hard, inedible
  fruit (except from a bird's-eye view!). Some have purple leaves.
  White-flowered varieties of either apples or crabapples are mostly
  edible, except for the Siberian Crab (*Malus baccata*). Full sun.

  Plant two different varieties that bloom at the same time to get
  fruit. In town the bees can probably find another apple tree on the
  same flight from the hive. If you are miles from a neighbouring
  apple tree, plant several varieties for cross-pollination. The fruit
  will not be a hybrid, only the seed inside the fruit.
- *Picea glauca*—White Spruce. 15–30 m (49–98 ft)
  Our most common native spruce tree. Full sun or part shade.
- *Picea pungens*—Colorado Spruce. 15–30 m (49–98 ft)
  Very symmetrical evergreen with larger needles than the white
  spruce. Very blue varieties are grafted. Needs lots of space. Water
  is essential to get it going.
- *Pinus aristata*—Bristlecone Pine. 10–40 m (33–131 ft)
  A slow-growing tree that lives to a great age. Long needles are
  flecked with white, giving a silvered appearance.
- *Pinus sylvestris*—Scotch Pine. 10–15 m (33–49 ft)
  Light brown bark, open habit, and long needles. A lovely tree,
  hardy and durable.
- *Populus*—Poplar. 60 m (197 ft)
  Not recommended for cities or near septic tank systems. Roots
  are very invasive. Poplars are the only trees that grow really fast in
  Alberta to provide shade in your lifetime! Good shelterbelt tree.
  Nursery-grown varieties are all males with no cotton fluff.
- *Populus tremuloides erecta*—Swedish Columnar Aspen. 10 m + (33 ft +)

Siberian Larch in its fall colours.

Narrow upright aspen. Use for accent or small spaces or to disguise an ugly power pole. Full sun.

- *Prunus maackii*—Amur Cherry. 7 m + (23 ft +)
  Beautiful bronze cherry bark. Needs to have its trunk in the shade of other trees to prevent sunscald. White blossoms in spring produce small, inedible black cherries (birds eat them).
- *Prunus padus commutata*—Mayday Tree. 12 m (39 ft)
  Large spreading tree prized for its spring blossoms.
- *Prunus virginiana*—Chokecherry. 5 m (16 ft)
  The variety named 'Schubert' is widely used for boulevard planting because of its neat habit, small stature, and purple leaves. It makes a fine specimen tree for a small lot. Its shiny black berries are loved by the robins.
- *Pyrus ussuriensis*—Ussurian Pear. 6–12 m (20–39 ft)
  White blossom and small, inedible pears. Very hardy and long-lived. Good orange fall colour. Slow-growing but imposingly large at maturity.
- *Quercus macrocarpa*—Bur Oak. 8–15 m (26–49 ft)
  Native to Manitoba. Slow-growing but rewarding. A most attractive tree in a sheltered location.
- *Salix pentandra*—Laurel Leaf Willow. 12 m (39 ft)
  This one keeps its leaves well into October. Needs lots of water to get it going.
- *Salix exigua*—Coyote Willow. 5 m (16 ft)
  Graceful, tall, shrubby tree. It waves in the wind like seaweed under water. Narrow, grey leaves. Suckering habit.
- *Sorbus americana*—American Mountain Ash. 6 m (20 ft)
  Flowers are white. Leaves turn orange in the fall. Reddish-orange berries stay on the tree well into winter. In Scotland a mountain ash, or "rowan tree," is planted near the entrance to the garden to ward off evil spirits or witches!
- *Sorbus aucuparia*—European Mountain Ash. 8 m (26 ft)
  Similar to the American Mountain Ash, but has red fall foliage.
- *Sorbus decora*— Showy Mountain Ash. 5 m (16 ft)

The hardiest mountain ash. A compact tree with larger flowers and fruit. Orange fall colour.

- *Syringa reticulata*—Japanese Tree Lilac. 7 m + (23 ft +)
  Very hardy, beautiful tree. Slow-growing but eventually needs a lot of room. Trusses of pure white flowers in midsummer. Full sun.

Mountain Ash (Sorbus).

Moving Mature Trees and Shrubs
by Anne Vale

This can be tricky, depending on the size, age, and location of the plant you want to move. Sometimes you realize that you have not chosen the right location for a tree or shrub and wish to move it to a better location within your yard, or else you want to take it with you when you move. Moving it successfully depends on age, size, and soil type. A tree growing in rocky or gravelly soil will lose most of the soil from the root ball during moving and the move is rarely successful.

Bigger trees are best done with a professional tree mover, but this is not always an option due to lack of access. They are best cut down and a stump grinder rented. Be careful in cities. There is sometimes a hefty fine for cutting down a tree, even on your own property.

If the tree or shrub is of a size that you can lift and handle, then for deciduous material you have about a two-week window in spring when the ground is not frozen and the plant has not leafed out, and again in fall before freeze-up and after leaves have fallen. If it has leaves

---

Helpful Hints

* When planting trees and shrubs, put a small shovelful of oats or barley in the bottom of the hole. The fermentation of the grain causes heat, which helps roots to form. Avoid heavy use of fertilizer—either manure or chemical fertilizer—at the time of planting, as it burns tiny roots that are essential to the survival of the tree or shrub.
* Water trees and shrubs well in late fall to prevent dehydration in winter. Spray anti-desiccant on trees on a warm day in late fall to protect from drying winds. Mulch after freeze-up.
* Junipers love lime, so sprinkle wood ashes around the base of them.

during these periods, then strip them off so they do not lose moisture from transpiration before the roots can replace it.

For conifers there is a longer period when they can be moved. The vulnerable time is when the new growth is expanding. During this period moving will probably kill them. Early spring works well or July through September. I have had the best success on a wet weekend in April. Tie a ribbon on the north side of the tree and replant it in the same compass direction. This does work. The late Frank Sharpe of Millarville gave me this valuable tip, and his old property is living testimony to his good advice.

Have the new hole dug before you start digging the tree out. Dig the hole much bigger and deeper than the root ball to leave room for new good soil under and around the roots. Use burlap or a tarp to help move it to its new location. Plant at the same depth. Tread it in firmly and water copiously and regularly until established in its new home.

Trees will need guy wires to keep them from rocking about in a wind and tearing the tiny roots loose.

Storing Trees and Shrubs Over Winter
by Norma Lyall

What do you do with those pots of trees and shrubs that you didn't get planted in time? In 1979 I had about thirty pots—some were spruce, there was an apple tree, northwest poplar, sharp leaf willow, and two flats of little pansies which I dug out of the garden to transplant but never did. Our problem was what to do with all these plants—let them die, or what.

One day I said, "Couldn't we put all these pots in this big pile of old wood shavings which we had stockpiled for further use?" So we hauled all the pots to the shavings pile and we started to set the pots tight together down in the shavings. We dug them in the full depth of the pots plus ten centimeters (four inches) on top of the pots with the tree or shrub sticking out above the shavings. The flats of pansies were put a foot deep in the shavings.

This was a success—everything survived. One or two of the pansies were in bloom and looked the same when we dug them out of the shavings in spring. There was no trouble with mice, as the shavings were wet.

Propagation of Woody Plants
Seed Propagation of Woody Perennials
by Pam and Ken Wright

The most probable deterrent to propagation of woody perennials by seed is the time involved to get a tree or shrub of noticeable size from a seed. This shouldn't be so; after all, many yards are dotted with seedlings of Manitoba maple (box elder), green ash, some elms, poplars, lilacs, and even a few conifers, to name a few plants that shed their seeds rather freely.

Every year many people plant vegetable and flower seeds quite successfully. This success can be matched with woody perennials (trees and shrubs), with a few extra steps. Some steps are the same as those taken by the ambitious gardener who saves the seed from the most outstanding vegetable or flower, to replant the following year.

Seed selection is the first step—any hardy and usually locally grown plant will make a good seed source. Take time to check the form of the plant, the colour of blossoms, leaf colour, and flavour of fruit (as with chokecherry, elderberry, and other edibles). Look to see if the plant has been attacked by insects, as some cultivars are more susceptible than others. Stay away from apples and named fruit trees—they are hybrids and do not breed true from seed. If the plants are proven hardy, they do make good windbreak or shelterbelt trees, but you won't get a Goodland apple from a Goodland apple seed.

Collecting seeds must by done at the right time; that is to say, before they are gone, taken by birds, animals, wind, or gravity. Cones can be plucked right from the tree before they are fully ripened, then dried and shaken to dislodge the seeds. Sometimes a rodent's cache can be found where cones are plentiful and ready for the taking. Dry seeds, such as lilacs or green ash, are easily collected by picking directly off the plant, or by spreading a sheet under the tree or shrub, then shaking the plant to dislodge the seeds. Break off any woody material that remains attached to the seeds. Fleshy fruits such as saskatoons, mountain ash berries, Nanking cherries, plums, chokecherries, elderberries, etc., must be taken from the plants before they start to dry, and cleaned to remove all fleshy material. This is easily done by breaking the skin by hand, then running water over all in a sieve, or similar utensil, to wash away the pulp, and placing on a paper or screen to dry. All seeds should be stored in paper bags or boxes, in a cool, dry, dark place, the same way you store vegetable seeds.

Woody perennial seeds, as a rule, have to undergo a stratification or moist chilling period in order to break dormancy. There are four factors involved in this: moisture, aeration, time, and temperature.

Moist peat moss is an excellent medium for seed stratification. Peat moss should be thoroughly mixed with water, wet to the point of almost dripping when a handful is squeezed. If it drips, it is too wet. If it is too dry, insufficient moisture is absorbed by the seed coat; too wet and mould problems arise. Mix seeds with two to three times as much peat as seed. Seal in plastic bags, which allow air exchange (the plastic works as a mulch). Then label accordingly and store in the root cellar or refrigerator, optimum temperature 2–7°C (36–45°F), for 60–90 days.

Seeds stratified in January or so are ready for planting in the spring. Sow your seeds outside in beds prepared the same way you would prepare beds for vegetables: uniform soil mixture, raked smooth, etc. The rules for seeding woody perennials are the same as for vegetables. Don't plant seeds deeper than three times the diameter of the seed. Keep moist during germination, as dry soil interferes with oxygen exchange. Keep those weeds under control. Allow for the fact that several years may pass before you move your seedlings.

This spring and summer, watch for the trees and/or shrubs that you would like to propagate. When the fruit matures, pick your seeds, just before the birds do.

One last note: Please label all of your seeds as to date, place, and kind picked, and time stratified.

Propagation by Cuttings From Woody Perennials
by Pam and Ken Wright

Propagation by cuttings is a very advantageous practice because the characteristics of the new plant are generally the same as the parent plant. There are several types of cuttings, and the plant to be propagated usually dictates the method to be used.

1. *Root cuttings*—red raspberry, aspen (*Populus tremuloides*)
2. *Stem cuttings*—a) from a soft, new wood: poplar, rose, willow, lilac; b) from a hard, older wood: spirea, rose, willow, poplar, currant, some conifers; c) semi-hardwood: junipers, conifers, aspen, arborvitae

The first step in propagating woody perennials (trees and shrubs) by stem cutting is to select the plant to be used for a cutting source, taking into consideration the characteristics of the plant, susceptibility to disease or insects, environment, and amount of cutting material (the newest growth). Cuttings at least 8 cm (3 in) long, 15–20 cm (6–8 in) being preferable, should be cut cleanly with sharp pruning clippers or shears that have been cleaned with household bleach. Cuttings root easier when the cut is made directly below a bud, having three or more buds on the length.

Suitable rooting mediums are:
1. *Sawdust* (not cedar)—is easily accessible, easy to keep wet, and easy to move when the cuttings have rooted
2. *Sand*—retains a lot of moisture, but not much air exchange
3. *Jiffy-7's*—fine for smaller cuttings of softwood if they call be kept constantly moist
4. *Perlite*—very hard to keep moist, but works well for juniper semi-hardwood cuttings
5. *The ground*—a fine medium for hardwood cuttings of easily rooted plants such as poplar and willow

The Art of Propagating a Shelterbelt
by Art L. Patterson

If you have longed to have a windbreak of hardy poplar trees glistening in the summer breeze, then start today and plan for one. A shelterbelt, envied and admired by all who see it, is a sight you will be proud of. The method I am about to describe to you will cost very little, as far as the cost of cuttings is concerned. The labour entailed in achieving this delightful windbreak can be charged to the labour of love. Without the initiative, the enthusiasm, and a constant effort in the care of these trees, things just don't happen, so be prepared to carry through from start to finish if you are to achieve the desired effect.

Method—Consider, visualize, and anticipate your dream of a windbreak as you would like to have it, taking into account the prevailing winds, the factors of drainage that may be used to your advantage, and the soil conditions. Obstacles have to be considered since no one plan will fit all circumstances.

Having considered these factors, make a start by preparing the land for planting. It is advisable to summerfallow a strip for two years, wide enough to accommodate the anticipated windbreak, bearing in mind that these little cuttings 15–20 cm (6–8 in) long will soon be stately trees up to 9 m (30 ft) tall. When planning the windbreak strip always bear in mind that trees must have room to grow, and as they grow must have cultivation, so leave 5–6 m (16–20 ft) between rows so you will be able to cultivate between with a tractor. They will need to be cultivated on both sides for three years and on the outsides for the next four years.

An ideal windbreak for this country would be a strip wide enough to accommodate a row of non-suckering caraganas on the outside, which are tough and will protect the poplars until they get started. Then two rows of Northwest, Brooks, or Russian poplars for fast growth and something to watch while a row of spruce trees, which are long-lasting but slower in growth, get established in the front row.

Cuttings and rooted trees can be obtained free by contacting your Provincial Department of Agriculture, providing that the land preparation requirements have been met, or you can take your own cuttings from cultivated poplar trees in your vicinity. Stay away from native varieties, e.g., trembling aspen.

When selecting cuttings, be sure to take them from male trees, as these trees are not fluff-bearing. It has been found that the female species of poplar are very beautiful trees, but they produce the seed fluff in the spring. (The female is always making a fuzz about something!) You can determine which are the male trees by observation in the spring. Male trees drop their catkins about three weeks before the females let go their fluff.

Cuttings should be 15–20 cm (6–8 in), taken from last year's growth which is limber and has buds appearing on the surface. A good cutting has three or four buds, is 15–20 cm (6–8 in) long, has the bottom cut at an angle, and has the top cut square off. One branch can give you several cuttings. Use a sharp hand pruner. Take these cuttings in March or before the sap starts to flow, and wrap them in burlap in bundles of twenty-five or so. Place them in a cool damp place, away from frost, always putting the tops or square cuts up. This will keep the cuttings dormant until planting.

The cuttings we used to plant our windbreak came from Indian Head, Saskatchewan. They arrived in the spring, and to say the least they looked very small and insignificant. Having never planted cuttings, I was a little skeptical, but we planted them just the same and were delighted with the result. Not more than ten died, out of the one thousand we planted. I was so pleased with the end result that I have been looking at them and talking about them ever since.

The method of planting these cuttings is important and holds some hints that are useful. This is what we did!

Steps to take:

1. The land is prepared and ready to grow.
2. The cuttings are at hand.
3. The time to plant is in the spring when the land is warm, the leaves are just bursting on the trees, and all things in nature have the urge to grow.
4. Establish the location of the row. Stake it out, leaving 5.5–6 m (18–20 ft) between rows, and 4–5 m (14–16 ft) between each set.
5. Take one or two bundles of cuttings from storage and place them in a bucket with a little water in it. This saves the cuttings from drying out while you plant.
6. Take one cutting and push it into the moist summerfallow on an angle of sixty degrees, pointing to the southeast. Only one bud should appear above the ground on the top side of the cutting, and this bud is at ground level. Place a second cutting about 25–30 cm (10–12 in) away from the first cutting. This establishes a set, thereby doubling your chances of ending up with one good tree in each spot. Planting the cutting at an angle enables you to pack the soil around it more firmly. The tighter it is packed, the sooner it begins to take root. The reason we place the cutting facing southeast is to expose the least amount of bark to the direct sunlight, and encourage the bud to grow straight up.
7. The following spring, remove the weaker tree from each set.

Our experience has shown that, for shelterbelts, cuttings are much preferable to rooted trees, because they don't need watering. Each cutting only puts up as much growth as its root system can support.

Our shelterbelt was planted twenty years ago, using this method. In five years, with no supplementary watering, the trees were 3.5–4.5 m (12–15 ft) high! They are now about 9 m (30 ft) tall, with 30 cm (12 in) trunks.

Roses
by Deb Francis and Anne Vale

Anyone who says you can't grow roses in Alberta should go and have a look at trial grounds in our own zone. The University of Alberta Botanical Garden at Devon, the campus at Olds College, Alberta Agriculture Special Crops and Research Centre at Brooks, and the Calgary Zoo Botanical Garden all have extensive rose gardens with varieties clearly marked, showing an amazing diversity of roses proving their suitability to our variable and rigorous climate. The best time to visit these gardens is from the end of June through mid-August. Although none of the above locations receives the extreme chinooks we get along the foothills, they are the closest demonstration gardens available to us. They provide a very good hardiness guide, and most of the roses that do well for them will grow here.

TIPS FOR PURCHASING ROSES

Give thought to what you like about roses. There is blossom type (form), frequency of bloom, fragrance, and height. Hips and foliage may also be a factor.

If you have not had any luck growing roses, choose a shrub rose that is described as having "cast-iron hardiness." Where possible obtain roses that are grown on their own roots and not grafted onto a different root stock. Not all root stock used by rose nurseries is prairie-hardy. Buy from a local supplier or catalogue that states the hardiness loud and clear.

GROWING ROSES

Roses need a minimum of six hours of direct sunlight daily. They will perform better in a sheltered location out of the wind. Grow in a rose bed or a mixed flower bed, with shrubs, as a hedge, in containers, or wherever you can find room.

HARDY SHRUB ROSES

These are the ones that need no winter protection here and very little pruning. They mature into big, vigorous bushes that fit in well with an informal country setting. They bear very little resemblance to the neat formal roses known as hybrid teas. Shrub roses usually flower for a short burst at the end of June and beginning of July with a profusion of bloom. Their perfume scents the whole garden. Most have ornamental rosehips that stay on the bush all winter and look good against the snow. This type of rose is very trouble-free. It is happy with our conditions, doesn't mind the chinooks, and needs very little pruning because it blooms best on the older wood.

Varieties usually are listed in catalogues under Hardy Shrub Roses but may sometimes be listed under Rugosa Roses. Many are the same varieties that have been grown in English cottage gardens for generations, and some were grown by Napoleon's Josephine in France. Empress Josephine was bent on making her gardens the finest in Europe and collected every known variety of rose, numbering about 250. Her official artist was Pierre-Joseph Redoute, whose rose paintings still appear on calendars, table mats, and flower prints in every department store today. Most of today's shrub roses are descended from these roses of the early 1800s. Others have been bred right here in Alberta using the hardiest shrub roses and throwing in a dash of our native rose for good measure.

Since the first edition of *Gardening Under the Arch*, the rose development program of Agriculture Canada has been producing an ever-expanding choice of hardy roses. These include the Parkland Morden series and the Explorer series, which is named for Canadian explorers such as David Thompson and Alexander Mackenzie. The Pavement series of roses includes strong, hardy rugosas. These are uniform, tidy bushes that make an easily controllable border for a garden path and are very fragrant. Other breeders of hardy roses of note are Georges Bugnet, Percy Wright, Dr. Frank Skinner, Robert Simonet, Robert Erskine, Dr. Niels Hansen, Dr. Griffin Buck, and John Wallis.

Hardy Roses	Flower Size	Fragrance	Height
Explorer Roses			
Capt. Samuel Holland. Red-pink. Excellent repeat bloom.	7 cm (2.5 in)	light	2–3 m (6–10 ft)
David Thompson. Medium-red double.	7 cm (2.5 in)	medium	1.2 m (4 ft)
Henry Hudson. White double. Intermittent bloomer.	6 cm (2 in)	strong	0.8 m (2.5 ft)
Henry Kelsey. Medium-red double. Repeat bloomer.	7 cm (2.5 in)	medium	2–2.5 m (6–8 ft)
John Cabot. Magenta, semi-double. Repeat bloomer.	7 cm (2.5 in)	medium	2.5–3 m (8–10 ft)
John Davies. Glowing medium pink. Exceptionally heavy repeat bloomer.	8–9 cm (3–3.5 in)	medium	1–2 m (4–6 ft)
John Franklin. Medium-red double. Repeat bloomer.	6 cm (2 in)	medium	2–3 m (6–10 ft)
J.P. Connell (Ottawa 1987). Lemon-yellow double. repeat bloomer. Takes 2–3 years to establish.	7.5–8 cm (3 in)	medium	0.9–1 m (3–4 ft)
William Baffin. Deep pink semi-double. Repeat bloomer.	6 cm (2 in)	light	2–3 m (6–10 ft)
Morden Parkland Roses			
Adelaide Hoodless. Deep red double. Many flowers to a stem. Repeat bloomer. Good for massed plantings.	7 cm (2.5 in)	light	0.9–1.5 m (3–5 ft)
Hope for Humanity. Blood-red double. Repeat bloomer.	8 cm (3 in)	none	0.5 m (1.5 ft)
Morden Blush. Pale pink-ivory double. Good repeat bloom.	8 cm (3 in)	light	0.6–0.9 m (2–3 ft)
Morden Centennial. Medium glowing pink double. Repeat bloomer.	7–8 cm (2.5–3 in)	light	1–1.5 m (4–5 ft)

Explorer rose: David Thompson.

Red leaf rose (Rosa rubrifolia).

Hardy Roses	Flower Size	Fragrance	Height
Morden Fireglow. Scarlet/orange double. Repeat bloomer.	6–8 cm (2–3 in)	none	0.9 m (3 ft)
Morden Snowbeauty. White semi-double. Repeat bloomer. Attractive grouped. Spreading habit.	6–8 cm (2–3 in)	light	0.9 m (3 ft)
Morden Sunrise. Yellow/orange blend, semi-double. Takes 2–3 years to establish well.	6 cm (2 in)	light	0.7 m (2 ft)
Prairie Dawn (Morden 1959). Salmon-pink semi-double. Repeat bloomer.	6 cm (2 in)	medium	1.5– 2 m (5–6 ft)
Prairie Joy. Medium-pink double. Repeat bloomer.	7 cm (2.5 in)	medium	1 m (4 ft)
Winnipeg Parks. Red-pink blend semi-double. Repeat bloomer. Takes 2–3 years to establish.	8 cm (3 in)	light	0.6 m (2 ft)
Hybrid Rugosa Roses. Pavement Roses. All extremely hardy.			
Foxi Pavement. Deep purple-pink single	-	strong	0.6 m (2 ft)
Pink Pavement. Semi-double. Repeat bloomer.	-	strong	0.6 m (2 ft)
Purple Pavement. Semi-double. Repeat bloomer.	-	strong	0.6 m (2 ft)
Scarlet Pavement. Semi-double. Repeat bloomer.	-	strong	0.6 m (2 ft)
Snow Pavement. Semi-double. Repeat bloomer.	-	strong	0.6 m (2 ft)
Other Hybrid Rugosa Roses. All extremely hardy.			
Blanc Double de Coubert. White double. Repeat bloomer.	8 cm (3 in)	strong	0.9–1.5 m (3–5 ft)

Hardy Roses	Flower Size	Fragrance	Height
Frau Dagmar Hartopp (Hastrup). Silvery rose-pink single. Repeat bloomer.	8 cm (3 in)	strong	0.6– 0.9 m (2–3 ft)
F. J. Grootendorst. Clusters of small, bright red double "fringed" blooms. Repeat bloomer.	3 cm (1 in)	none	1.5– 2 m (5–6 ft)
Grootendorst Supreme. Clusters of small, crimson double blooms. Repeat bloomer.	6 cm (2 in)	none	1.5– 2 m (5–6 ft)
Hansa. Magenta-red double. Repeat bloomer.	8–10 cm (3–4 in)	strong	1.5–2 m (5–6 ft)
Marie Bugnet. White double. Repeat bloomer.	6 cm (2 in)	strong	0.9–1 m (3–4 ft)
Pink Grootendorst. Clusters of small, pink fringed blooms.	3 cm (1 in)	none	1.5–2 m (5–6 ft)
Sir Thomas Lipton. White double. Repeat bloomer.	6 cm (2 in)	strong	0.6–0.9 m (2–3 ft)
The Hunter. Medium-red double. Repeat bloomer.	8 cm (3 in)	medium	1.5 m (5 ft)
Theresa Bugnet. Medium-pink double. Repeat bloomer.	8 cm (3 in)	medium	1.5–2 m (5–6 ft)
Miscellaneous Hardy Roses			
Damask Rose. Madame Hardy (1832). White double. Large flowers. Blooms late June to mid July.	10 cm (4 in)	strong	1.5 m (5 ft)
Rambler Rose. The Polar Star. White semi-double, vigorous. Good in sunny locations. Blooms late June to early July.	2 cm (1 in)	none	2 m + (6 ft +)
Rosa harrisonii. Harrison's Yellow. Deep yellow semi-double. Blooms in early summer for 3–4 weeks.	7 cm (2.5 in)	light	1–2 m (4–6 ft)

Hardy Roses	Flower Size	Fragrance	Height
Rosa foetida bicolour: Austrian Copper. Yellow/orange single. Blooms in early summer for 3–4 weeks.	6 cm (2 in)	light	1 m (4 ft)
Rosa gallica: Empress Josephine. Medium pink, very fully double. Blooms early summer only.	8–10 cm (3–4 in)	strong	0.9 m (3 ft)
Rosa gallica: Rosa mundi (1851). Crimson and white stripes. Blooms in early summer only.	7 cm (2.5 in)	strong	0.9 m (3 ft)
Rosa glauca: The Redleaf Rose. Small, single pink, red-purple tinted leaves. Red hips all winter. Blooms in early summer.	3 cm (1 in)	none	3 m (10 ft)
William's Double Yellow (Scott's hybrid rose). Deep yellow double. Blooms late June.	5 cm (2 in)	medium	0.3 m (1 ft)

Explorer rose: J.P. Connell. *Rugosa rose: Blanc double de Coubert.*

Explorer rose: John Cabot.

Rugosa rose: Harrison's Yellow Rose 'Prairie Traveller's Joy.'

TENDER ROSES

Hybrid tea roses can be grown here but require much special care and winter protection. Their blooms do not reach the size and magnificence that they achieve in more temperate climates. Our Alberta air seems to suck the moisture out of them, and in most cases they are disappointing and short-lived. However, Eileen Jameson recommends the following methods for protecting tender roses in winter.

Method One—Hill up the soil around each plant and cover with paper cones.

Method Two—Trim rose to fit a large cardboard box, fertilize and soak, then place a cardboard box over the rose with the flaps open at both ends and fill with peat moss. The lower flaps are covered with soil, and the upper flaps are left open until the ground is frozen. Then they are closed in and another box is placed over the top to prevent the melting snow from running through and dampening the peat moss. This method has enabled us to save Queen Elizabeth and Peace roses for twelve to sixteen years.

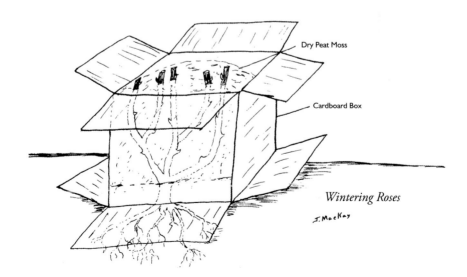

Dry Peat Moss

Cardboard Box

Wintering Roses

J. MacKay

When purchasing hybrid tea roses or other tender types of rose
that you intend to keep over the winter, you should be careful to order
only those which are grown on hardy rootstock. Catalogues that supply the prairies should state this. Beware of falling for glossy pictures in
catalogues from other regions. These hybrid teas are unlikely to winter
here. Certain cultivars are hardier than others, however, and provided
they are on prairie-hardy rootstock they should be worth a try, given
suitable winter protection.

Tender roses (tested and proven reasonably hardy given winter
protection):

Tender Roses	Flower Size	Fragrance	Height*
Hybrid Teas			
Fragrant Cloud. Orange/coral red blend double. Repeat bloomer. One of the most fragrant roses in the world.	12 cm (4.5 in)	strong	0.9–1 m (3–4 ft)
Mr. Lincoln. Deep crimson-red velvety double. Repeat bloomer.	13 cm (5 in)	strong	1 m (4 ft)
Peace. Soft yellow edged with rose-pink, double. Repeat bloomer. Perhaps the most famous rose in the world, named by the Americans to celebrate the end of WWII.	15 cm (6 in)	light	0.9 m (3 ft)
David Austin English Roses			
Abraham Darby. Apricot-copper, double. Repeat bloomer. Comes back from below ground each spring. Very vigorous and a show-stopper.	10 cm (4 in)	strong	1–2 m (4–6 ft)

* Heights shown are the average in the Chinook Zone and do not reflect potential growth in milder
climates.

Tender Roses	Flower Size	Fragrance	Height*
Constance Spry. Light- to medium-pink double. Blooms in late June to early July. The blooms resemble peonies. Have patience with this rose. Slow to establish, it will reward you by the third year.	15 cm (6 in)	strong	1–2 m (4–6 ft)
Ground Cover Rose			
White Meidiland. Small, creamy-white double. Repeat bloomer. Dark green, shiny leaves.	2.5 cm (1 in)	light	0.3 m (1 ft)
Hybrid Perpetual			
Ferdinand Pichard. Carmine and white striped semi-double.	9 cm (3.5 in)	strong	0.9–1 m (3–4 ft)
Floribunda			
Chuckles. Deep pink semi-double. Repeat bloomer. Makes an outstanding show planted in a group.	3.5 cm (1.5 in)	light	0.5–0.6 m (1.5–2 ft)
Iceberg. Purest white semi-double. Petals have a pink tinge when nights are cool. Prolific repeat bloomer. Effective in groups. One of the most popular roses in the world.	7.5 cm (3 in)	medium	0.9–1 m (3–4 ft)
Nearly Wild. Medium pink single.	3.5 cm (1.5 in)	light	0.3–0.5 m (1–1.5 ft)
Shrub Rose			
Bonica. Medium pink semi-double. Prolific repeat bloom.	6 cm (2 in)	slight	0.9–1.5 m (3–5 ft)

* Heights shown are the average in the Chinook Zone and do not reflect potential growth in milder climates.

MINIATURE ROSES

Modern miniature roses are reasonably winter-hardy but they do require covering with at least 30 cm (12 in) of soil by mid-October. Do not use the soil from close to the bush, which would expose the roots. The lilac/mauve colours appear to be less hardy than the others. Miniatures should be on their own roots, not grafted. They are easily planted, not needing such a deep hole, and they will bloom most of the summer.

Miniature Roses	Height
Angela Rippon. Rose-salmon pink double. Repeat bloomer.	46 cm (18 in)
Cupcake. Medium-pink double. Repeat bloomer.	36 cm (14 in)
Little Artist. Red with white markings, semi-double. Repeat bloomer.	30 cm (12 in)
Popcorn. White semi-double.	30 cm (12 in)
Rise and Shine. Golden yellow, double.	40 cm (16 in)
Starina. Orange/red blend, double.	36 cm (14 in)
Hot Tamale. Orange-red single.	30 cm (12 in)
Golden Beryl. Golden yellow, double.	46 cm (18 in)

CLIMBING ROSES

Unfortunately there is, as yet, no true climbing rose that is hardy in Alberta. Such roses bloom on stems that are at least one year old, and the canes are too tender to survive the winter. They will put up nice, long canes the first year, but by the following summer when you expect clouds of bloom they will have winterkilled. If you have one you may try burying the canes in fall, but they are usually a disappointment.

Some of the hardy shrub roses will grow quite tall and can be trained up a pillar or fence, but even these benefit from being laid down for winter and covered for winter protection. Flax straw works well or a commercial nursery blanket. See list of Hardy Roses for the taller recommended varieties.

PLANTING ROSES

Two main methods work well for planting roses in this area. In both cases make sure there is adequate drainage. Roses love water but do not appreciate growing in a puddle.

Method A (Upright)—Dig a hole that is twice as wide and twice as deep as the container, or the bareroot rose. Ideally a planting hole for a rose is 0.6 m (2 ft) wide by 46 cm (18 in) deep. Put a handful of bone meal in the hole. Place the rose in the hole upright, spreading the roots around a mound of soil in the bottom, leaving the junction between roots and stem 15 cm (6 in) below the soil surface. Gently refill with good soil by hand, watering well at the half-full stage. Continue to fill, covering the crown of the plant 15 cm (6 in) deep. Leave a depression around the drip line to retain water. Water again to overflowing.

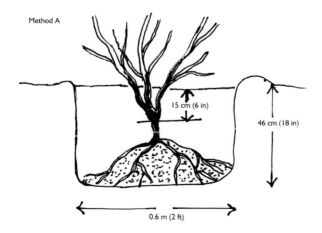

Method A

15 cm (6 in)

46 cm (18 in)

0.6 m (2 ft)

Method B (Slanted)—This is a good method to use where your topsoil is very shallow. You can still get the crown of the plant 15 cm (6 in) under the surface, and although the slanted stems look weird for the first year or two, new stems will shoot straight up. The planting hole does not have to be so deep but should be much wider. This method has been used successfully in the shallow soil of prairie gardens for many years. Follow remaining directions as for Method A above.

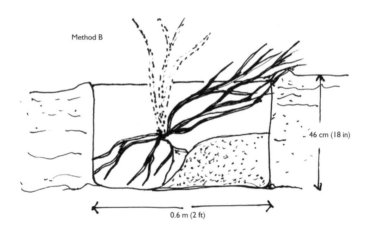

These two methods hold good for all types of roses (with the exception of miniatures) when planting in harsh climates. Note: If your container-grown roses have already leafed out, do not disturb the roots. Dig the hole as described and plant the rose. Pop it out of its plastic pot intact. Make sure there is good soil to fill the hole so the roots have somewhere to expand.

Roses grown in an above-ground container must either be planted in the ground before the onset of winter or the whole container moved into a building to keep it from freezing over the winter.

SOIL

For the best results, take time to prepare the soil. The best advice is that success lies all in the soil. In good soil roses become healthier, stronger, and more disease-resistant, and consequently less work. Roses prefer a rich, acidic soil with a pH of 6.2 to 6.5. To adjust the pH downwards, amend your soil with peat moss or sulphur-based fertilizers. Horticultural sulphur is also available at most garden centres.

Roses are heavy feeders. A generous supply of well-rotted manure, compost, and coarse peat moss is beneficial. The final mixture should consist of equal parts of soil, manure, compost, and peat moss. Try to aim for at least 30 cm (12 in) of topsoil in your rose bed. Continue to add compost each fall and fertilizer in early spring. This all sounds like tremendously hard work, but after the initial preparation maintenance is much easier. Each spring add more compost on top of the soil and in the fall use the last of the lawn mowings, complete with fallen leaves mulched by the lawn mower. This decomposes quickly and makes wonderfully healthy soil. Even hardy roses prefer snow cover, and in the Chinook Zone this can vary from day to day. Shredded leaves with grass clippings provide a little extra protection with a shovelful of soil to weight them down.

PRUNING

- *Tender Roses and Hybrid Teas*—Wait until early May to prune. If more blooms are the aim, do not prune too severely. If exhibition flowers are what you want, cut the branches back to about 10–15 cm (4–6 in) in length. This will give you fewer but larger blooms. Remove any dead wood entirely and cut live branches back to an outfacing bud. Deadheading promptly promotes formation of new flower buds.
- *Shrub Roses*—Shrub roses do not need much pruning except to remove any dead wood and any very ancient, unproductive branches from the base of the bush. Do not be too hasty in removing branches in spring until you are sure they are dead. Start trimming from the tip until you find green wood. Those with very

decorative hips or leaves should not be deadheaded. Any which do not have fancy hips can be deadheaded to encourage a second flush of bloom.

Roses occasionally produce suckers. These need to be removed. Suckers are vigorous shoots that appear from below where the union was made with the cultivated rose and the root stock. The sucker will appear quite different from the flowering parts of the bush. Scrape the soil away until you can cut off the sucker where it grows from the root. They will not bloom and instead just sap the energy from the rose you are trying to grow.

Don't confuse suckers with offshoots, which may spring from roses grown on their own roots. These will be identical to the parent plant and are a good method of propagating your rose bush.

WATERING

Water newly planted roses frequently until well established. Continue watering deeply once a week through the summer, even if you have to pack the water. Water individual bushes at the base of the plant. Avoid overhead sprinkling, which can spread disease. Stop watering in early September to allow the wood to harden off before winter. By mid-October or just before freeze-up give them another good soak. This enhances good winter survival.

FERTILIZING

Recommendations from the experts differ from rigid weekly applications to once a season. Experience teaches us to start with a low dose. You can always add more but it's pretty hard to remove an overdose. Start with a one-time application of granular rose fertilizer in early May. Keep adding humus (compost, manure, peat moss) when you think it necessary. Rugosas and other shrub roses prefer organic fertilizer rather than chemical. Stop fertilizing by July 31 to slow growth in preparation for winter.

Where soil is extremely alkaline, give each rose bush a handful of

Epsom salts (magnesium sulphate) placed around the drip line. Applied in late April and mid-July this assists with maintaining acidity and also enhances rapid growth of new canes. Rugosa roses show immediately if the pH is too high: leaves turn a chlorotic yellow with darker veins. A shot of Epsom salts, and they recover within a week or ten days.

Pure alfalfa pellets or meal make a great natural fertilizer. Use about 1 L (1 qt) per plant in early April. When alfalfa breaks down it releases tricontanol, which acts as a powerful organic fertilizer.

PESTS AND DISEASES

Generally shrub roses are a tough bunch, but a little care and common sense can prevent a host of problems. Keeping the bushes free of diseased foliage and removing fallen debris is a must, as is identifying the problem and taking prompt action.

Encouraging birds to visit your yard will take care of a lot of insect problems. Ladybugs and green lacewings and even wasps will consume an enormous quantity of larvae and adult insects.

In some instances pesticides are absolutely necessary, but only spray the problem spot, never the whole yard. Even insecticidal soap will stunt the growth of some roses, especially rugosas.

PESTS

- *Aphids*—The first line of defence is a sharp spray of water from the hose, or the good old finger-and-thumb method.
- *Rose curculio beetles*—These red and black beetles with the pointy snout will pierce holes in rosebuds to lay their eggs. They are a problem in some gardens. Proximity of wild roses is usually a factor. Pinching off rosebuds with holes in them will take care of some larvae, and picking off the adults in the early morning while they are sleepy and slow helps. By midday they are too agile to catch.
- *Spider mites*—These are sometimes a problem in very hot, dry summers. Infested leaves will appear freckled on top. Look for the spider mites under the leaves. Strip off affected leaves. Remember

that spider mites are not an insect, and insecticides will not kill them. A special miticide is available but try water first. Spider mites hate wet conditions and can't swim worth a darn.

DISEASES

- *Black spot*—This fungal disease looks like ink spots on the leaves. A cool, wet period makes it worse. Prevention is easier than a cure. Dusting sulphur around the base of susceptible plants is helpful. In London, England, where air pollution from burning coal was a factor years ago, the sulphur in the air prevented the occurrence of black spot, whereas further from industrial centres black spot was rampant. Yellow roses are more prone to black spot. Although not an organic method, Lysol aerosol spray on the soil under the plant (but not on the plant itself) seems to help. Remove and destroy the infected leaves promptly.
- *Rust*—Bright orange spots appear on the bushes usually in late spring. Amongst other carriers, the wild species of rose can contaminate certain cultivars. A strong baking soda solution of 60 ml (4 tbsp) of baking soda in 4 L (4 qt) of water sprayed on the bush and then rinsed off after two hours is helpful.
- *Mildew*—First ensure that the roses are receiving adequate sunshine and air circulation. Water only early in the day so that leaves are dry by nightfall. Spraying twice a week with diluted skim milk can prove effective. Use one part skim milk to nine parts of water.

Helpful Hints

✻ When planting hybrid tea roses in spring, plant early according to directions but hill them right over with loose soil. Leave it on for two weeks and then remove carefully by hand.

Vines—Clematis
by Theresa Patterson and Anne Vale

This family of climbing vines is sensationally beautiful once established. They bloom over a long period from June to September, producing hundreds of blossoms. They will thrive in almost any exposure, although for best results they prefer their feet in the shade and their heads in the sun. To help the roots stay cool, either grow small plants around the base to provide shade, or use rocks or a small shrub. They seem to like the lime from basement walls, so do not add peat moss to the soil. Compost or leaves will not have such an acidifying effect. Chicken wire will stop the leaves from blowing away.

Plant new clematis about 15 cm (6 in) deeper than they were in the pot and hill them up with soil about 20 cm (8 in) deep. This soil can be gently removed by hand in June or when all danger of frost is past. Once the roots are firmly established and the plants are growing strong this will not be necessary.

Be sure to keep them well-watered all summer to freeze-up and beyond, especially if they are right next to a concrete foundation. After the ground is frozen, cover them well with light, branchy material or leaves.

Fertilizer is best applied in the form of bone meal or blood and bone meal. This organic fertilizer will not burn the roots. It is slow-acting and long-lasting, only needing to be applied every five years or so. Clematis do not like fish fertilizer, chemical fertilizers, or manure.

The vines need a sturdy trellis to climb on. Be sure to make it 3–3.5 m (10–12 ft) high. Plastic-coated chain-link fence makes a dandy support for them. Wooden trellises tend to break down over time, and wood stain burns the tender new shoots and really offends the vines when they touch it.

Clematis look very effective when allowed to scramble up through a shrub or small tree. Imagine a red twig dogwood covered in large purple flowers!

Clematis are divided into three main pruning groups. The groups that most interest us are Group 1(A) and Group 3(C). Group 2(B) is not suitable for this area. Although the roots of the Group 2(B) clematis are hardy, the wood is not and will winterkill, leaving the plant with no old vines on which to bear the first crop of flowers. By the time the new vines have grown up from the base and are just budding up, the first early frost gets them.

This leaves us with some excellent clematis in both Group 1(A) and Group 3(C).

GROUP I (A)

These are usually small-flowered species clematis which do not need to be cut back. They will bloom early on the old wood that does not die back in winter. These are very vigorous and hardy. Most of them will bloom in sun or shade and are not fussy about soil type.

- *Clematis x 'Prairie Traveller's Joy'*—This was developed by Hugh Skinner in Manitoba, hybridizing with the Western white clematis, which it closely resembles. It can climb 6–9 m (20–30 ft) up through a poplar tree. It produces clouds of little, starry, white flowers, each 1.5 cm (0.5 in) across.
- *Clematis ligusticifolia* (Western White Clematis)—A native to southern Alberta, growing on dry, steep slopes in rocky soil. Similar to 'Prairie Traveller's Joy' above.
- *Clematis verticellaris var. columbiana* (Blue Clematis)—The vines with their pretty blue, bell-shaped flowers 5 cm (2 in) across are to be found in woodland sites in part shade throughout southern Alberta. The height is variable depending on soil nutrients but can grow as tall as 3.5–4.5 m (12–15 ft).
- *Clematis alpina*—A dainty, bell-shaped flower 5 cm (2 in) across covers this hardy vine. It will bloom equally well in sun or shade, and is very hardy. Suggested varieties to try: Pamela Jackman, Willy, Helsingborg.
- *Clematis macropetala*—This is similar in habit to the alpina species, and very hardy, grows anywhere and will bloom in sun or

Clematis x ligusticifolia.

shade. It blooms right through June in various colours. Recommended varieties include Blue Bird, Rosie O'Grady, Markham's Pink Double, and White Swan. Vines can reach a height of 4.5 m (15 ft) or more and do not need pruning. Flowers are 5 cm (2 in) across.

- *Clematis tangutica* (Yellow Clematis)—This is very tough and independent, and has self-seeded to the point of being a weed in some areas. If you are having trouble growing clematis, try this one. Its charming, bell-shaped, yellow flowers 4 cm (1.5 in) across are followed by a spectacular cloud of feathery seeds.

Clematis macropetala 'Markham's Pink'.

Clematis tangutica.

Clematis viticella 'Madame Julia Correvon.'

GROUP 3 (C)

This is our best source of large-flowered clematis. The roots are very hardy but the vines need to be cut back to the ground in winter to make room for the new growth that bears the flowers in July through August. This pruning group also includes the bush-type herbaceous clematis, such as integrifolia and recta. The well-known Jackmanii belong to this group. Any exposure will do except deep shade where they may not bloom much.

Recommended varieties include:

- *Jackmanii*—One of the hardiest and an old favourite. Flowers are 12–15 cm (4.5–6 in). It comes in the most common purple as well as white or red. (3.5 m/12 ft)
- *Perle d'Azure*—The best light blue, very heavy bloomer and vigorous. Flowers are 10–12 cm (4–4.5 in) across. (3 m/10 ft)
- *Ville de Lyon*—Bright crimson-red, with a long blooming period. Flowers are 10–15 cm (4–6 in) across. (3 m/10 ft)
- *Ernest Markham*—Magenta flowers, tried and true old favourite. Blooms July through August and grows to 3.5 m (12 ft) high.
- *Huldine*—Pure white, medium-sized flowers, 10–15 cm (4–6 in) across. Very hardy and reliable. Will reach 3 m (10 ft) tall.
- *Clematis viticella*—The flowers are a little smaller, 3–5 cm (1–2 in) wide, sometimes bell-shaped, but others are more open-faced, such as *C. viticella* Madame Julia Correvon, *C. viticella* Etoile de Violette, or the double-flowered *C. viticella* 'Purpurea Plena Elegans.' This needs a very sheltered location.
- *Clematis integrifolia*—Forms a bush and does not climb. Vibrant blue flowers in abundance appear in July. Reaches a height of 76 cm (30 in). Full sun is best for this one.
- *Clematis x durandii*—A hybrid derived from the bush-type integrifolia but with a more upright habit. It does not cling naturally and needs support, but is great grown by a low fence or through a rose bush. The bell-shaped flowers are bright blue, 8 cm (3 in) across.

Mandarin Honeysuckle.

- *Clematis recta*—A bush clematis that is herbaceous. The starry white (2–3 cm/1 in) flowers are wonderful in a mixed border. They will bloom in sun or shade. *C. recta* Purpurea has purple leaves. The bush gets to about 1 m (3 ft) tall and dies back in winter like the rest of Group 3(C).

Clematis are sometimes hard to establish, but well worth the effort. Once they are into their third year they are well on their way. If you lose one, don't grieve over it—go buy another one.

OTHER HARDY PERENNIAL VINES

- *Celastrus scandens* (American Bittersweet)—Although bittersweet is hardy here, the growing season is not long enough for it to bloom, which is its main attraction.
- *Aristolochiar durior* (Dutchman's Pipe)—Huge, heart-shaped leaves but insignificant brown flowers under the leaves. This is not likely to be successful in the more difficult growing areas, but there are some nice mature specimens in protected locations. It will climb pillars or a trellis and will grow in sun or shade.
- *Solanum dulcamara* (Deadly Nightshade)—This relative of the potato is indeed deadly with very tempting orange berries. If children are a part of your life, stay away from it in spite of its ease of cultivation and pointy purple flowers. All parts of the plant are poisonous. If you are determined to have one, your best bet is to get a cutting from a friend.
- *Lonicera* (Honeysuckle)—Blooming vines with a tall twining habit, honeysuckles will climb a trellis, or cover an old shed or tree stump. They bloom in early summer, attracting the hummingbirds. They will winter better if planted where their roots will not dehydrate against a scorching south wall. Mulch is beneficial.
- *Lonicera x brownii* 'Dropmore Scarlet'—Proven ultra-hardy over many years, this honeysuckle was developed by Skinner's Nursery in Manitoba. It has a very long flowering season and grows to 3 m (10 ft) or more.

- *Lonicera* 'Mandarin'—Introduced by the University of British Columbia, this is a beautiful honeysuckle which does well in a sheltered location. It appears to be not quite as hardy as Dropmore Scarlet, but has better glowing orange colour. Its leaves are an attractive bronze-green in early summer, aging to dark green. Reaches a height of 4.5 m (15 ft) in favourable locations. Roots should be mulched.
- *Lonicera dioica var. glaucescens* (Native Twining Honeysuckle)—This one is native to our area and can be found growing wild in woodlands along the rivers and in the foothills. Abundant yellow flowers with a reddish tinge are sweetly scented. It grows readily from seed and transplants well when dormant.
- *Humulus lupulus* (Hops)—This hardy vine shaded the verandahs of many a homestead and, like the pioneers who planted them, can handle tough times. The most common one has green leaves. There is also a golden one (*H. lupulus* aureus) with bright yellow leaves if planted in full sun. It looks amazing near evergreens. Hops need support from trellis or wires and will shinny up a power pole right to the top in one season. Remember that hops die back to the ground each year and should be cut back and tidied up before new growth starts again.
- *Parthenocissus quinquefolia* (Virginia Creeper)—This one needs support to climb. It has five-fingered leaves which turn red in the fall if planted in full sun. Small greenish-white flowers produce bunches of blue berries by midsummer.
- *Parthenocissus quinquefolia* 'Englemann Ivy' (Virginia Creeper)—This is the self-clinging one with little sucker feet which cling well to wood, brick, or stucco. The leaves are smaller and turn bright fiery-red in fall.

The plant known as *Parthenocissus tricuspidata* (Boston Ivy) is not hardy in our area.

Golden Hops.

ANNUAL VINES

A quick and easy way to add a vertical dimension to your garden is with annual vines. These grow very quickly from seed to cover a trellis, or climb up strings against a fence or on twiggy branches stuck in the ground (tied together to make a bushy support). In fall just pull them out and add to the compost pile.

- *Beans, Kentucky Pole*—Vigorous vines, white flowers, produce great long green beans. 2 m (6 ft)
- *Beans, Scarlet Runner*—Large, heart-shaped, green leaves and bright scarlet flowers that bring the hummingbirds. Edible pods of delicious beans for slicing french-style if the growing season between frosts is long enough. 2 m (6 ft)
- *Eccremocarpus scaber* 'Tresco' (Chilean Glory Vine)—Spikes of tubular, orange-red flowers adorn this smaller vine in profusion all summer. 1 m (4 ft)
- *Ipomea tricolor* 'Heavenly Blue' (Morning Glory)—Does best against a sunny wall with a trellis. Huge, intense blue trumpet flowers. 2.5 m (8 ft)
- *Rhodochiton atrosanguineus* (Purple Bells)—Reddish-purple pendant flower with prominent black calyx hanging down from the bell. Twining stems and leaves trail down from a planter or climb up a window screen. 1 m (3 ft)
- *Sweet Peas*—See article by Tom Davenport on page 183.
- *Thunbergia alata* (Black-eyed Susan Vine)—Small, trumpet-shaped yellow, white, and deep-orange flowers with a black eye. Leaves twine around any support. Likes a warm, sunny location. 1–1.5 m (4–5 ft)
- *Tropaeoleum majus* (Nasturtium)—Tall, climbing, or trailing variety. Will quickly screen an ugly view or give privacy to a deck. Needs a trellis or something for support. Brings the hummingbirds. Prefers partial shade. 2 m (6 ft)
- *Tropaeoleum peregrinum* (Canary Bird Vine)—A relative of the nasturtium, this airy vine has dainty divided leaves and yellow flowers resembling birds in flight. Prefers partial shade. 2 m (6 ft)

TRAILING VINES

These will hang down amazingly quickly from a hanging basket or window box. The more soil they have, the faster and longer they will grow. You may have to hang them quite high.

- *Dichondra* 'Silver Falls'—Sold as a started plant or basket stuffer, two or three in a hanging basket will create a stunning stalactite-like effect.
- *Glechoma hederacea* (Creeping Charlie)—This one would sooner trail than climb but makes a spectacular waterfall of a plant from a hanging basket.
- *Lamiastrum galeobdolon* (Yellow Archangel)—This is a hardy perennial when planted in the ground but doubles as a good trailing basket plant. In fall, cut back and plant in the garden.
- *Lysimachia nummularia* (Creeping Jenny)—Green or golden leafed varieties with small, yellow, buttercup-like flowers. Will trail over retaining walls effectively. 1 m (3 ft)
- *Vinca major* (Periwinkle)—A reliable trailing plant that will take a lot of frost. Glossy leathery leaves in green or variegated form will trail effectively from baskets or window boxes.

Purple Bells (Rhodochiton atrosanguinea).

4

Perennials

Gardening with Perennials
By Anne Vale

PLANNING

It is a great art to plan a perennial border well. The blooms are spectacular and colourful, but each has its own blooming period of three to six
weeks; then it is finished for the season. Some bloom in early summer,
and others don't start until late July or August. Another group does not
begin flowering until September but these are usually too late to be
worthwhile planting in this area. You should draw a plan on paper to
figure out heights, blooming times, and colours, as well as the mature
size of the plants. Either blend the colours and varieties so that there
is always something blooming, which can give a rather spotty appearance, or else have a spring display and a summer bed so that there is a
great mass of colour with several types of plants all doing their thing at once in a certain area. Remember that
only people make straight lines. Nature prefers curves.

Leaf shape and texture also add a lot of interest to
the perennial bed. Sword-shaped leaves of the iris contrast
well with more bushy greenery. A few grey-leaved plants, such
as artemesia or pinks, add an interesting colour variation.

Perennial border—lupins in foreground, silver Sea Holly (Eryngium giganteum) and scarlet Maltese Cross (Lychnis chalcedonica) behind.

The most important requirement perennials have is good drainage. Usually they do not require any particular type of soil, and most do well in full sun or semi-shade.

PROPAGATION

Perennials can be started from cuttings, division, or seed. If you plan to start seed indoors, bear in mind that many perennial seeds take a very long time to germinate. Do not give up on them too soon. Some perennial seeds require a period of chilling to break dormancy. A lot depends on their country of origin. If the plant grows naturally in a cold climate, when seeds fall from the parent plant to the ground they will not start to grow until repeated frosts have broken down the seed coat. The freeze/thaw cycle wears away the germination inhibitor that prevents the seed from coming up too soon. Such seed will benefit from a prolonged cold period after planting. The temperature can vary between −5°C to +5°C (23°F to 41°F) for a period of six to eight weeks. This process is known as stratification. If you do not have ideal conditions to accomplish this, sow the seed in a nursery bed outside in late fall, or early spring when the soil has warmed up. Be sure to label securely so you don't forget what and where they are. In a year or so the resulting plants can be moved to their permanent location.

Perennials not easily started from seed and better propagated by division or cuttings include peonies, iris, bleeding hearts, trollius, and grasses. Those which germinate readily without stratification include campanula, dianthus, poppies, lupin, Jacob's ladder, Maltese cross, centaurea, and shasta daisy.

Take note of the blooming time of each perennial before making plant divisions. It is a general rule that perennials which bloom in spring, such as bleeding heart or oriental poppies, should be divided in early fall to give them enough time to develop roots before the ground freezes. Summer-blooming perennials should be divided in spring as soon as the soil has warmed up, but before growth is too far advanced. Iris should be divided three weeks after blooming, usually mid-August. When dividing perennials, preserve as much root as possible from the outer perimeter of the clump and discard the old, worn-out centre portion. Do not allow the fibrous roots to dry out. Tubers and rhizomes should be divided with a very sharp knife and the cut allowed to callous over before replanting. When you obtain plant divisions, check for disease, pests, and weeds, which must be removed before planting. Some gardeners recommend soaking the roots in a bucket of lukewarm water before planting as the best method of cleaning the plants of weeds, grass, and pests.

CULTURE

In the spring you should cultivate the soil surface around your perennials manually and carefully. Perennials usually grow better if left undisturbed. Seedlings usually do not appear until late May or June. Some perennials reproduce well from seed, so be careful not to hoe out any seedlings you wish to keep. At this time you will see if any plants are growing out of bounds and can control them before they take over. It is also a good time to remove any weeds. The most effective way to remove quack grass is by painting a systemic weed killer on the leaves, taking extreme caution not to drop any on the surrounding plants. Be sure to wear rubber gloves. Do not use systemic weed killer near roses, as they will become distorted.

Wind and rain can do a great deal of damage to your taller perennials, so it is wise to stake them. The best time to do this is before too much growth has taken place. The leaves will then grow and conceal the stakes and ties. You can use the traditional bamboo stakes and twine or green acrylic knitting yarn but a natural effect is hard to achieve. Instead, save your woody shrub prunings and stick them into the soil around the perennial you wish to stake. No twine is needed. The twiggy branches will be mostly hidden by the emerging plant and look very natural besides giving good support. Peony rings or tomato cages also make good supports.

When watering your perennials it is better to give them a deep watering once a month than a sprinkle on the surface frequently. If the soil is damp deep down it will encourage deep root growth and water will not be necessary so often. Group drought-resistant plants together, and keep those which prefer more moisture to an area where water collects naturally or at least where you can accommodate their needs more economically.

WINTER CARE

Not all the perennials grown in our area are fully hardy if left exposed to chinook winds in winter. Those which retain their leaves through the winter are particularly susceptible; thus, without winter protection they will not survive. This category of perennials, such as dianthus or sweet william, should receive only a light trim.

In the fall, after hard frost has stopped all growth, other perennials may be cut back and cleaned up. Leave about a 20 cm (8 in) stubble to catch the snow and to hold your protective mulch. Some gardeners prefer to leave the decorative seed heads and grasses standing

This well-sheltered water garden thrives in a rural yard.

until spring. If they are strong enough to stay upright through wind and snow this adds to the look of your winterscape far more than mulch. Only the tender perennials which would otherwise winterkill need mulch. By far the majority are best left to spend the winter in the open. Some perennials reseed themselves but a thick mulch will bury the seeds too deep to germinate.

Mulch can be a 10 cm (4 in) layer of well-rotted manure, compost, or shredded fall leaves. This will eventually be pulled down into the soil by earthworms, improving the texture of the soil, and does not need to be removed in spring. Removable mulches, such as flax straw or fallen leaves, are more work but they are effective. This kind of mulch will blow away unless held down by loose branches or chicken wire. Other types of straw have drawbacks, as one of our members points out: "It attracts mice which burrow in it, which inevitably results in the destruction of my best plants." If you do use straw or leaves, wait until the ground is completely frozen. Mice will not be so keen to move in on top of frozen soil.

Note: Iris rhizomes will rot if covered with compost or manure. Peonies will stop blooming if the crowns are buried more than 5 cm (2 in) deep. Dianthus need only a thin layer of leaves or branches to catch the snow.

HARDY PERENNIALS AND ZONING

Many types of perennials are grown successfully in our very difficult growing area. Some of them are listed below. To mention them all is not possible in one chapter. Do not be afraid to push the zoning. Although most of us here live in Zone 2 or 3 this is only a guide, not a rule. Some very hardy plants have been designated Zone 4 or 5. Plants in that category are worth a try but Zone 6 and higher are definitely on the tender side.

- *Achillea millefolium*—Yarrow. 60 cm–1.0 m (24–39 in)
  Ferny leaves, flat-topped flowers in many different shades. Dried seed heads stay attractive all winter.

- *Achillea ptarmica*—'Bridal Wreath.' 60 cm (24 in)
  Clusters of white pompom flowers. Very invasive.
- *Aconitum napellus*—Monkshood. 1.5 m (5 ft)
  Blue or blue/white bicolour. Flowers in August/September. Very hardy. Poisonous. Sun or shade.
- *Alchemilla mollis*—Lady's Mantle. 40 cm (16 in)
  This is a flower arranger's dream. Lemon-lime fuzzy flowers. Round leaves that hold the dew like a pearl. Sun or part sun.
- *Aquilegia*—Columbine. 10 cm–1 m (4 in–3 ft)
  Blooms in early summer. Wide range of species, heights, colours, and habits. Does not like being moved. Flowers last longer in the shade but happy in the sun also. Leaves are sometimes attacked by caterpillars. Dust with Deritox, a safe larvicide. Susceptible to mildew in late summer. If this happens cut to the ground.
- *Artemisia ludoviciana*—'Valerie Finnis.' 50 cm (20 in)
  Taller, elegant, silvery leaves. Try with Nepeta 'Six Hills Giant' or anything else blue and spiky.
- *Artemisia schmidtiana*—'Silver Mound.' 30 cm (12 in)
  Neat silvery cushions.
- *Artemisia stelleriana*—'Silver Brocade.' 20 cm (8 in)
  Perennial dusty miller.

All artemisias are extremely drought resistant and prefer full sun.

- *Aster alpinus*—'Goliath.' 25 cm (10 in)
  Single blue daisy.
- *Aster alpinus*—'Marchenland.' 25 cm (10 in)
  Double aster, mixed colours.
- *Aster tongolensis*—'Wartburg Star.' 30 cm (12 in)
  Blue aster with yellow centre which blooms over a long period June—August.

Asters like full sun. These three will bloom early enough for us. Other asters are usually too late for our short season.

- *Bergenia cordifolia*—Elephant Ears. 30 cm (12 in)
  Evergreen leaves turn red in fall. Pink hyacinth-like blooms in spring. Sun or shade.
- *Brunnera macrophylla*—Siberian Bugloss. 30–40 cm (12–16 in)
  Spring blooming cousin of pulmonaria and mertensia. Brunnera blooms in the shade and comes in blue or white and also a variegated leaf form.
- *Campanula carpatica*—Carpathian Bellflower. 20 cm (8 in)
  Neat mound of heart shaped leaves/ Blue or white upfacing bells in July/August.
- *Campanula cochlearifolia*—Fairy Thimbles. 15 cm (6 in)
  Tiny blue or white bells. Self seeds.
- *Campanula glomerata*—Cluster Bellflower. 40 cm (16 in)
  Vivid purple. Very invasive. Grows anywhere.
- *Campanula persicifolia*—Peach leaf Bellflower. 1 m (3 ft)
  Tall clumps. Spires of blue or white flowers in August.
- *Centaurea macrocephala*—Globe Centaurea. 1.3 m (4 ft)
  Tall, stiff and sturdy. Makes a big clump with huge bright yellow bachelor buttons on top. Great cut and dried.
- *Centaurea montana*—Mountain Bluet. 45 cm (18 in)
  Very early bloom. Rather floppy but makes a wonderful splash of blue from large bachelor button flowers. Full sun.
- *Chrysanthemum coccineum (Tanacetum coccineum)*—Painted Daisy. 60 cm (24 in)
  Formerly known as Pyrethrum, this daisy is colourful and early. Shades of red, white, and pink. Self seeds. Full sun.
- *Dianthus arenarius*—Grassy Pinks. 15 cm (6 in)
  Starry white flowers in June.
- *Dianthus caesius*—Cheddar Pinks. 15 cm (6 in)
  Pink or red fragrant flowers above cushion of blue green leaves.
- *Dianthus deltoides*—Maiden Pinks. 10 cm (4 in)
  Spreading carpet of red flowers in July.
- *Dianthus plumaris*—Clove Pinks. 20 cm (8 in)
  Scented. Resembles a small carnation.

All dianthus above are hardy but better with snow cover. The evergreen leaves will rot under a heavy wet mulch. All need a well-drained location in full sun. Chicken wire is a good protection from deer in winter.

- *Delphinium hybrids*—1–2 m (3–6 ft)
  Plant out of the wind. Pacific Giants will need staking. Magic Fountains are shorter but still need staking. Sun or part shade. Watch for caterpillars devouring the flower buds in early spring. Wood ashes sprinkled around base of plant will help repel bugs, or use Deritox, a safe larvicide, in powder form.
- *Dicentra eximia* 'Luxuriant'—Fern Leaf Bleeding Heart. 25 cm
  Blooms almost all summer. Small, rose-pink flowers. Sun or partial shade.
- *Dicentra spectabilis*—Bleeding Heart. 1 m (3 f t)
  Blooms in early summer. Needs soil rich in humus. Useful in shady places, but will grow anywhere. Pink or white.
- *Doronicum orientale*—Leopard's Bane. 25–50 cm (10–20 in)
  Very early blooming yellow daisies for the shade. Leaves die back by midsummer. Drought-tolerant after the leaves disappear.
- *Echinops bannaticus* 'Blue Glow'—Globe Thistle. 1 m (3 ft)
  In spite of its common name, echinops is not related to the thistle family. It is a well-behaved plant that stays where it's put. 'Blue Glow' has bright blue, round flower heads which dry well for winter arrangements. Full sun.
- *Echinops sphaerocephalus*—2 m (6 ft)
  This one is taller and has steely blue flowers.
- *Erigeron speciosus*—Fleabane. 70 cm (28 in)
  Many-petalled daisies in shades of pink, blue, and purple. Extremely hardy everywhere. Very pretty and non-invasive. Butterflies love them. Full sun. Drought-resistant.
- *Eryngium giganteum* 'Miss Wilmott's Ghost'—70 cm (28 in). Silvery-blue flowers that dry well to a bleached bone colour. Miss Wilmott was a famous gardener in Victorian times who had no luck persuading her friends to try this plant so she travelled with

a pocketful of seeds and scattered them in her friends' flower beds when they were not looking. Wherever she had been, up they came, hence the name 'Miss Wilmott's Ghost.'

- *Eryngium planum*—Sea Holly. 1 m (3 ft)
  Very hardy and drought-resistant. Prickly blue flowers in sprays. Dries well for winter display. Full sun.
- *Euphorbia polychroma*—Cushion Spurge. 40 cm (16 in)
  This useful, drought-resistant plant is beautiful in three seasons. In early spring it has yellow flowers, all summer it behaves like a neat mounded small shrub of dark green leaves, which in fall turn a blazing red. Although it is officially a Zone 5 it is perfectly happy in Zone 2. Full sun. No care.

Ferns

This climate is a little dry for ferns. By far the most reliable and successful is the ostrich fern or fiddlehead fern (*Matteuccia struthiopteris*). This one multiplies fast and is very spectacular. Tall fronds will grow to 70 cm (28 in). All ferns must be in the shade. Other ferns worth a try in the right location are: Dryopteris filix-mas (male fern), Adiantum pedatum (maidenhair fern), Athyrium filix-femina (lady fern), Athyrium niponicum metallicum (Japanese painted fern). Ferns will grow under spruce trees if given plenty of water.

- *Filipendula rubra* 'Venusta'—Queen of the Prairie. 2.5 m (8 ft)
  Likes a boggy spot. Flowers look like pink candyfloss. Tall, stately plant. Needs no staking. Full sun.
- *Filipendula ulmaria*—Meadow Sweet. 1 m (3 ft)
  Coarsely divided leaves. Tall stems of small, creamy white flowers in clusters. Likes moist soil. Full sun or part shade. Very hardy.
- *Filipendula vulgaris*—Dropwort. 60 cm (24 in)
  Ferny leaves. Tall, loose clusters of tiny, white flowers. This one does not need as much water as other filipendulas. Long blooming and very hardy. Sun or part shade.

- *Geranium* x 'Brookside'—50 cm (20 in)
  A long blooming season. Clear blue flowers. Very hardy and reliable. Full sun.
- *Geranium cantabrigense*—'Biokovo.' 20 cm (8 in)
  Pretty light pink flowers. Blooms and blooms and blooms. Makes a good-hardy ground cover. Full sun to part shade. Does not set seed.
- *Geranium dalmaticum*—15 cm (6 in)
  Soft pink flowers crown this little plant. Quickly spreads to make a big patch. Very hardy but must have a well-drained site in full sun.
- *Geranium magnificum*—60 cm (24 in)
  A handsome plant that blooms for a long time from June through July. Bright blue-purple, large flowers. Leaves turn red in fall. Full sun.
- *Geranium sanguineum*—30–40 cm (12–16 in)
  Many named cultivars in an assortment of colours from this one. For example, 'Max Frei,' 'Appleblossom,' and 'Album.' All are very hardy.

These geranium hybrids (cranesbill) are sterile and will not grow from seed. Many cultivars and species are available from alpine types to taller bolder plants. Cranesbills will grow in sun or part shade, and are very drought-resistant and colourful. The ones mentioned here are the hardiest of them all.

- *Gypsophila paniculata*—Baby's Breath. 60 cm (24 in)
  Blooms in midsummer. Clouds of tiny, white flowers. Needs space and sun. Drought-resistant.
- *Heliopsis helianthoides*—False Sunflower. 1 m (3 ft)
  Double yellow flowers in July/August. Needs to be staked. Full sun.
- *Hemerocallis hybrids*—Daylily. 0.5–1 m (1.5–3 ft)
  Easy to grow. Requires lots of space, moist soil, good drainage. Yellow and peach varieties bloom profusely and grow fast. Fancy colours are slower to develop.
- *Heuchera sanguinea*— Coral Bells. 35 cm (14 in)
  Dainty red or pink flowers. Needs protection if no snow cover. Full sun or part shade.

- *Hosta hybrids*—Plantain Lily. 30–45 cm (12–18 in)
  Hostas struggle along here in the more exposed locations. They like the shade, and of course in the shade the ground does not thaw out very fast in the spring, giving hostas a slow start. Try planting hostas under a late-leafing deciduous tree or shrub so that the ground warms up faster and the leaves shade the hosta in the hot summer days. In a sheltered microclimate in the city they do better than in more rugged rural conditions.
- *Iris germanica (Rhizomatous)*—Bearded Iris. 46–91 cm (18–36 in)
  The old garden varieties are the hardiest. Search in local horticultural society sales or from a neighbour. The Intermediates (46–91 cm/18–36 in) are tougher than the taller ones. A well drained site is essential.

Iris germanica 'Wild Ginger.' The large-flowered iris needs perfect drainage.

- *Iris pumila (Rhizomatous)*—Dwarf Bearded Iris. 20–40 cm (8–16 in)
  Very hardy and multiply quickly. Many colours. In all the above
  types of iris the pink shades are least hardy.

Rhizomatous iris need a very well-drained site. They need dividing
every four to five years, three weeks after they finish blooming. Plant
the rhizomes at the surface. Full sun. Mulch of any sort that will bury
the rhizomes will make them rot. Use bone meal or granular fertilizer.

- *Iris sibirica*—Siberian Iris. 61–91 cm (24–36 in)
  This one has a fibrous root system and likes quite different conditions to the rhizomatous irises. They love moisture and need rich,
  deep soil. They should be divided every four to five years to keep
  them blooming prolifically. Provide surface mulch or compost an-
  nually. Flowers in shades of blue, purple, cream, and white. Tall,
  grassy leaves. Blooms in July. Full sun.
- Leucanthemum superbum—Shasta Daisy. 30 cm–1 m (12–39 in)
  Easily grown from seed. Tall, hardy plants providing showy white
  daisies midsummer through fall. Prefer rich heavy soil. Many varieties. Full sun.
- *Liatris spicata* 'Blazing Star.'— 1.2 m (4 ft)
  This is the old-fashioned one which soars happily to 1.2 m (4 ft)
  tall. Stiff spikes of bright pink. Slow to come up in spring so don't
  give up on it until June. It is very hardy, just slow to wake up. It
  blooms in August. Full sun.
- *Liatris spicata* 'Kobold.'—50 cm (20 in)
  A modern hybrid of more manageable size. Vivid pink. A white
  one, 'Floristan,' is also available. Full sun.
- *Ligularia dentata*—(a) L. dentata 'Othello.' 1 m (3 ft)
  (Great Leaved Golden Ray). Dark green leaves, reddish underside
  and stems. Sprays of orange daisies in August.
- *Ligularia dentata* 'Przewalskii.'— 1.5 m (5 ft)
  Tall, narrow spires of yellow flowers in July/August. Leaves are
  deeply divided.

Good planning and maintenance make this country garden special.

- *Ligularia stenocephala* 'The Rocket.'—1.5 m (5 ft)
  Very similar to 'Przewalskii' above; leaves are toothed but not so deeply cut as its cousin.

  Ligularias demand deep, rich, moist soil and partial shade.

- *Lilies*—See Lily article page 164.
- *Linum perenne*—Flax. 50 cm (20 in)
  Delightfully dainty plant which blooms in the mornings. Will self-seed, so cut after seeds form but before they ripen, if you don't want too many of them. Hates to be moved.
- *Lupin polyphyllus*—60 cm (24 in)
  Lupins do not like lime. They prefer heavy, acidic soil and do not transplant well when full grown. Tend to be short-lived but self-seed prolifically. Full sun. See Soils section on acidifying your soil.
- *Lychnis arkwrightii* 'Vesuvius'—45 cm (18 in)
  Leaves have a dark, chocolatey tone which sets off the shocking orange flowers.
- *Lychnis chalcedonica*—Maltese Cross. 1 m (3 ft)
  Clusters of star-shaped, bright red flowers in July/August. Hummingbird magnet. Full sun and lots of moisture.

- *Lychnis coronaria atrosanguinea*—Blood Campion. 55 cm (22 in) Silvery, hairy leaves. Contrasting blood-red flowers in midsummer. Full sun and poor soil preferred.
- *Lychnis viscaria*—German Catchfly. 45 cm (18 in) Very easy, showy, and hardy. Bright pink flowers have sticky stems under each flower, hence "Catchfly." Full sun.
- *Malva moschata*—Musk Mallow. 1 m (3 ft) Mallows are from the hollyhock family. They come in pink or white and are very hardy. Easy to grow in full sun.
- *Monarda didyma*—Bergamot or Bee Balm. 25 cm–1.5 m (10–59 in) Many varieties include red, pink, purple, or white varieties, and also some dwarf ones. They prefer full sun and lots of water.
- *Papaver nudicaule*—Iceland Poppy. 40 cm The Lake Louise poppy. Blooms all summer. Easily grown from seed planted directly in the ground. Hates to be moved.

Pink Oriental poppy.

- *Papaver orientale*—Oriental Poppy. 60–90 cm (24–35 in)
  Hairy leaves. Very large blooms in May/June. Shades of pink, plum, red, or white. Bees love them. Leaves die down by July. Plant with later perennials such as daylilies, liatris, or rudbeckia to fill the gap.
- *Peony*—Consult Index for separate article.
- *Phlox paniculata*—Tall Garden Phlox. 60–80 cm (24–31 in)
  Most modern varieties are mildew-resistant, which is a common problem with this plant. The old, white variety *P. carolinia* 'Miss Lingard' is still one of the best.

For short creeping phlox see the chapter on groundcovers.

- *Platycodon mariesii*—Balloon Flower. 30 cm (12 in)
  Blue flowers in early August. Buds are balloon-shaped. Full sun.
- *Polemonium caeruleum*—Jacob's Ladder. 60–80 cm (24–31 in)
  An easy perennial. Blooms in June/July. Blue or white. Sun or part shade. Cut back after it sets seed to prevent mildew.
- *Primula* species. The primula, listed below are completely hardy here. There are some for sun, others for shade, and some for boggy spots.

Sun Lovers	Shade Lovers	Bog Lovers (shade or sun if sufficient water)
P. auricula	P. alpicola	P. alpicola
P. cortusoides	P. elatior (oxlip)	P. chungensis
P. denticulata	P. luteola	P. florindae
P. marginata	P. pulverulenta	P. sikkimensis
	P. veris (cowslip)	

- *Pulmonaria longifolia* 'E.B. Anderson' or 'Cevennensis'—Lungwort 30 cm (12 in)
  Lance-shaped leaves, dark green, spotted. Flowers are blue.

- *Pulmonaria mollis*—Lungwort. 30 cm (12 in)
  P. angustifolia is very similar. Unspotted green leaves. Blooms as soon as the ground thaws. Eye-catching peacock blue. Extremely hardy but very subject to mildew later in summer. Trim back to the ground as soon as mildew appears.
- *Pulmonaria officinalis* 'Sissinghurst White'— 30 cm (12 in)
  Neatly spotted leaves and white flowers.
- *Pulmonaria rubra* 'David Ward'— 35 cm (14 in)
  Variegated leaves; light red flowers. Needs partial shade.

All pulmonaria will grow in sun or shade and are very hardy.

- *Rudbeckia laciniata* 'Gold Quelle.'—1–2 m (3–6 ft)
- *Rudbeckia laciniata* 'Golden Glow.'—2 m (6 ft)
  Tall yellow daisies that bloom in August. Full sun.
- *Rudbeckia occidentalis* 'Black Beauty.'—80 cm (31 in)
  Stunning black cones, ringed with yellow stamens. No petals. Blooms in August. Full sun.
- *Salvia nemorosa* 'May Night.'—50 cm (20 in)
  Very hardy. Deep blue spikes of flowers in midsummer. 'Blue Hills' light blue version of 'May Night.' Full sun.
- *Salvia verticillaris*—'Purple Rain.' 60 cm (24 in)
  Long loose panicles of soft purple flowers in June/July. Hummingbird magnet. Very hardy. Full sun.
- *Scabiosa caucasica* 'Fama'—Pincushion Flower 60 cm (24 in)
  Sun-loving plant with attractive light blue flowers in mid summer.
- *Scabiosa ochroleuca*—75 cm (30 in)
  Light yellow pincushion flowers for a long period in August/September. Self-seeds rampantly.

All scabiosa like full sun and alkaline soil. They also attract butterflies.

- *Sidalcea candida* 'Bianca.'—80 cm (31 in)

Sidalceas are from the hollyhock family. 'Bianca' is perennial in habit and a very useful, long-blooming, white addition to the perennial garden. Full sun.

- *Sidalcea malviflora* 'Party Girl,' 'Stark's Hybrids,' 'Sussex Beauty,' 'Little Princess'—Prairie Mallow 1.2 m (4 ft)
  These are various shades of pink or red. All sidalceas like full sun and lots of room to grow. 'Little Princess' is only 40 cm (16 in) tall.
- *Solidago hybrid* 'Crown of Rays,' 'Super'—Goldenrod 0.5–1 m (20–39 in)
  Goldenrod does not cause hay fever. The culprit is ragweed. Goldenrod is a useful, drought-tolerant plant which blooms in August and is totally hardy anywhere. Full sun. Some cultivars, such as 'Laurin,' bloom too late for our area.
- *Stachys macrantha (grandiflora)*—Big Betony. 40 cm (16 in)
  Striking large, pink flowers which resemble hyacinths. Very hardy. Blooms June/July. Drought-resistant. Full sun.
- *Stachys officinalis*—Wood Betony. 45 cm (18 in)
  Stiff stems bearing thumb-sized clusters of pink flowers on top of long, bare stems. July/August bloomer.
- *Thalictrum aquilegifolium*—Meadow Rue. 1.2 m (4 ft)
  Fluffy clouds of light purple flowers in early summer. Sun or partial shade.
- *Thalictrum flavum ssp. glaucum*—1.5 m (5 ft)
  Blue-green leaves and fluffy sprays of light yellow flowers. Sun or partial shade.
- *Trollius europeum (cultorum)*—Globeflower. 30–40 cm (12–16 in)
  These are the early blooming ones for May flowers. Large orange or yellow buttercup-like flowers. Prefer cool moist soil and some shade.
- *Trollius ledebourii (chinensis)*—Globeflower. 60 cm (24 in)
  These bloom in July and are taller with a tuft of narrow, upright petals in the centre of the bloom. Mostly yellow.
- *Valeriana officinalis*—Common Valerian or Garden Heliotrope. 2 m (6 ft)

Globeflower (Trollius cultorum).

Very tall and stately plant. Clusters of small, white flowers in Au-
gust. Sun or shade.
- *Veronica incana*—45 cm
  Grey, hairy leaves. Small spikes of contrasting blue flowers in Au-
  gust. There are many other veronicas worth a try, from groundcovers
  to taller varieties. All like full sun and will tolerate many soil types.
- *Veronica spicata*—Speedwell. 15–60 cm (6–24 in)
  Narrow, green leaves. Showy spikes with masses of tiny flowers.
  Many colours available in blue, white, or shades of crimson and
  pink.

Helpful Hints
❋ Nylon stockings or J-cloths make good ties for tall plants. Green yarn is
  good as well and is inconspicuous.

Biennials
By Anne Vale

Plants that take two seasons to complete their growing cycle are called biennials. They die after blooming and producing seed. However, as they self-seed they can continue to bloom year after year. All biennials stay green over the winter and should be protected as described under perennials. Biennials commonly grown in our area are as follows:

Hollyhocks thrive in full sun at Nanton.

- *Alcea rosea*—Hollyhocks, 2 m (6 ft)
  Plant in sunny, sheltered spot. Doesn't like wind. Summer blooming. Needs staking. Old-fashioned single kind is hardiest; the hybrid doubles not always surviving the winter without adequate protection. Colours: red, white, pink, and yellow. A shorter annual kind can be started in March indoors and will bloom the first year.
- *Campanula calycanthema*—Canterbury Bells, 0.6 m (2 ft)
  Can be grown from seed. During the first summer will grow as green plants. Will bloom second year and reseed themselves. Colours range from blue and pink to white.
- *Dianthus barbatus*—Sweet William, 76 cm (30 in)
  Likes a sunny spot. Loves lime. Blooms in early summer. Must be covered for winter. Sprinkle wood ashes around plants.
- *Hesperis matronalis*—Sweet Rocket, 76 cm (30 in)
  Grows all over Christendom. Purple, strongly perfumed flowers.
- *Myosotis*—Forget-Me-Nots, 20 cm (8 in).
  Blue blooms in early June at the same time as tulips.
- *Viola tricolor*
  Prolific. Small variety called Johnny Jump-up. Can become a nuisance—will grow anywhere.

Helpful Hints

❧ To keep a supply of biennials such as Canterbury bells, hollyhocks, pansies, etc. leave some blooms to go to seed. The following spring you will find seedlings around the old mother plant. Transplant as many as you need and hoe out the rest or they will take over your garden.

Hardy Ornamental Grasses
by Deb Francis

This group of plants performs spectacularly well in the Chinook Zone. Tolerant of the short season and cool nights, named varieties grow as vigorously as in more favourable climates.

Grasses are growing in popularity as gardeners have experimented and realized the diverse ways this group can enhance their gardens. Requiring minimal care, they will reward the grower with a year-round interesting display. Ornamental grasses provide texture and form, and easily fit into any landscape design. Large or small, there is always a place where they will just "fit" and look good. Another bonus is that there are no fussy soil requirements, as they need only average garden soil and adequate drainage. A few ideas that have worked well are shared here.

Ornamental grasses fit well in a late-blooming bed with achillea and Joe Pye weed.

Ornamental grasses mix well in the perennial garden. An example is the blue oat grass (*Helictotrichon sempervirens*) which, when placed near a silvery artemesia or sea holly, creates an outstanding group. A wavy design of blue fescues (*Festuca glauca*) can be made to emulate a stream bed, or a clump of blue fescues simulates a pool of blue. At the back of the border a hedge of stately 'Karl Foerster' (*Calamagrostis x acutiflora*) provides a dramatic background.

Besides the mannerly, clump-forming ornamentals, make room for the invasive grasses. Do not be put off by the description "invasive." These have their uses in garden creation. An example of an invasive ornamental is blue lyme grass (*Elymus arenarius*). Spreading quickly with an extensive root system, it has turquoise leaves. On a large property it could be used as a massed planting. Planted, for example, between the landscaped grounds and wild untouched native areas, it draws the eye to a sea of blue. Another use for invasive grasses with their spreading roots is soil binding on slopes and difficult terrain, thus controlling erosion.

'Skinners Golden' brome grass creates its own patch of sunshine.

Remember, for invasive mass planting, that even difficult sites require soil preparation. All existing grasses or plants must be eliminated. Do not expect all invasive grasses to take over totally. A quick, fail-safe method is to place red or black plastic sheeting over the area to be prepared. Start in early spring and leave the plastic on for several months until unwanted vegetation is fried. By August or the following spring plant the ornamental grass. Plant close together to decrease the chance of weed infestation. Small roots and shoots of these grasses are ideal for this method. Water well the first season and remove weeds immediately.

Calamagrostis x acutiflora 'Karl Foerster' stays upright all winter and combines well with late-season perennials.

Mulching or landscape fabric is not recommended, as this will retard the rapid growth and soil coverage.

Unless otherwise listed, all named varieties prefer full sun, and after the first year when they have become established, moisture that falls from the sky is adequate.

As most ornamental grasses remain interesting to look at year round, they can be left almost unattended until spring. A trim may be in order in late July for some cool-season grasses. In spring the fescues should be sheared 8–10 cm (3–4 in) from the ground. Fescues should also be divided after two to three years when the centre starts to hollow out. Blue oat grass needs combing! This is easily done with gloved hands, running them through the plant. The old, dead foliage is combed out and a fresh plant is ready for the season. The tall feather reed grass (*Calamagrostis*) needs cutting down to 20–25 cm (8–10 in). An efficient way to chop this monster down neatly is to bind the clump with twine firmly in its middle, then use a weed wacker, shears, or hedge trimmer to cut the base. The result is a tidy stack, as opposed to a myriad of grass stalks left to be picked up. All other ornamental grasses can be cut down in early spring. Save the tall stems for use in dried arrangements.

The terms "cool-season" and "warm-season" are used to describe grasses. These terms simply refer to the growing pattern. The cool-season grasses grow well in the cooler spring weather, but sulk or remain static in the heat of the summer. Warm-season grasses are slow to start in the cool spring and then race ahead in the heat of summer.

Blue Oat grass with Scabiosa caucasica 'Fama' in a hot, sunny location.

The following ornamental grasses have performed well in the Chinook Zone.

Name	Description	Height	Width
Arrhenatherum elatius spp. bulbosum *(Bulbous Oat grass)	Not invasive. White and green striped leaves. Likes dry summers and cool nights. Full sun or part shade.	30 cm (12 in)	30 cm (12 in)
Bromus inermis (Brome grass) Named variety: 'Skinner's Gold'	Spreading habit (cool season, so can be cut back in early summer). Golden/green variegated blades.	61 cm (24 in)	-
Calamagrostis x acutiflora *(Feather Reed grass) Named Varieties: 'Karl Foerster' 'Overdam' (variegated)	Tall; clump-forming. Does not require staking. Pinkish seed heads in summer.	2 m (6 ft)	0.6 m (2 ft)
Elymus arenarius *(Blue Lyme Grass)	Extremely invasive spreading habit. Great for erosion control. Blue-grey, sharp steel blades. Bluish-green flower spike rising above leaves. Will overwinter in a large planter.	5–7 cm (2–2.5 in)	-
Festuca glauca (Blue Fescue) Named varieties: 'Azurit,' 'Blue Fox,' 'Elijah Blue,' 'Pepindale Blue,' 'Sea Urchin'	Clump-forming. Seed heads on stalks in summer.	30–46 cm (12–18 in)	30–40 cm (12–16 in)
Helictotrichon sempervirens (Blue Oat grass) Named variety: 'Sapphire'	Clump-forming. Tan-coloured seed heads.	1m (3 ft)	60 cm (24 in)
Koeleria glauca (Blue Hair grass)	Early cool-season grass. Clump-forming. Neat, tidy, upright little grass, with light brown, narrow, erect seed heads.	0.6 m (2 ft)	-
Phalaris arundinacea var. picta (Ribbon Grass) Named variety: Feesey's form	Invasive spreading habit. Variegated green and white leaf. Cool-season grass, so can be cut back in early summer.	1 m (3–4 ft)	-

* Suitable for dried arrangements.

A meadow of native grasses with a mowed pathway glows in the evening light.

Native Grasses in the Landscape
By Beryl West

I have often mused how wonderful it would be to live surrounded by a vast sea of native prairie. How extraordinary a sight it must have been for those first travellers from the east: hundreds of miles of grassland interwoven with flowers. A little bit like this evening, perhaps. On my way home from the Homestead gardens I came across a quarter section of native prairie where the crocuses are just beginning to bloom through the grass. Heaven.

There is much being said these days about the use of various grasses in the landscape, whether it is for one's garden beds, as meadows, or as an alternative to the traditional lawn. I believe all grasses and grass-like plants to be worthy of introduction, and given our present concerns with water consumption, the amount of available time on our hands, and the quantities of chemicals used in the upkeep of the traditional lawn, native grass species offer an extremely viable addition to our plant lists.

The natives are already extremely well adapted to our soils, the crazy chinook weather patterns, the available moisture levels or lack thereof, and, more often than not, less than ideal growing conditions. There are grasses for every type of environment: alkaline sloughs; dry, sun-baked disturbed slopes; open grasslands; aspen woods. Some are clump-forming, while others are rampant spreaders with strong rhizomatous root systems. Half green up as soon as the daytime temperatures rise above freezing, while the other half wait until summer is definitely here before showing any signs of green at all. The choices are many and varied.

SITE PREPARATION

If one is planting native grass in the border, one only need marry the border conditions with the requirements of the grass, keeping in mind that the majority of the natives will thrive in less than ideal conditions in terms of soil and moisture. Larger specimens are now becoming more widely available, allowing them to be planted much like a perennial. Care must be taken to select a grass that will not become invasive either through seed or root.

If one is intending to create a meadow and/or lawn, site preparation is the most crucial component. Native species are ill equipped to compete with our introduced grasses such as Kentucky bluegrass, quack, and brome grasses. The site must be as clean as possible of invasive grasses and weeds.

From experience I have learned that eighteen months or more is required to prep the site. Patience is indeed well rewarded here. At this point I feel I must say that, although I find it very difficult to recommend to fellow gardeners the use of herbicides in the garden, one of the ways to clear the site is to apply a non-selective herbicide that will not persist in the soil late in the summer while the grass is still actively growing. Come the following spring, it will be easy to see which areas one missed or where the herbicide did not take. Apply the herbicide to these areas again and wait.

At this stage one has several options: The area can be cultivated or left as dead sod. A word of caution at this point. Cultivation will bring to the surface the seed bank resident in the soil, whether it is desirable or not. If you decide to cultivate, water the area after cultivation to promote new growth, which again will be treated with herbicide. Continue on this pattern until the ground is clean and well tilled.

If by this time it is fall, one can wait to seed until the spring or seed now. There are several advantages to fall seeding, I think, particularly if you live on an acreage and are converting a large area to native grass. The ground is drier in the fall, making it easier to work. With our moisture arriving naturally over the course of the winter and into the spring, a lot of water and time spent watering could be saved. After seeding, the ground must be rolled twice at right angles to each other to ensure soil/seed contact. If one decides to leave the sod, a thin layer of topsoil (2.5–5 cm/1–2 in) is spread over the area, which then becomes the seed bed.

If one is looking to prep an area without using herbicides there are several options, but one must keep in mind that you might not achieve a kill of one hundred per cent. This is due primarily to invasive root systems, and so the total area to be seeded/planted to native may have to take place over a longer span of time. One method is to cover the area with old carpets turned upside down, which, over the course of one growing season, will kill the plants under it. Then the sod layer could be stripped, cultivated, or covered with soil. One could also use black plastic. This summer, I am experimenting with a thick layer of newspapers, dampened and then covered with soil or sand. The advantage of both the carpet and the newspaper/soil method is that the wind will not carry them away.

After seeding, the area must be kept moist until the majority of seeds have germinated. Gradually decrease the watering. It is most important during the first season to have the natives become well established, keeping in mind that the majority of their growth is below the surface (⅓ above, ⅔ below). Annual weeds will no doubt appear; however, by mowing off the flower heads before they go to seed, by the second and third seasons, the grass will take over. As for perennial weeds, weeding by hand, deadheading, or the selective use of a herbicide will be necessary.

In addition to seeding, grass plugs are also an option, as they are relatively inexpensive, cover a large area, and will give you something to look at while the rest is starting to grow. Native wildflower seeds can also be added to the seed/plug mixture. The Alberta Native Plant Council publishes a source list of seed and/or plant suppliers. Their address is Garneau P.O. 52099, Edmonton, AB T6G 2T5; www.anpc.ab.ca; email: info@anpc.ab.ca.

QUALITIES

Natives possess the characteristics of all grasses. In terms of form and texture, they add a very different quality to the garden with their fine textures and loose form. This in turn allows the gardener to play with the infinite combinations and contrasts possible using the elements of stone, water, plants, structures, and various objects. Grasses add the dimension of movement and sound. The slightest breeze will cause a stirring and rustling. And then there is the quality of the light. Ephemeral. Glistening. Sparkling. Translucent. Glowing. Nothing really compares.

THE GRASSES THEMSELVES

Short Grass (ankle height)

- *Buchloe dactyloides*—Buffalo Grass. Warm season; sod-forming, spreads by runners on surface; foliage grey-green, fine textured, 10 cm (4 in); flowers July–Sept; full sun; well-drained soil; tolerant of extreme heat and drought; greens up late June–early July; new cultivars developing in the U.S. for lawn use; early spring bulbs look great with this grass.
- *Bouteloua gracilis*—Blue Grama Grass. Warm season; clump-forming; foliage light green, fine textured, 15–20 cm (6–8 in); flowers June–Sept; also known as mosquito grass, referring to the seed

heads; full sun, extremely drought-tolerant; very useful as a short lawn that is not mowed.

Mixed Grass (knee height)

- *Beckmannia syzigachne*—Slough Grass. Cool season; upright, clump-forming; green foliage, medium textured, 30–40 cm (12–16 in); flowers June–July; seed heads resemble stacks of plates, unusual and interesting; prefers moist soils, e.g., streams, ditches, shallow marshes.
- *Deschampsia caespitosa*—Tufted Hair Grass. Cool season; mounded, clump-forming; foliage dark green, fine textured, 30–60 cm (12–24 in); flowers May–July to 90 cm (35 in); moist, fertile soil; full sun to light shade; tolerates dry conditions; magnificent in flower but will self-seed everywhere, so weed in early spring.
- *Festuca idahoensis*—Idaho fescue. Cool season; vase-shaped clump-forming; foliage fine blue/blue-green, 20 cm (8 in); flowers May–June; average to poor soil; full sun, drought tolerant, avoid moist soil; a tiny, perfect grass of intense colour; good in the alpine garden or anywhere it can be readily seen.
- *Festuca campestris*—Foothills Rough Fescue (Alberta's provincial grass). Cool season; densely tufted mounds forming large tussocks to 50 cm (20 in); foliage grey to blue-green, sheaths purplish at base; flowers June–July; full sun to part shade; found on montane slopes; a dominant species of the foothills fescue grassland.
- *Festuca ovina*—Sheep's Fescue. Cool season; tufted bunch-grass with blue-green spiked leaves, 20 cm (8 in); flowers May–June; full sun to partial shade; very easy to establish; the softest grass you will ever lie in!
- *Hierochloe odorata*—Sweet Grass. Cool season; sod-forming rhizomatous grass; fresh green foliage, 20 cm (8 in); flowers May–June; full sun to partial shade; appreciates moisture; from the Greek *hieros*, sacred, and *chloe*, grass, also known as holy grass;

Little Bluestem (Andropogon scorparius) *with colour-coordinated friend.*

scent is very evident where it grows and stays with the plant for
years after it has been dried; the first grass to flower.

- *Koeleria cristata/macrantha/pyramidata*—June Grass. Cool season;
  upright clump-forming; foliage light green, almost glaucous, finely textured, somewhat succulent to the touch, 30 cm (12 in); flowers mid-June; full sun, well drained soil; a delightful addition to a
  low- to medium-height lawn when in flower.
- *Nassella viridula (a.k.a. Stipa viridula)*—Green Needle Grass. Cool
  season; upright, clump-forming; foliage green, finely textured, 40
  cm (16 in); flowers June reaching 1 m (3 ft); full sun to partial
  shade; drought-tolerant, tough and resilient; self-seeds readily;
  looks brilliant in a meadow or in the border.
- *Oryzopsis hymenoides*—Indian Rice Grass. Warm season; upright,
  clump-forming; foliage grey-green, finely textured to 50 cm (20
  in); flowers August–September; full sun, found on dry, exposed,
  eroded slopes; drought-tolerant; from *oruza,* rice, and *opsis,* a suf-

fix meaning "like," referring to the seeds; a beautiful container plant because of the cloud of seed heads.

- *Pascopyron smithii (a.k.a. Agropyron smithii)*—Western Wheat Grass. Cool season; strong upright spreader with extensive rhizomes, 45–65 cm (18–26 in); foliage steel blue, medium texture to 40 cm (16 in); flowers June–July; full sun; common in grasslands, especially in low-lying areas and heavy alkali soils; a reclamation species; a slow, steady spreader in the meadow with that intense blue hue.
- *Schizachyrium scoparium*—Little Bluestem. Warm season; upright clump-forming; foliage green with reddish stalks, fine textured, 40–50 cm (16–20 in); flowers July–Sept; full sun to light shade; appreciates moist, fertile soil; tough and hardy; puts on a brilliant display of colour in the fall.
- *Spartina gracilis*—Alkali Cord Grass. Cool season; sod-forming rhizomatous grass; foliage spring-green lying in graceful woven mounds to 70 cm (28 in); full sun; excellent for riverbanks, ditches, and low areas.

Tall Grass (waist height)

- *Andropogon gerardii*—Big Bluestem. Warm season; sod-forming; foliage blue-green with reddish-mauve stalks, fine to medium textured, 100–200 cm (39–79 in); flowers August–September with a three-pronged seed head, hence the name "turkey tracks"; moist, fertile soil; full sun, part shade; drought-tolerant once established, long-lived and showy; I find it to be at the edge of its natural habitat and thus not as robust.

Native grass Big Bluestem (Andropogon gerardii) shows off its "turkey-track" seed heads.

- *Calamovilfa longifolia*—Prairie Sand Reed/Sand Grass. Warm season; sod-forming, strongly rhizomatous; foliage spreading, thick, firm, and persistent, light green to 50 cm (20 in); flowers August–September to 100 cm (39 in); full sun, sandy soil; good reclamation species; brilliant used in a meadow (requires a large area); seed heads hold up over winter months.
- *Elymus canadensis*—Canada Wild Rye. Cool season; vase-shaped clump-forming; foliage coarse in texture, to 120 cm (47 in); flowers August–September; very ornamental seed heads with long awns and threads off each seed; full sun to partial shade; found along edges of woodlands, as well as open areas.
- *Glyceria grandis*—Tall Manna Grass. Cool season; strongly rhizomatous; foliage green, tinged yellow, medium texture to 150 cm (59 in); flowers July–August reaching 200 cm (79 in); very ornamental; full sun, moist, fertile soil; found along streams, on shores, in wet meadows.
- *Panicum virgatum*—Switch Grass. Warm season; sod-forming, slow spreader; foliage green, medium textured to 150 cm (59 in); flowers late summer to frost, reaching 200 cm (79 in); moist, fertile soil; full sun; adaptable to a wide range of soil conditions; I have found this to be another grass at the edge of its range, and due to our sometimes short summers, it will not have time to flower.
- *Phalaris arundinacea*—Reed Canary Grass. Cool season; rhizomatous; foliage light green to 60 cm (24 in); flowers June–August reaching 100 cm (39 in); a wetland species.

A new young rockery showing soil covered by 10 cm (4 in) of washed pea-gravel.

Rockeries
By Anne Vale

There is no getting away from it: Rockeries are a lot of work. Why have a rockery? One reason is that it is a great way to tier a sloping garden or make good use of a natural contour. Another is to provide a setting for alpine plants that require a well-drained situation. Rockeries need not necessarily be on a bank but can equally well be laid out like an alpine meadow provided you have really well-drained soil that never collects puddles.

The rockery should be situated in the open, away from interfering tree roots. A shallow, north-facing bank that gets oblique sun in summer but does not lose its snow in winter is ideal. East-facing is the next best location. If facing due south on a slope that is at right angles to the midday sun, you will find that it bares off and dries out too quickly in winter and you will lose a lot of valuable plants.

Nature's rockery.

A flat rock in the mountains designs its own rock garden.

Big rocks store heat and water.

A south-facing rockery needs big rocks to keep the soil cool and damp.

The very first thing you have to do is make a plan on paper. Pace off the area you are going to develop and try to draw it to scale on paper. Plan your plantings. Take a picnic up in the mountains and study how wild plants trail over rocks and fill crevices. With both types of rockeries, remember to provide steps or pathways so that you have easy access to tend your plants.

The site should be prepared very carefully, since once your rocks and plants are in place it is very hard to get at the soil underneath to correct any problems. It does not get dug and manured at regular intervals like other flower beds and the soil must last the plants for the lifetime of the rockery. You should start by deeply digging the site. If quack grass is anywhere in the vicinity, you must clean it all out with the use of a systemic weed-killer that will not contaminate the soil. You must also provide a physical barrier to prevent it creeping back in again. Do not add manure or fertilizer to your soil. Alpines thrive on poor soil and will grow too big and coarse on rich soil.

Choose your rocks carefully. They should be large and porous with a flat surface. Field stones are not too good, as they are round, slippery, and non-porous. If you can find some sandstone with attractive lichen already growing on it, so much the better. Remember that smaller porous rocks tend to be split by frost and will disintegrate.

ROCKERY ON A SLOPE

Set the rocks well into the soil with their flat surface uppermost, sloping them backwards so that any rainwater falling on them will drain off back into the slope, instead of cascading off and taking valuable topsoil along with it. Only about one-third of the rock should be visible. Pockets of soil between the rocks should extend at least 30–46 cm (12–18 in) back into the bank, providing a cool root run for the alpine plants. The rocks will hold warmth and moisture deep in the soil and insulate the plants from sudden changes of temperature. Avoid setting the rocks on end, which tends to give a "jaws" or "tombstone" impression, and looks most unnatural.

ALPINE MEADOW ROCKERY

Make sure your soil is really well drained, and construct a rolling contoured effect with low, broad mounds of soil, large doghouse-sized rocks, and a few shrubs. Use only very large rocks for focal points and flat rocks or gravel for pathways. Carpet-

Hen and Chicks are happy in a rock crevice.

ing plants or ground covers (See section on Ground Cover) may be used instead of grass in low-lying areas to connect mounds planted with alpines. This plan should provide a suitable environment for many plant preferences.

When all the rocks are securely positioned, the weeds have been controlled, and the whole thing has settled over the winter, you are ready to begin planting. Try to make your rockery look as natural as possible. Use a variety of plants and do not regiment them in rows. Determine their ultimate expected spread and height. Plan blooming times so that

Woolly thyme flows over sandstone rocks like a waterfall.

there is always a point of interest in your rockery. Use dwarf shrubs and junipers for height and texture variation and evergreen effect. Do not neglect the smaller bulbs for spring colour. Low annuals are useful for filling gaps and providing bold splashes of bright colour. Stay away from any plant that will be too invasive and take over the whole thing. Provide coarse limestone grit (available from a feed store) for those plants that prefer alkaline conditions and dry surfaces. If you have sloped your rocks correctly, your rockery should store sufficient water from the annual rainfall and snowmelt, but in times of severe drought you may water it deeply but gently. The rocks will act as a reservoir.

A white pasqueflower (Pulsatilla vulgaris alba) in early spring.

You may try any hardy plant that is short and likes well-drained conditions. I recommend a visit to the Calgary Zoo Botanical Garden or the University of Alberta Devonian Garden at Devon, Alberta to study a well-built and planted rockery on a grand scale. The following list recommends some easily grown and readily obtainable plants. There are many others with which the keen gardener may experiment.

Suggestions for Rock Garden Plants

Perennials	Perennials	Perennials	Perennials
Alyssum montanum	Bergenia cordifolia	Gentiana paradoxa	Pulsatilla vulgaris (Pasqueflower)
Alyssum sulphureum	Campanula carpatica	Geranium dalmaticum	Saponaria (Soapwort)
Arabis caucasica (Snow Carpet or Compinkie)	Dianthus (many varieties)	Iris germanica, pumila	Saxifrage
Artemesia schmidtiana (Silver Mound)	Dodecatheon (Shooting Star)	Leontopodium (Edelweiss)	Sedum (Stonecrop— many kinds except Sedum acre)
Aster alpinus	Festuca glauca (Blue Fescue)	Phlox (Creeping varieties)	Sempervivum (Hen and Chicks)
Aubretia (Purple Rock Cress)	Gentiana acaulis	Pulsatilla patens (Prairie Crocus)	Thyme
			Veronica prostrata
Bulbs	Shrubs	Not Recommended (too invasive)	
Allium (any short variety)	Dwarf conifers	Aegopodium podograria (Goutweed)	
Chionodoxa (Glory of the Snow)	Potentilla	Cerastium tomentosum (Snow-in-summer)	
Iris reticulata, danfordiae	Spirea froebelii 'Gold Mound'	Sedum acre (Yellow Stonecrop)	
Scilla siberica			
Tulip—dwarf varieties and species tulips			

Lily of the Valley
carpets the shady, dry area
under evergreens.

Ground Covers
by Anne Vale

Ground cover is a term used to describe any plant, including grass, that will spread to form a solid mat over the ground.

They are useful where mowing is difficult, such as on a steep bank, under a tree, or around a rock. They can also be used in bold, sweeping patches to reduce the amount of mowing necessary or to fill in an awkward space. They may be combined with larger plants, boulders, or driftwood as a focal point. Once established they require minimum care and can be an attractive addition to your landscape.

It is very important to prepare the site properly. The ground should be cultivated, raked smooth, and cleaned of all weeds. It is best to first prepare the area intended for ground cover plants and let it lie fallow the first year so that you may control any weeds with a systemic weed killer of a type that will not persist in the soil. Covering the site with a firmly anchored sheet of black plastic in the summer months will also eliminate weeds without using chemicals.

If your ground cover area borders a lawn it will be necessary to provide a barrier to prevent the grass roots creeping into the ground cover or vice versa. A border of 5 x 15 cm (2 x 6 in) treated lumber set on edge flush with the ground will do the job. Various types of edging are on the market today. We recommend the 15 cm (6 in) width. The appearance of these may be disguised with the clever use of rocks or bricks.

Ground cover plants will not win the battle with existing weeds, but given a clean bed and good well-prepared soil they will grow so closely together that after the first couple of years no new weed will be able to get a foothold. Therefore it is most important to start with clean soil and keep it weeded until your young ground cover plants have become firmly established. Please bear in mind that in disturbing the soil, dormant weed seeds will be brought to the surface and may germinate.

Suitable plants vary from shrubby material such as juniper, kinnikinnick, or clematis to succulents like hen and chicks or stonecrop or even strawberries. Some spread further and faster than others, and you

Thyme makes a great ground cover for sunny spots. It loves the heat from the rocks.

should determine their mature spread and plant them a little closer than their ultimate expected spread, so that they mesh closely together and form a dense mat. Stonecrop will spread a long way in one year, and so will goutweed, but others which are very attractive as ground covers are not so invasive and will need closer planting to be effective within two years. To cover a large area with bought plants can be very expensive, but a lot can be accomplished with seed, or by starting your own slips in a nursery bed the first year while you are waiting for your ground to be free of weeds.

Most of the ground cover plants will not like being walked on but you can solve the problem by the clever use of stepping stones to make a path, or with a prickly bush to stop people from cutting a corner.

Some of the ground covers that will survive light traffic are creeping thymes, potentillas, veronicas, Irish moss, and pussytoes.

There are plants to suit a wide variety of situations in the sun or shade, light or heavy soils, dry or damp locations.

PERENNIAL GROUND COVERS

Key to Propagation below: C—cuttings; D—division; L—layering; S—seed.
Key to Soil Types below: 1—sandy, well drained; 2—heavy, moist; 3—any well drained.

Plant	Propagation	Soil Type	Sun or Shade	Space Apart
Aegopodium podograria (Goutweed or Snow-on-the-Mountain). Variegated green/white leaves, lacy white flowers. Very invasive.	D	2	Shade	46 cm (18 in)

Plant	Propagation	Soil Type	Sun or Shade	Space Apart
Ajuga reptans (Bugleweed). Shiny leaves either green or bronze, blue flowers	C, D	2	Shade	15–30 cm 6–12 in
Anemone sylvestris (Snow-drop Anemone). Beautiful big white flowers in early summer. Extremely invasive.	D	3	Either	25 cm (10 in)
Arctostaphylos uva-ursi (Kinnikinnick). Leathery, dark, shiny, small evergreen leaves; insignificant white flowers; red berries and red leaves in fall.	L, C	3	Either	30 cm (12 in)
Artemisia frigida (Pasture Sage). Aromatic silver filigree leaves. Very durable.	D	1	Sun	20 cm (8 in)
Asarum canadense or europeum (Wild Ginger). Heart-shaped leaves.	D	2	Shade	30 cm (12 in)
Cerastium tomentosum (Snow-in-Summer). Grey-leaved spreading plant with white flowers in midsummer.	S, D	3	Sun	46 cm (18 in)
Convallaria majalis (Lily of the Valley). Broad green leaves. Fragrant white flowers in May/June. Will grow under evergreens.	D	2	Shade	46 cm (18 in)
Cornus canadensis (Bunchberry). Leaves turn red in fall; white dogwood flowers. Floral emblem of B.C. Red berries in fall. Will grow under spruce trees.	D	3	Shade	30 cm (12 in)
Dianthus deltoides (Maiden Pinks). Creeping mat of dark green leaves. Red or pink flowers in June. (Many other dianthus species make good ground covers.)	S, D	1	Sun	30 cm (12 in)
Epimedium rubrum (Barrenwort). Stiff, papery leaves turn red in fall. Red flowers.	D	3	Shade	30 cm (12 in)

Plant	Propagation	Soil Type	Sun or Shade	Space Apart
Festuca glauca (Blue Fescue). Tufts of fine blue fescue grass.	D	3	Sun	20 cm (8 in)
Fragraria 'Pink Panda' (Strawberry). Carpet of strawberry leaves, turning red in fall. Pink flowers and small edible fruit.	C	3	Sun	30 cm (12 in)
Gallium odoratum (Sweet woodruff). Whorls of pointed leaves. White flowers.	D	2	Shade	30 cm (12 in)
Geranium (Cranesbill) himalayense; cantabrigense, maccorhizum, sanguinium, dalmaticum. These species come in many cultivated varieties and will spread quickly.	C, D	3	Either	30–46 cm (12–18 in)
Juniperus horizontalis (Spreading Juniper). Many hardy cultivars are available in varying textures and colours.	C, L	3	Either	1 m (3–4 ft)
Lamiastrum galeobdolon (False Lamium) Yellow flowers in May; green/silver leaves. Can become invasive.	C, D	2	Shade	30 cm (12 in)
Lamium maculatum (Dead Nettle). Green/silver variegated foliage. 'Beacon Silver' and 'Chequers' produce pink flowers in May.	C, D	2	Shade	30 cm (12 in)
Lysimachia nummularia (Creeping Jenny). Buttercup-like flowers in June/July. Quickly forms creeping mat. Can become invasive.	S, L	2	Sun	46 cm (18 in)
Persicaria bistorta 'Dimity' (Fleece Flower). Shiny evergreen leaves. Pink, candle-like flowers.	C, D	3	Sun	30 cm (12 in)
Phlox borealis (Arctic Phlox)	C, D	3	Sun	30 cm (12 in)
Phlox douglasii	C, D	3	Sun	30 cm (12 in)

Plant	Propagation	Soil Type	Sun or Shade	Space Apart
Phlox subulata (Moss Phlox). All of the above phlox form mounds and are covered with starry little flowers in shades of pink and purple. Leaves are unattractive in winter.	C, D	3	Sun	30 cm (12 in)
Polemonium caeruleum (Jacob's Ladder). Will grow under spruce trees.	S	3	Sun/Shade	20 cm (8 in)
Sagina subulata (Irish Moss). Mossy plant with tiny, white flowers.	C, D	2	Shade	30 cm (12 in)
Sedum acre (Yellow Stonecrop). Small, fleshy leaves and yellow flowers in midsummer. Forms a low, close-knit mat. Very invasive.	D, S	3	Sun	30 cm (12 in)
Sedum hybridum. Yellow flowers; red/orange seed heads. Forms a carpet quickly.	C	3	Sun	30 cm (12 in)
Sedum kamtschaticum (Kamtschatica Stonecrop). Green or variegated leaves. Orange/yellow flowers in midsummer.	C, D	3	Sun	30 cm (12 in)
Sedum reflexum (Reflexed Stonecrop). Recurved fleshy leaves resemble spruce needles. Forms dense mat very fast. Yellow flowers in August.	C, D	3	Sun	30 cm (12 in)
Sedum spurium ('Dragon's Blood,' 'Bronze Carpet,' or 'Fuldaglut'). Bronze leaves, pink blooms in midsummer. Very hardy.	C, D	3	Sun	30 cm (12 in)
Sempervivum (Hen and Chicks). Fleshy-leaved succulent. Very hardy. Bronze or green leaves; occasional tall blooms are produced.	D	3	Sun	20 cm (8 in)

Plant	Propagation	Soil Type	Sun or Shade	Space Apart
Thymus lanuginosa (Woolly Thyme). Woolly grey leaves form tight, low mat. Dull purple flowers.	C, D	3	Sun	30 cm (12 in)
Thymus praecox (Creeping Thyme). Very flat growing. Ideal between paving stones.	C, D	3	Sun	30 cm (12 in)
Thymus serphyllum (Mother of Thyme). Heat-loving, creeping plants. Purple blooms in July.	S, C	3	Sun	30 cm (12 in)
Veronica whitleyi (Whitely's Veronica). Creeping habit. Masses of small blue flowers with white eye in early summer.	D	3	Sun	30 cm (12 in)
Vinca minor (Periwinkle). Long, trailing stem, almost evergreen. Blue flowers.	C, D	2	Shade	30 cm (12 in)

Peonies
by Theresa Patterson

Peonies have been favourite perennials in gardens for hundreds of years. They originated in China and Japan. They are among the most beautiful, reliable, and long-lived plants that you can grow. In bloom they are magnificent but even after blooming the lush green foliage is lovely. They are available in pots or dry rooted in garden centres almost everywhere in the spring.

If you have to move an established peony, do it in late August or September when the plants are dormant. They have large, tuberous-like roots and resent being moved from place to place. They come in a variety of types and colours.

The singles have one or more rows of true petals and a centre of bright yellow or white stamens.

The Japanese peonies have five or more outer guard petals and a centre of stamens that do not produce pollen. They come in early to mid-season in lovely shades of pink, white, and a cerise pink (P. Gay Paree).

Single Japanesse peony 'Romance.'

Peony lactiflora are the familiar heirloom and old-fashioned varieties. They include the big doubles and bomb types. The blooms are fully double with stamens seldom visible. The most common are white, pink, or red. A true yellow has been developed (P. Goldmine). They are very rare and expensive so far.

Peony 'Festiva Maxima' is very fragrant.

The bomb types have distinct outer petals surrounding a pompon tuft of dense petals. Flowers are large and full.

The fern-leaf peony is one of the earliest peonies. It is very expensive but worth it. It is hardy with red flowers held close to its finely divided ferny foliage about 35 cm (14 in) high.

The tree peonies are not really herbaceous perennials, as they only bloom on old wood like a shrub. They require a sheltered location and some winter cover to be successful in this area. It may take several years of

Fern-leaf Peony, P. tenuifolia plena.

careful attention to coax them into bloom. These, too, are expensive but worth a try.

Peonies like a sunny, well-drained location, preferably on the level, as they need to have their crowns about 2.5–3 cm (1 in) below ground level, and this depth is hard to maintain on a slope. Find out the mature size of the peonies and allow them enough room to develop to their full potential. They need good air circulation to help keep them disease-free. They can tolerate partial shade but need several hours of full sun each day.

Peonies are not fussy about soil as long as it is well drained, but of course they do best in fertile soil. They dislike competition from tree roots. They can live in the same place for many years without division, so be kind to them and give them a good start.

Dig a hole big enough to accommodate the root system, 30–60 cm (12–24 in) wide and deep. Add bone meal, well-rotted compost, and alfalfa pellets. Plant your peony in the hole positioning the eyes 2.5–3 cm (1 in) below the soil surface—no more or they will not bloom. Fill the hole, firm the soil, and water thoroughly. At no time use fresh manure. Some winter protection the first year is advisable. Remove the cover carefully in the spring before active growth occurs. Do not over-fertilize. Peonies can live for years without much help. Deep watering in times of drought is necessary for good blooms.

In the fall cut back the tops after a hard frost kills them back, and remove all old foliage. This helps to prevent botrytis, which causes buds to fail to open.

Some form of support for big plants is necessary. Stakes and string can be used, and wire peony cages are available which are inconspicuous and work well.

SINGLES

- P. A la Mode is early, white with a pompon tuft of bright, golden-yellow stamens.

- P. America is early to mid-season with dazzling scarlet flowers, strong stems, and outstanding foliage.
- P. Chiffon Clouds is early, soft pink; holds up well in wet weather.
- P. Lights Out is early, with deep dark red single blooms.
- P. Romance is early, pink with big tufts of white stamens.

Red Charm.

DOUBLES

- P. Felix Crousse is a lovely red.
- P. Festiva Maxima is white flecked with crimson, introduced in 1851, very durable, long-lasting, and wonderfully fragrant.
- P. Sarah Bernhardt is late, a deep rose-pink, very beautiful.

BOMB TYPES
(These are a few to look for.)

- P. Angel Cheeks is tall, deep pink.
- P. Pink Lemonade has an outer ring of pink with pink, yellow, and cream. Fragrant.
- P. Raspberry Sundae is two-tone pink and cream.
- P. Red Charm is tall and needs staking. Explosion of dark red petals.

FERN-LEAF

- P. tenuifolia rubra (single) or P. tenuifolia rubra plena (double): Both have ferny leaves and red petals. Early.

Tree Peonies are generally not successful here. Although the roots are hardy and the plant will grow, the plant will bloom only on old wood. Since the top growth is killed to the ground every winter the plant never gets a chance to bloom.

Pink Asiatic Lily 'Wanda.'

Lilies
by Betty Nelson

Most lily bulbs are planted in the fall just before the ground freezes. Plant where there is good drainage (if water puddles around them the bulbs will rot). Lilies like a good humusy soil, well prepared (no manure unless it is very well rotted). Plant the bulb as soon as you get it—don't let it dry out. Plant small bulbs about 30 cm (12 in) apart and cover with 8–10 cm (3–4 in) of soil; large bulbs 46 cm (18 in) apart and covered with 10–15 cm (4–6 in) of soil. Water as soon as planted. Fertilize plants with fertilizer high in nitrogen during the early growing season and later with fertilizer high in potassium for flower and bulb growth. Stake so the wind doesn't break them and don't let them get too dry. They like cool feet so mulch around plants or grow low annuals around them to shade the base. Remove dead lily flowers; don't let them go to seed. If cutting lilies for cut flowers, leave two thirds of the stem and leaves to feed the bulb (if you cut too much stem the bulb will die). I fall mulch with leaves, etc. to keep the ground from freezing and thawing.

Lilies take at least a month longer to produce bloom here, so if the seller says they are June bloomers they will bloom in July; July in August. The so-called August and September bloomers will be frozen while still in the bud stage. By planting varieties with specific blooming dates you can have lilies in bloom all summer. If they grow well in your location clumps will become crowded and will need to be divided up. They like a sunny location.

For further information on growing lilies I recommend the book *Let's Grow Lilies* by the North American Lily Society. (www.lilies.org)

ADDENDUM TO 2006 EDITION
Anne Vale

The following lilies are very hardy here and can be left in the ground to multiply.

- *Lilium philadelphicum*—A heritage lily popular with pioneer gardeners and shared with neighbours resembled the native "tiger lily." It has never been available in stores but is still happily ensconced in old gardens. It is a strong up-facing orange Asiatic type. Get some from a neighbour.
- *Lilium tigrinum*—Tiger lilies. Reflexed "turk's cap" petals; several colours are available, usually spotted. They quickly make a big clump.

Yellow Tiger Lily.

Martagon Lily.

• Asiatic lilies. Absolutely hardy anywhere. They need good drainage and full or part sun, and come in many different colours and heights. Most are up-facing; some out-facing or down-facing.

• L.A. Hybrids. Longiflora and Asiatic breeding combines the ultra-hardiness of the Asiatics with larger flowers, stronger stems, and longer-lasting qualities of the Longifloras. Many of these have a delightful perfume.

• Martagon lilies. The aristocrats of the lily world, martagons are tall, graceful lilies with turk's cap petals. They prefer shade and hate to be disturbed. Good drainage is essential. An old, established clump of martagons is a showstopper. Patience is required. Mark the spot where you planted them, as they may not come up for a couple of years.

*Up-facing
Asiatic Lily.*

- Orienpet or O.T. lilies. These are a hybrid between Oriental and Trumpet, neither of which is hardy, but their offspring seem to have some hybrid vigour and are much hardier than either of the parents.
- Oriental lilies, such as the well-known Stargazer, are not truly hardy and will disappear after a year or two.

Hardy Bulbs
by Anne Vale

As soon as your annuals are cut down by the first heavy frost you should be planting your fall bulbs. The earlier you can get them in, the better the flowers will be next spring. It is no good waiting until spring and then going to your garden centre when you see your neighbour's bulbs in bloom. The first bulbs come on the market sometime in September, and the sooner you get there the better choice of colour and type you will have. Budget-minded gardeners can pick up half-price bargains late in October, but by that time you may have to chisel a hole in the ground with an ice pick to plant them.

Bulbs like rich soil which is well drained. They will not tolerate sitting in a puddle in the spring. They will grow in sun or shade but those planted in full shade will bloom much later

The Kaufmannia tulip is one of the first to bloom.

than the ones basking in full sun. If they are planted up against a basement wall, they will be awakened too early by the hot days in early spring and the flowers will be frozen. A little bit away from the wall is advisable, or out in the open away from the house. They will also be in less danger of drying out than if they are right against a south wall.

Of the bigger bulbs, tulips are most satisfactory. Daffodils are nearly always a disappointment. It is possible to grow them, but they bloom at the same time as the dandelions, and their full yellow glory is lost. Hyacinths have been coaxed into bloom by some green thumb gardeners but are only borderline hardy. Tulips are easier and a sure-fire success, even for beginning gardeners. If you choose your varieties carefully they will show colour over a period of six to eight weeks in spring.

The first to bloom are the Kauffmania tulips. They are quite short with striped leaves and will bloom almost as soon as the snow melts. They are followed by the Fosteriana hybrids which include the familiar Red Emperor, a large-flowered brilliant scarlet, which does better out of the wind, as it is rather tall. A better choice for a windy place is the sweet little Red Riding Hood or the peacock tulips, both only 15–20 cm (6–8 in) high. They bloom very early, the same time as the scillas.

Species tulips, the wild tulips from different parts of the world, are also very early and make a lovely miniature rockery plant of great charm. Many have four or five flowers on one stem. The better bulb catalogues list quite a few hardy varieties well worth a try. Tulipa tarda multiply rapidly and are completely hardy. They are only 10 cm (4 in) tall and covered in small, yellow, star-like blooms.

Following these in bloom are the single earlies, double earlies, and Triumph tulips. About ten days later again the Darwin hybrids bloom, and then the Darwin tulips and cottage tulips round out the season. Another later flowering tulip is the lily flowering tulip with elongated, pointed petals.

Plant your tulips at least 20 cm (8 in) deep. This way they will not come up too soon in the spring and will have a much longer life, only needing to be dug and divided about the fifth or sixth year. Otherwise they can be left in the ground and will reappear each spring without much help from you. At planting time you may give them a little bone meal, which they enjoy, but they don't need fertilizer at this stage and manure will only make them rot. The time for using a high phosphate fertilizer is after they have bloomed to build up the bulb for the following year. The leaves should not be removed until they have yellowed naturally.

Glory of the Snow (Chionodoxa lucillae) is an early-blooming spring bulb.

When you have planted them, water the bed very thoroughly right till freeze-up and cover with a protective mulch so that it does not freeze too soon. Leaves raked from the lawn do very well as a mulch for bulbs. Twigs or chicken wire on top will stop it blowing away and it can be raked off again just before the leaves of the bulbs begin to poke up in spring.

Alliums are flowering onions of various kinds, and most are completely hardy. There is a yellow one, 30 cm (12 in) tall, blooming in June (Allium moly), and a very attractive white allium (A. neopolitanum) also 30 cm (12 in), June blooming. A strikingly different one is Allium caeruleum, 0.6 m (2 ft) tall with blue balls on top. Allium ostrowskianum is a pink one, 30 cm (12 in) tall, blooming in July and is very hardy. They don't smell like onions unless you pinch them.

Three early-blooming blue beauties are Scilla siberica (Siberian Squills), Chionodoxa (Glory of the Snow), and Muscari (Grape Hyacinths). They bloom one after the other in very early spring, and if you mix all three of them together in a paper bag and then plant a patch somewhere you will have a sky-blue carpet for at least six weeks in early spring. They are all about the same height and colour and multiply fast. Scillas and Chionodoxa will naturalize happily in a lawn and bloom before you cut the grass.

Snowdrops are not too successful. They want to bloom so early that they are tempted to come up in a chinook in January with the inevitable result. Aconites (Eranthis hyemalis) suffer the same way.

There are some dwarf iris that are grown from a true bulb, not a rhizome. These are completely hardy and will pop up through the snow and bloom in late April. Iris reticulata (violet) and Iris danfordiae (yellow) are both only 10 cm (4 in) high.

Lilies are given their own section in this book and I need not describe them here except to say there are many hardy varieties which are grown in the foothills with great success.

Crocuses do well against some shelter. Mine are planted in front of a big rock which reflects the heat to them, and they just love it. Stay away from the yellow ones. There again, they bloom at the same time as the dandelions and don't show up as they should. In other climates they come much earlier and miss the competition provided by May dandelions. I have tried English bluebells (Scilla campanulata) several times but never had any success with them. I think it probably is too dry and cold for them. Anemones are not hardy over winter and must be started early in spring, the same as gladioli bulbs.

As a general rule of thumb, plant all types of bulbs at a depth of four times the diameter of the bulb.

5

Annuals

Gardening with Annuals
by Anne Vale

Many members of the Millarville Horticultural Club start a number of their annual flower seeds indoors, which enables them to grow a larger variety of annuals as well as getting them to bloom earlier than if they were sown directly into their garden.

Sowing seed indoors or in the greenhouse is easy. Both methods follow the same set of rules. The greenhouse provides ideal conditions, but the windowsill method has to be adapted to survive the excess heat and lack of light encountered in the average home. If you have large, bright basement windows with wide sills, the seedlings will thrive in the cooler conditions. West- or east-facing basement windows are perfect. Supplementary light in the form of fluorescent lamps is a great help to indoor growing. These should be hung 15 to 45 cm (6 to 18 in) above the seed, and should be turned on for sixteen hours a day. A timer device is helpful.

For beginner growers trying the indoor method it is advisable to stick with the varieties that need only a short period of time to grow to transplanting size. Marigolds, asters, alyssum, cabbage and tomatoes are quick and easy. You may use any shallow container with good drainage holes. Commercial seeding medium works well and contains no soil,

Annual garden.

consequently avoiding soil-borne fungus diseases. The base for the mixes should be peat moss with the addition of some perlite. Very fine mixes are good for sowing very tiny seed but a coarser mix is good for larger seed which needs to be covered up.

SEEDING METHOD

Sow the seed just as thin as you can in straight lines about 2–3 cm (1 in) apart. The bigger seeds can be covered with a thin layer of your mixture, just enough to hide the seed, but the smaller seed should not be covered at all. Most of the smaller seed needs light to germinate, and covering it will severely delay and reduce germination.

When the seed has been sown into the damp, peaty mixture, it should be watered gently and carefully with room temperature water. A watering can with a fine rose is ideal. Spray bottles tend to whoosh all the seed to the edges if you are not careful. No fungicide is necessary. Over-use of chemicals can be harmful to the germinating seed.

The seeded containers can then be placed under a clear plastic tent and left in a warm location until germination occurs. It is most important not to let them dry out during germination or the embryo inside the seed will die. Damp, not soggy, is the rule. Some seed prefers to germinate warm at a constant 20°C (68°F) night and day. Direct sunlight shining on the plastic tent will raise the temperature to cooking level. Cover your tent with a layer of newspaper or a white cloth to keep the temperature more stable.

Once the seedlings appear, they must be removed promptly from your little tent and placed in a light, bright, cooler location (15°C/59° F). Watch them closely and continue to water gently with room temperature water when the soil begins to dry on top. Try to keep them on the dry side, with a temperature of about 12°C (54°F) by night and 15–20°C (59–68°F) by day. When the seedlings have two pairs of leaves, or are big enough to handle, whichever occurs first, seedlings should be transplanted to larger container where they will have plenty of room to develop. Any container at least 6 cm (2.5 in) deep may be used, provided it has good drainage.

At this stage, one third soil may be added to your peat moss/perlite mixture if that's what you are using, and you may begin fertilizing with plant starter 10–52–10. This will encourage root development. Don't use a heavy nitrogen feed, as that would produce lots of greenery on top which you don't need at this stage. If your seedlings get too tall you may pinch out the top to develop side shoots, but if you have been able to maintain a temperature of 10–15°C (50–60°F) they will stay stocky of their own accord. Remember, you can better control growth with cultural conditions than with chemicals. If you can run them cool, hungry and dry, you can produce a better plant. If growth is too slow and you want to speed them up, apply heat, water and fertilizer and you will get startling results.

Towering annual, Nicotiana sylvestris.

Seeds of annuals are very different in their individual requirements, some insisting on darkness to germinate and others benefiting greatly from sixteen hours of supplemental light. Germination times and light and temperature requirements for a few of the most common annuals are listed further on in this section.

Planting outside must be preceded by a period of acclimatization or "hardening off." Set plants out in the shade all day when the temperature is over 4°C (40°F), and put them somewhere cool at night. Don't bring them back into the house where they will be "nice and warm" or put them in the basement until you can plant them out. All they need is protection from actual freezing, such as an unheated garage. During this period, water only sufficiently to prevent wilting. Withholding water helps to toughen the tissues and produce a dark green, stocky plant that will be able to withstand stress conditions. The east side of the house or a shed is best, where they will be protected from wind and

Keep pansies dead-headed for continuous bloom.

late afternoon heat. A cold frame is the ideal situation, where they can have the lid closed on them at night and opened all day, rain or shine. Don't baby them too much.

When the time comes to plant out, do so in the evening or on a cool day. Water immediately. You may add fertilizer to the water such as a tablespoon of 10–52–10 per 3½ litres (one gallon) of water. Once you have placed your seedling in the garden, firm up the soil around it, and if the weather clears or the wind comes up, cover it with an overturned flower pot to protect it, for hot sun or strong winds can devastate young transplants. Anytime you notice your seedlings are wilting, cover them for a few hours until they are strong enough to withstand the weather. In more unprotected gardens, encircle your transplant with a milk carton or tin can from which both ends have been removed, and leave on until the plant outgrows it.

Some annuals can be sown directly outdoors in the spring. These are noted in the list of recommended types of annual flowers further on in this chapter. For those who do not have the space or the time to start seeds indoors, and who do not wish to go to the expense of purchasing bedding out plants, these annuals will be of great service to them.

Location of your flower beds is an important consideration for all flowers have different needs. Some like full sun, others prefer a moist area. Nearly all need some shelter, so awareness of the prevailing winds in your area is important. If you have flower beds on each side of your house, consider the following factors. The south and west walls of your house receive the most sun, while the east wall receives the early morning sun and is warmed up first. The north wall receives very little. Thus your north bed is good for shade-loving plants; your east bed for plants requiring a long day, semi-shade and good protection from the wind; your south bed for annuals loving hot, dry conditions; your west bed for flowers which will tolerate afternoon heat. Your house will also offer some protection against frost, as houses lose heat through their walls, which flows out over the adjacent flower beds.

Petunias thrive in full sunshine.

Cineraria is happy in a shady cool spot.

Sunflowers turn their heads to face the sun.

The colour of your home can modify the available light. White walls can bounce a lot more light around on the shady side, enabling plants requiring more light to be successfully grown there. Conversely, a dark brown log or shingle wall will absorb the light, causing plants to lean away towards the light.

When trying to determine where to locate flower beds in gardens located away from your house, consider the amount of shelter they will receive, the degree of shade, and the drainage provided by each location. We suffer from late spring and early fall frosts in our area, so it is a good idea not to put beds in low-lying areas, as that is where frost will settle.

At the end of the growing season remove dead annuals from your beds, as they may contain insect eggs. Add fresh loam, well-rotted manure, and peat moss and sand if your soil is too heavy. Dig the garden roughly to allow for greater moisture absorption. Large clumps of soil should be left, as winter's frost will break them down. In the spring, when the soil is dry enough, remove any debris and dig the beds well to thoroughly mix in your fall coverings of manure, etc. Smooth the beds with a rake to help maintain the moisture level.

The following is a list of recommended annual flowers grown successfully in our area. (Those marked with * are self-seeding and will come up year after year if conditions are favourable.)

Type	When to Plant	Location
African Daisy	indoors, early May	dry area, full sun
Ageratum	indoors, early April	full sun
Alyssum	indoors, early April	full sun
Aster	indoors, late March	full sun
Baby Blue Eyes (Nemophilia)	seed directly in garden	full sun
*Bachelor Button	seed directly in garden	grows anywhere
Bartonia	seed directly in garden	full sun
Bells of Ireland	indoors, early April	full sun
*Calendula	seed directly in garden	full sun
California Bluebell (Phacelia)	seed directly in garden	full sun
*California Poppy	seed directly in garden	poor soil, full sun
Calliopsis	indoors, early April	full sun
Candytuft	seed directly in garden	grows anywhere
Clarkia	seed directly in garden	full sun or semi-shade
Convolvulus Tricolour	indoors, mid March	full sun or semi-shade
*Cosmos	seed directly in garden	warm spot
Dianthus	indoors, early April	dry area, poor soil
Dusty Miller	indoors, mid March	grows anywhere
Gazania	indoors, mid March	full sun
Gloriosa Daisy	indoors, early March	full sun
Godetia	seed directly in garden	sunny position
Larkspur (annual)	seed directly in garden	full sun or semi-shade
Linaria	seed directly in garden	grows anywhere
Livingstone Daisy (Mesembryanthemum)	indoors, early April	full sun, poor soil

Type	When to Plant	Location
Lobelia	indoors, early March	cool location
Marigold	indoors, see chart p.181	full sun
Mimulus	indoors, early April	full sun or semi-shade
Mignonette	seed directly in garden	full sun or semi-shade
Nasturtium	seed directly in garden	full sun or semi-shade
Nemesia	indoors, early April	full sun or semi-shade
Nicotiana	indoors, early March	semi-shade
Ornamental Kale	indoors, mid April	grows anywhere
Pansy	indoors, early March	grows anywhere
Petunia	indoors, early March	full sun or semi-shade
Phlox	indoors, early April	semi-shade
Pincushion Flower (Scabiosa)	indoors, early April	full sun or semi-shade
Portulaca	indoors, mid March	full sun, warm spot
Queen Anne's Lace	seed directly in garden	full sun
Rudbeckia	indoors, early April	full sun
Salpiglossis	indoors, early April	full sun or semi-shade
Schizanthus	indoors, early April	full sun or semi-shade
*Shirley Poppy	seed directly in garden	dry area
Snapdragon	indoors, late March	full sun
Stocks	indoors, early April	full sun
Strawflower	indoors, early April	sunny position
Sweet Pea	sow early in garden	full sun or semi-shade
*Tidy Tips	seed directly in garden	full sun
Verbena	indoors, mid March	full sun
Viscaria	indoors, mid March	full sun

It is too cold in this region to grow plants commonly recommended for shade, such as coleus and impatiens, which is why they are not on the above list. We recommend nicotiana, pansies and other annuals on the list which state semi-shade.

A MEMBER'S SOWING DATES FOR ANNUAL SEEDS

Planting dates for starting annual seeds indoors are as follows. Note that anyone growing plants for sale would have to start their seeds earlier in order for their plants to be large and attractive enough to sell. For your own use, smaller plants will set out and grow better than bigger plants.

When Planted	Flowers
March 10 to 15	Pansy, single petunia, snaps, wallflower, lobelia
March 18 to 25	Asters, statice, larkspur, dianthus, salpiglossis
April 1 to 5	Nicotiana, mimulus, scabiosa, calliopsis, cosmos, rudbeckia, quaking grass, phlox, nemesia
April 10 to 15	Stocks, strawflowers, gilia, lavatera, large marigolds, marigold, paprika
April 20	Calendula
May 1	Dwarf marigold, african daisy
When Planted	Vegetables
March 10	Celery, leeks, Spanish onions
April 1	Lettuce, early tomatoes
April 15	Cauliflower, brussels sprouts, broccoli

VIABILITY OF SEEDS

It is not a good idea to keep your leftover seeds more than one year. Usually you can use them up the second spring in any case. Germination percentage and vigour of seedlings decrease with each year and depend greatly on type of seed and storage conditions.

Fresh seed should be stored in a cool, dark, dry place in a cardboard box or paper bag. If stored in airtight tins or polyethylene bags before they are cured and dry, condensation will form and they will rot. Dampness is fatal. Mark the year of purchase or collection on each stored packet.

Old seed should be given a germination test three weeks before sowing the main batch. Fill a jar half full of damp soil and put ten seeds on a piece of damp paper towel on top of the soil. Put the lid on tight, set in good light, and see how many germinate. It is not necessary to grow them any further than the germination stage. This saves discovering too late that they will not germinate and missing three weeks of our short growing season while you wait to be certain they are not coming up.

It is hard to generalize because each kind of seed has different requirements. Some need to be fresh from the plant for successful germination. Others need six months of rest or a freezing period to break dormancy. Some stay viable for many years, and indeed seeds found deep within a glacier, having been deep-frozen for hundreds of years, have germinated upon being sown.

The following list names some seeds which I have found to lose vigour very quickly and which should be used their first year.

Flowers

Alyssum	Hollyhock	Nicotiana
Canterbury Bell	Kochia	Portulaca
Delphinium	Nemesia	Salvia

Vegetables

Chives	Lettuce	Onions

These seeds I have found to last for more than two years. Seedling vigour did not decrease noticeably and germination was extremely good up to four years.

Flowers

African Daisy	Marigolds	Snapdragon
Cosmos	Pansy	Sweet Pea
Daisy	Petunia	

Vegetables

Beans	Cabbage	Radish
Beets	Cauliflower	Spinach
Broccoli	Pea	Swiss Chard

Nearly all seeds will germinate at a fairly good percentage the second year, provided they have been stored under the proper conditions, but to keep them longer is asking for problems.

GERMINATION TIMETABLE FOR POPULAR ANNUALS

Variety	Light Requirements	Days to Germinate	Soil Temp. to Germinate	Temp. to Grow Seedlings	Weeks to Grow**
Ageratum	Light	5	21 C/70 F	16 C/60 F	10
Aster	*	8	21 C/70 F	16 C/60 F	6
Alyssum	*	5	21 C/70 F	10 C/50 F	10
Dusty Miller	Light	10	24 C/75 F	16 C/60 F	16
Dianthus	*	4	21 C/70 F	10 C/50 F	8
Dahlia	*	5	21 C/70 F	10 C/50 F	6
Lobelia	*	20	21 C/70 F	10 C/50 F	16
Marigold (Tall African)	*	5	21 C/70 F	10 C/50 F	6
Marigold (French Dwf.)	*	5	21 C/70 F	10 C/50 F	8
Marigold (Large fl. Dwf.)	*	5	21 C/70 F	10 C/50 F	10
Nemesia	Dark	5	18 C/65 F	10 C/50 F	12
Nicotiana	Light	20	21 C/70 F	16 C/60 F	8
Pansy	Dark	10	18 C/65 F	10 C/50 F	20
Petunia (Single)	Light	10	21 C/70 F	13 C/55 F	12
Petunia (Double)	Light	10	21 C/70 F	13 C/55 F	16
Portulaca	Dark	10	21 C/70 F	16 C/60 F	10
Snapdragon	Light	10	18 C/65 F	10 C/50 F	12
Verbena	Dark	20	18 C/65 F	10 C/50 F	10
Cabbage Family	*	5	21 C/70 F	10 C/50 F	6
Onions	Dark	5	24 C/75 F	10 C/50 F	20
Tomatoes	Dark	10	24 C/75 F	10 C/50 F	8

*Will germinate in either light or dark
**This means weeks from sowing of seed until plant is ready to set out in the garden. These figures are for greenhouse conditions. For windowsill gardens, reduce the time by one third.

OUTDOOR SEED SOWING AND TRANSPLANTING GUIDE

Although May 24 is widely used as a guideline for when to sow seeds, the region covered by our book may experience frost at any time of the year, and conditions may vary greatly from year to year. Some plants are able to take far more frost than others, and the earlier the tough ones are set out or sown, the greater use they will make of the extra days to build a good root system. The following timetable works pretty well:

When these are in full bloom	Sow these	Plant out these
Buffalo beans	Lettuce	Onions
	Peas	Pansies
	Sweet Peas	
	Poppies	
Saskatoons	Broad Beans	Petunias
	Carrots	Snapdragons
	Turnips	Cabbage
	Beets	Broccoli
	Spinach	Potatoes
	Calendula	
	Clarkia	
Lilac	Green Beans	Marigolds
	Corn	Lobelia
	Zinnias	Nemesia
	Squashes	Alyssum
		Tomatoes
		Salvia
		Dahlia

Helpful Hints

❉ Danger times for frost are when the sky clears off after a rain, and at the full moon.

❉ Newspaper, paper or cloth make better frost protection than plastic.

Sweet Peas
Tom Davenport's Method

Plant seed around April 10–15. Before planting, soak seeds for twenty-four hours, by which time most of them will be swollen. Break open any that are not are nicked on the side opposite the lifeline.

Plant in 8 cm (3 in) peat pots containing a mixture of potting soil, peat moss and vermiculite. Put three or four seeds in each pot 1 cm (0.5 in) deep and cover with soil. Water well, cover with black plastic, and put in a warm place until the seeds germinate and you can see green tips peeking through the soil (ten days to two weeks). Remove immediately to a cooler spot (around 10°C/50°F). You may wish to separate the plants in the peat pots into individual pots before transplanting outdoors. When four leaves have formed, plant tips should be pinched off after selecting one strong shoot to remain as a leader; or, if you only have a few plants of one colour, let two shoots grow. Plants may be hardened off in a cold frame.

Select a fairly sunny spot with a good depth of topsoil for planting your sweet peas. Dig a trench 30–46 cm (12–18 in) deep and add well-rotted manure and bone meal to the bottom of the trench, mixing it well with the soil as you fill it in. Add bone meal alone to the top 20 cm (8 in), mixing it in well also. Let it settle before transplanting your plants.

Sweet peas need a support fence on which to climb. Chicken

Sweet Peas on an east-facing wall on a high windy hill.

wire stretched between posts set in at each end of the row works very well. Rows should run north to south and on either side of each support fence so that two rows can be supported by one fence. Between the double rows you should leave 1 m (3 ft) of space to the next double row.

Sweet peas should be planted 5 cm (2 in) deeper than required. Fill in the trench as they grow. Transplanted sweet peas should be planted at ground level. Plants should be 20 cm (8 in) apart in the row.

In order to grow beautiful, long-stemmed sweet peas, carefully remove the tendrils and fasten the stems to the support fence with tie-ons or attach them with fine metal rings which you can purchase. This must be done each morning. Removing the tendrils allows more strength to go into the bloom and also makes for straighter stems.

When the plants are approximately 46 cm (18 in) tall, carefully loosened the ties from the supports and plants, and lay the vines on the ground for about half their length. Bend the other half gently back up again and retie to the support fence. This process, called layering, gives the plants greater strength and is said to improve the quality of the bloom.

Sweet peas like lots of water, so don't spare the hose.

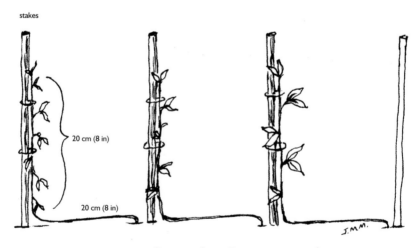

Layering Sweet Peas

Helpful Hints

🌸 On frosty mornings, water at daybreak to save plants.

🌸 Use rocks to hold heat.

🌸 To beat frost, sow seeds early and cover with newspaper on cold nights in late May or June. It is much easier to cover small plants in spring than big plants in late August, e.g., corn, beans, zinnias, potatoes.

🌸 When seeds are cured and dry, use canisters from 35 mm film to save your seeds, as they are airtight. (Fresh seed contains too much moisture and might rot in an airtight container.)

Tender Bulbs and Tubers

Tuberous Begonias
by Dessa Macklin

Tuberous begonias are among the most satisfactory plants. They provide beautiful blossom continuously through summer and fall.

There are two types, one having large blooms, both double and single, and the pendulous, a smaller hanging variety. The latter is most suitable for hanging baskets of any kind. Begonias have a wide range of beautiful colours ranging from pink to red, various shades of yellow, orange, and of course white. They also vary in form. Some resemble carnations, others roses, still others camellias, which are large and exotic.

A good time to start these plants is in late March whether by planting individual tubers or by putting several in a large container. They start very well in peat moss in a warm place, such as on top of the refrigerator, where the temperature will not go over 27°C (80°F). When growth is 10 cm (4 in) or so, each begonia can be replanted into a larger pot, basket, or a well-sheltered spot in the garden. Begonias like a rich planting mixture: one third well-rotted manure, one third good

Tuberous begonia 'Sunburst Picotee.'

garden loam and the rest peat moss with leaf mould if possible. Plant tubers firmly and cover with about 2.5 cm (1 in) of soil. They like an eastern exposure, which provides morning sun. Protection from wind is essential, as they break very easily. They need fertilizer about every three weeks. All-purpose plant food, 15–30–15, or fish fertilizer will do nicely. They take a lot of water in hot weather and will bloom continuously until it is time to bring them in to escape frost. Allow tubers to dry out in their own soil, which they will do after foliage dries off. Remove, shake off soil, and spread out to dry for a few days. Before storing, dust tubers with a good bulb dust. Put in separate plastic bags covered with dry peat moss, seal, and store in a cold room until the following spring. Remember to label as to colour and variety.

Dahlias
by Betty Nelson

Start dahlia tubers about the middle of April in a soil mixture of two parts soil, one part perlite and one part peat moss in containers with good drainage. Before planting, divide up roots, being sure to leave a growth eye on each piece. Plant in a milk carton laid horizontally with one side cut out for the top and drain holes punched in the bottom. Plant so the growth eye on the tuber is at one end. If the tuber starts to sprout in mid-winter, it will exhaust the parent tuber, but a cutting may be taken from the tip of this new growth, from which you

Betty and Leonard Nelson's garden.

Dinner plate Dahlia.

may start a new plant. Tip cuttings may also be taken from any small growth sprouts which have appeared when you come to divide the tubers before planting. This way you get twice as many plants.

Plant in the garden about May 24. Dig a hole larger and deeper than the milk carton, remove the plant by cutting the side out of the carton, and slide the plant and soil into the hole, trying not to disturb the roots.

Place a support stake just behind the plant before filling in the hole, and leave a depression around the plant to hold moisture. Cover on cold nights, as plants will be about 20 cm (8 in) tall by this time and are susceptible to frost. Fertilize with 10–52–10 at half strength every three weeks or so. In dry weather, water deeply once a week. Gradually fill in the depressions around the plants and, as they grow up, tie their stems to stakes for a wind can easily break them. Dahlias do best in a well-drained, fertile soil in full sunlight. They must also be in a sheltered spot. Cut off dead flowers and watch for pests, as dahlias are bothered by aphids, mites and some bug that nips the buds out just when they start to form.

When the tops have died down after frost, cut them off leaving about 5 cm (2 in) top growth. Take up the tubers by digging well back from the plant, because tubers will have grown sometimes 30 cm (1 ft) long under the soil surface, mostly horizontally.

Remove as much soil as possible. Turn the plants upside down to drain their hollow tops and dry. When dry take ordinary household scissors and cut off any small roots. Place in dry peat moss or perlite in labelled plastic bags and store in a cold room.

Helpful Hints

❋ Cuttings from dahlias can be taken from the tips of sprouts that form in late winter or early spring—a good way to increase your stock of plants.

Gladioli
by Mary Poffenroth

Glads do best when planted in full sun. A light sand loam is ideal but they grow satisfactorily in almost any garden soil that has been enriched with compost, leaf mould or peat moss. A 5–10–5 fertilizer may be added. Avoid animal manures, as they encourage bulb rot.

In this region, bulbs should be planted in early May. For earlier blooming they may be soaked in water for about a week. Plant the bulbs about 10–15 cm (4–6 in) apart, covering them with 10–15 cm (4–6 in) of soil. A double row of bulbs is sometimes advantageous. I have found it successful to dig a trench 20 cm (8 in) wide, put leaf mould and bone meal (15 mL/1 tbsp per bulb) in the trench, and make the double row by staggering the bulbs to achieve the proper spacing. Fertilize when the flower spikes appear and again after the flowers are picked.

When plants are about 30 cm (12 in) tall, hold them erect by "hilling up" the earth around the stems. Otherwise glads should be supported with stakes.

When picking the flowers, leave four or five leaves on the plant so that the bulb can mature. To ensure stronger bulbs for another year, permit only one flower to mature on each stock.

Dig up the bulbs, preferably about four weeks after frost. Cut off the tops and let the bulbs dry in an airy place out of the sun for two or three weeks. Remove the dried parts of the old bulb, dust with a combination insecticide/fungicide bulb dust and store in a cool place. Old nylon stockings make excellent storage bags, as they can be hung up to allow air to circulate around them.

Gladiolus flowers are available in many sizes and in early, medium and late flowering varieties. It is seldom worthwhile in this region to plant anything but early flowering bulbs.

Helpful Hints

※ Heat treatment helps to cure gladiolus bulbs. Hang bulbs in nylon stockings over a heat register for ten days.

6

Planters

Gardening Without a Garden
by Grace Bull

There are several reasons for gardening using pots, hanging baskets, planters and window boxes. Lack of space for a conventional garden, featureless house lines, short growing season, predators, old age or disabilities—all these can be overcome with container gardening. The main disadvantage is the fact that planters, etc. tend to dry out quickly and are usually placed where they receive little or no rain, so frequent watering is necessary.

Soil requirements are much the same for any container. A good potting mixture is half good rich soil, one quarter peat moss to retain moisture, one quarter perlite for porosity and a bit of bone meal or dried steer manure. All containers must have good drainage. Drainage can be achieved with a good layer of gravel or broken clay pots, covered with leaves or clean straw. It is better not to set containers on grass or bare ground since worms and other undesirables can invade the pots if there are drainage holes. A cement or gravel base is ideal. Large containers become very heavy when filled with soil—platforms of wood on casters can be

Recycled work boots have a new purpose.

used if you want to move planters from place to place. Some planters can be set on cement blocks for a tiered effect.

If a greenhouse or well-lighted basement is available, it is advantageous to plant up your planters early so that by the time the danger of frost is over you can put out an instant garden. In the fall the shelter and warmth of the house will give you blooms much longer than in the open. Smaller containers can be moved inside for protection from that first early frost. Perennials and small shrubs or trees are not successfully grown in pots in our climate. Remember that if you leave ceramic pots filled with soil outside in the winter, freezing and thawing are apt to break them.

HANGING BASKETS

These are used under eaves, under covered porches or patios, or anywhere else you fancy. A windy location is not desirable. Hanging baskets can be of many types—sphagnum peat lined wire baskets are attractive but tend to dry out rapidly; plastic or wooden baskets are probably best. Be sure the hooks are solid and the wires or fine chains are secure. The best way to water hanging baskets is to place them in a tub of water until bubbles cease. If this is not convenient, there are long handles with breaker nozzles which can be attached to your garden hose.

Some good plants for hanging baskets in full sun are ivy geraniums, African daisies, petunias (especially the cascade type), trailing lobelia and alyssum. Others that prefer shade are asparagus fern, nasturtiums, pendulous begonias, pansies and schizanthus (dwarf variety). In fact, it is surprising how many garden flowers will trail if hanging, which under normal growing conditions would not do so. In a well-protected spot, many houseplants will benefit from a summer outside.

TUBS AND PLANTERS

Most any container can be used if it is of fair size. Clay pots and plastic pots are ideal, but five gallon cans or tree containers from nurseries can also be used. Roses, small dahlias, some of the more exotic but tender

Any convenient container will do!

lilies, tiger flowers, etc. can be grown in tubs. Lilies and dahlias can be lifted in the fall and stored over winter. Vegetables such as tomatoes, cucumbers, herbs and climbing beans can all be grown in containers. Many seed houses offer special patio types of vegetables. Any number of flowers can be used, depending on your location. Some of the better varieties for sun are geraniums of all types, African daisies, marigolds, petunias and in shady areas begonias and schizanthus. Don't forget to use alyssum, lobelia (both trailing and compact kinds) and dusty miller (dwarf variety such as silverdust) to fill in the pots around the edge and to trail over the sides.

WINDOW BOXES

Window boxes not only add interest to the outside of the house but also have the advantage of being seen from within. Window boxes should be at least 23 cm (9 in) deep and about 30 cm (12 in) wide, fastened securely and tipped slightly toward the back. Cedar and fibreglass are excellent. The inside of wooden boxes may be treated with a wood preservative and the outside only can be painted. Use the same type of soil as for other containers. Plants in individual pots can be set in the box and the area around filled with moss.

Remember, the rules for successful container gardening are: rich soil, good drainage and adequate water as well as the proper choice of plants for their location.

Containers, Hanging Baskets, and Potted Plants
by David Teskey

CONTAINERS

With today's busy schedules and little time for gardening in flower beds, one can still have a wonderful show with lots of variety in containers. Some of the advantages of container gardening are portability and advance planting, which gives a longer grow time for our short summers. Weeds are easily removed when their roots can't travel under rocks, sidewalks and retaining walls. "Watering made easy" techniques such as drip hoses and soaker hoses installed in planters; and gels retain water and stop soil shrinkage.

Let's take a look at a planter 30 x 90 x 24 cm (12 x 35 x 9 in). This planter should have a plastic liner, such as a garbage bag with drain holes at the bottom, with 5 cm (2 in) of gravel for drainage. For a good growing medium, combine one third each of perlite, peat moss, and sterilized soil. Use good humus (black topsoil) treated with steam to kill weed seeds and soil-borne worms and pests. Sterilized soil can be purchased at garden centres or you can get creative and steam your own. Do not overfill your planters with medium. You must leave a good 5 cm (2 in) at the top of this planter for water to be applied. Otherwise it will run off and defeat your efforts.

Soilless mixes require regular applications of fertilizer, as they have no residual nutrients. Slow-release pellets are also helpful, but be careful, as it is easy to overdose and you cannot remove them. Real soil not only makes a good anchor for tiny root hairs to attach themselves, but also is a good source of minerals for most plants. Never reuse soil medium. You will get better results by starting fresh every year. Do you like leftovers? Put used planter medium into compost—they both get a treat.

Frequently, waterings are done in haste with only the top 3 cm (1 in) of soil receiving moisture, leaving the rest a dry, unhappy planter. In this planter I recommend cutting the bottoms off three 1 L (32 oz) water bottles. Place these upside down with their lids still on. Space them evenly along the planter. Allow a 3 cm (1 in) lip of the bottom to protrude to stop soil from working its way into the bottle. A sharp knife can be used to make vertical slits in the bottle at all levels. This allows the water in the bottles a chance to diffuse slowly into the area where the roots congregate. Extra water runs off through the drainage rocks in the bottom. I call it good plumbing.

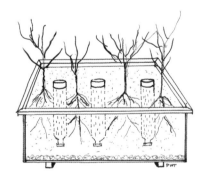

Next we can look at large patio pots. Again make an upside down water bottle for the centre of each. The water gets to the roots, our ultimate goal. Within a week or two the plants will hide the bottle. For those who must plant a spike in the geographic centre of the pot, insert two smaller water bottles tipped slightly to the sides equidistant, from the centre.

As well, a spaghetti drip system can be supplying water continuously with a roll of pipe and some clamps. Drip irrigation with all hanging baskets, pots, and planters can be plumbed with a minimum of effort. These can be adjusted to their location requirements: Sunny and hot, more drips per minute; shady cool areas, fewer drips per minute. It takes a couple of weeks to regulate the water drip to the correct amount. As the season wears on, your plants will talk to you about their requirements. If you get abundant growth and lots of flowers, you are on the right track. If some areas look sparse and dried out, allow more drips per minute. Remember, always monitor the plants to see how they are reacting. The beauty of the drip system is that even when you aren't there in person, the plants are getting water. It's a good feeling. Plants love it, too.

HANGING BASKETS

These are really portable. If you are going away for a short holiday, take your hanging baskets down and find a shady place to give them some protection from hot sun, wind, etc. The harsh elements make for some pretty tired-looking baskets. Without proper moisture in the soil, the growing medium shrinks, allowing air to dry even more between the pot and the soil. This dry gap allows water to rush down the side and out the bottom, barely wetting the soil. Have you watered the pot well or not at all? The whole premise is to water the pot well, not just the top 2 cm (1 in).

Big pot for a hot spot. Purple Wave petunias with Canna Lily.

A wide range of new plants that will go the distance in containers is upon us. I put these into two main groups: "Torture Plants" for sun and wind, and "Sheltered Plants" for shady areas where a lot of light isn't available.

TORTURE PLANTS

With the advent of the Wave series petunias, large baskets can be created with abundant colour and vigour. Larger containers are needed for the Waves, as a larger upper growth is supported by an equally large root ball. These petunias *must* be fertilized weekly to keep up the massive blooming. They tolerate, in fact love, hot sun and wind. The Waves are not hurt by the first frost. Often they cheer right up and continue for another month or so. New, larger types of trailing lobelia in many new colours are also available. The Bacopas (like small, trailing white strawberry blooms) are wonderful to have cascading out of baskets. These are very heat tolerant. Plant breeders have also come out with pink and soft purple bacopas as well. Trailing greenery such as creeping jenny, Kenilworth ivy, lotus vine, and variegated vinca vine also make graceful baskets. A wide variety of trailing verbenas in blues, purples, pinks, and whites abound.

SHELTERED PLANTS

Next we have the shady ladies with the old standbys—fuchsia, impatiens and begonias. As someone who grows plants for a living, I always marvel at clients who come with large, open eyes and declare that they can't grow these varieties. Here before them is a large, beautiful basket in full bloom. They don't have to grow them; I do that. The customers just have to water, fertilize and enjoy. "Illumination" begonias or trailing types just hang around and get better and better. They require lots of light, but not full blazing sun. If blooming stops, they need more light. Remember, in a hanging basket these plants can be moved every second week to a brighter place for a boost. They love morning sun. Hanging baskets also give you a chance to turn the basket to allow the backside to get some more sun.

To make my shady plants a place for more light, I hang a 3 m (10 ft) piece of pipe in a sunnier location for rest and more sun. It works both ways: less sun for torture plants and more sun for shade baskets. Neutral ground, so to speak.

When your baskets start to improve in the time-out area, reintroduce them to your favourite spots and bring another group in for rest and recuperation. Each hanging basket will have its need for a rest, and this method works well. Remember, when you are out in the sun, if it gets too hot, where do you go? Into the shade for a drink. Your plants watch you. They too would like to head for some shade and a drink. Bottoms up! They're portable.

Helpful Hints

※ Put a layer of plastic in the bottom of moss hanging baskets to keep them from drying out so fast.

Winter Planters
By Patty Webb

The first sign of trees and shrubs taking on fall hues indicates it is time to gather material to make winter arrangements or planters.

SELECTING A CONTAINER
1. Almost anything that has a cavity large enough to hold a firm support. (see below)
2. Larger containers or raised planters are a wise choice, as the height will prevent the arrangement from being overwhelmed with snow.

3. Ceramic or terra cotta pots should have an inner liner to protect them from the expansion and contraction of freezing, which will crack the container.

SUPPORTS
(The base in which materials are held in place)

1. Old soil, sand, and floral foam blocks are best because they will absorb the water, keeping evergreens and branches fresh.
2. Add water to supports. This will eventually freeze, giving weight and stability to the base.

CHOOSING MATERIALS
Dried materials (flower heads, pods, cones, grasses, etc.)

1. Harvest solid, dense flower heads. Hang upside down to dry in a dark airy place to cure and keep their colour.
2. Choose strong stems that will hold the weight of snow and withstand strong winds, e.g., yarrow, sedum flower heads (autumn joy), veronica, hyssop, alliums, sunflower, statice (Sinuata and German), heliopsis (false sunflower).
3. Pods, e.g., oriental and peony poppy, iris pods, and flax.
4. Wild sage or artemisia (Valerie Finnis).
5. Inexpensive spray paint can give dried materials a colour lift.

EVERGREENS

1. Evergreens add a rich contrast against dried material.

This winter planter is impervious to frost or snow.

2. Prune evergreens while still accessible before deep snow arrives. (juniper, pine, spruce, fir.)
3. Mist and put in plastic bags to keep moist.
4. Keep cool or freeze until ready to use.

BERRIES

1. Berries on branches or grouped into clusters create interest with combinations of shape, texture and colour.
2. Good choices are rosehips, mountain ash, cotoneaster, snow berries, silver wolf willow, juniper, ornamental fruit trees such as crabapple, etc.

BRANCHES

1. Branches will give height and balance creating linear movement.
2. Any branches with colour or unique form, e.g., dogwood, buffalo berry, silver wolf willow.

MISCELLANEOUS MATERIALS

1. Let your imagination guide you to experiment with unconventional materials such as sempervivum (hen and chicks).
2. Soak wooden skewers in water, and then pierce them into the base of the plant, giving you a longer stem to insert into planter.
3. Wooden skewers can also be inserted into hollow stems to make them stronger.

GRASSES AND GRAINS

1. Group stems together and insert a wooden pick or skewer into the middle of the base and secure around the outside of the bundle with a pipe cleaner. This grouping creates a light, wispy effect.
2. Cattails and sedges give an interesting contrast in shape and texture.
3. Spray with lacquer to prevent shattering.

Winter planter of dried garden plants.

CONES

1. Small cones can be wired together in clusters, like grapes. Larger cones can be wired onto wooden picks or skewers, making it possible to insert them into the arrangement.

GLYCERIZED FOLIAGE

1. Cut mature foliage with woody stems in early September, e.g., sage (artemisia), saskatoons, spirea, aspen.
2. Put stems into a solution of equal parts warm water and glycerine. After absorbing the solution, the leaves will remain very supple.

ACCESSORIES

1. Incorporating accessories adds visual interest and a new dimension to the planter.
2. Trellis, driftwood, birdhouses, birdfeeders, bird's nests and garden décor.
3. Artificial flowers—a few can be added to produce a theme, e.g., poinsettias for Christmas, tulips or daffodils for an early touch of spring.

Have fun and let your imagination inspire you.

Geraniums
by Norma Lyall
(Written for the original edition in 1982)

PROPAGATION BY CUTTINGS

You will need soil, perlite, peat moss, labels, a sharp knife or razor blade, rooting powder, pen, pencil, and enough plastic bags to cover cuttings in pots. Use two parts soil, one part coarse or medium perlite, and one part peat moss which has been soaked in hot rain or snow water, and mix them together. This mixture should be quite moist so it will hold its shape when you squeeze it, yet will still fall apart.

Fill clean pots with moist soil mixture and clap the side of the pot to settle the soil. Put two cuttings in each 5 cm (2 in) pot or four cuttings in each 10 cm (4 in) pot. This way, if one dies you will still have plants in each pot.

Before you start taking cuttings, separate all your colours and make sure you have enough labels for your pots so you know which colour is in each pot. Otherwise, if your geraniums are not in bud when it comes time to transplant them outdoors, you will have no way of knowing what colour they are.

Cuttings may be made from February to September if they are in good sunlight. They should be taken from strong, healthy plants from which you have kept blooms and buds cut off so that all the strength has gone into the plant. Cut about 0.5–1 cm (¼–½ in) below the node or leaf stem and remove all lower leaves and flower buds. A cutting only needs to be 5–10 cm (2–4 in) long. Dip cuttings in rooting powder about 0.5 cm (¼ in) deeper than they will be set in the soil, tapping off any excess powder. Taking the blunt end of the pencil, make a hole in the soil large enough to cover the node. Insert the cutting and press soil around it to remove any air pockets. Cover the pot and cutting with a plastic bag and close with a twist

Geranium Cutting

Appleblossom geranium.

tie. Place in a warm room with indirect light for two to four weeks.

When cuttings have started
to root or when you see leaves
or shoots starting to appear, remove the bags and put the plants
near sunlight. Check every day to
make sure they are moist, for they
must not be allowed to become
dry. Geraniums don't like to be
wet so don't over water.

I have also had good luck
starting cuttings in a tumbler of
rain or snow water. In May of
1962 I received from my aunt a
5 cm (2 in) cutting off a red and
white geranium. I put it in water and in three days it had a nice
thick root on it. This was unusu-
al, though, as most times it takes seven days or more in water. As soon
as roots are about 1 cm (½ in) long cuttings should be planted. Take
great care not to break off these tender roots when planting. Use some
potting mixture as described above and put the newly potted plants in
plastic bags for two or three days. By the way, the red and white geranium from my aunt had flowers on it by the end of June when I put it
outside. I still have it—it has been a gem to me.

My mother grew lovely geraniums and she always used soil from
pocket-gopher mounds. Some say nothing will grow in this soil, but
Mother always said gophers wouldn't dig in anything but good soil and
her geraniums seemed to prove it.

GROWING AND STORAGE

Before you put your tender new plants out in the garden you should
harden them off by putting them in a cold frame or a porch where they

won't freeze if we should have the odd frost at night. Geraniums seem to do very well on the east side of a building or fence. You may put them in the open if they are sheltered from winds. You should fertilize about every two weeks. Some people think fish fertilizer is the best and I do use it. I also use 20–20–20, 5 mL per L (1 tsp per qt) of water. Make sure you water first with clear water, or you can set your pot in a pan of fertilized water and leave it until you can see or feel moisture on top of the soil. You then know the roots are moist and the fertilizer got to where it was needed. This method is fine if you only have a few plants. There are lots of good liquid plant foods, such as 10-15-10, which you may use with every watering if you make sure you follow the directions on the label. If you wish to keep your plants over winter, do not fertilize after late August, because the plants should be allowed to slow down and get ready for their dormant period.

If you have a greenhouse or a sunny room in which you can keep your plants blooming all winter, you can bring them in, fertilizing about once a month. If your plants are not already in pots or planters, dig them out of the garden and pot them. Keeping your favourite plants over winter saves money, and most of the time they do better than new plants. If your plants do well the way you are treating them, keep up the good work. If not, try new ideas or methods to make your plants happy.

Some plants I put in the basement in the dark, some I put in light, and I have four or five pots in a south window which I use for cuttings. Some plants I put in our well, which is like a root cellar. I leave them right in their pots. If the frost freezes these, I still have some plants in the basement. I water the plants I keep in the basement when they are dry, which is about every two weeks. I make sure not to get them too wet, as the roots will rot. The plants in the well I don't water, as it is very cool and damp there already.

Sometimes I cut plants back to about 15–20 cm (6–8 in) when I bring them inside in the fall so they don't take up as much space. When little shoots start to appear in January or February, I put them in indirect light for a couple of weeks and then move them to direct sunlight later. If the sun is hot it will kill the tender sprouts. Don't forget to water at all times when needed, but as I said, don't get the plants too wet. A real good watering that gets to the roots is better than a little bit on top each day. Test to see if the plant has enough moisture by putting your finger in the soil about 1 cm (½ in). If soil sticks to your finger or you can feel moisture, then remove the pot from the pan. A good practice is to water from the bottom once in a while by setting the pot in a pan of warm water. You may use half-strength fertilizer on these plants about every three weeks after they get 5–10 cm (2–3 in) of growth.

If plants start to wilt, they either need water, have too much water, or are getting too much heat. I like to shape my plants by pruning them early in spring with a good sharp knife or sharp pruning shears. Even though I have two pairs of these, I use them so much that sometimes I can't find either of them. The cuttings you trim off your plants can be put back in the same pot. By trimming your plants, you ensure they get a lot bushier and stand up to the wind much better than tall plants.

In the fall, dig up geraniums, shake dirt off roots, tie several plants together, and hang them upside down in the dark in your root cellar or cold room. In February put in individual pots and cut them back to about 13–15 cm (5–6 in). Water and leave in the dark in the cold room for about a week. Gradually bring plants into the light. These plants may be put back in the garden in early June. If they are too woody, cut off the tops for cuttings and throw the old plant away.

Good luck with your geraniums!

Fuchsias
by Anne Vale

These beautiful plants are surprisingly easy to grow. The secret is to give them as nearly Vancouver-like conditions as possible. They like to be outdoors and do not make a good houseplant. Indoors they will get long and straggly in growth and their flower buds will drop off. Find a location in part shade, such as under a tree or on the east side of the house, out of the wind. If you have such a location, success is assured.

Fuchsia 'Dark Eyes.'

Start hardening them off in early spring by bringing them into a cool place that is protected from frost at night and setting them outside in the daytime. Gradually they will become used to cold nights with this treatment and be able to withstand several degrees of frost without harm. They like to be rained on, and should be hosed down regularly if no rain appears.

Soil mixture should be two parts soil, one part sand, two parts peat moss, and should be kept on the damp side and fertilized at weekly intervals all summer with 20-20-20 fertilizer at a dilution of 15 mL to 3.7 L (½ tbsp to 1 gal) of water.

In the autumn they should be brought in after the blooms and new growth have been exposed to a killing frost, and pruned hard back to the old wood. Let them dry out and keep them cool and dark, watering only enough to avoid dehydration to the point of no return. A root cellar or cold room is an ideal place for wintering fuchsia. If you have a greenhouse, bring them out in March or earlier, put them in light, and feed and water them so they will start into growth again. Pinch back the new growth when it is about 15 cm (6 in) long and grow as cool and dry as possible until it is time to start hardening them off outdoors once more. If no greenhouse is available, put them in the house in your coolest, lightest place.

Fuchsias are very prone to pests. Hosing regularly will help, but if you notice whiteflies or aphids, put a pest strip among the branches, cover with a lightweight plastic bag and put in a shady place for a day or two.

Fuchsias root easily from cuttings taken in early spring. When pinching back the new growth, save the top 5–8 cm (2–3 in), remove the bottom pair of leaves, trim off neatly at a node, dip in rooting hormone and stick the cutting in a mixture of peat moss, perlite and sand. Pull a plastic bag over its head and put in a warm place until rooted, which should take about three weeks.

Single varieties of fuchsia seem to bloom more prolifically than the doubles. There are many superb colour variations on the market.

7

Lawns

A Ground Cover to Walk and Play On

Lawns tie the garden together and lead the eye restfully from one area to another. There is without a doubt satisfaction in having a green, healthy lawn that is free of disease and weeds. However, each gardener has to decide for herself how important the lawn is and how much time she wishes to spend on it in comparison to the rest of the yard and garden. There are some basic things that will help you to have a good lawn without too much effort.

PREPARING THE SITE

To prepare a site for a new lawn, for either seed or sod, it needs to be graded, cultivated, raked and cleaned of roots, rocks, etc.

Major grading should be done first, before the topsoil is added. Slope the drainage away from the house and fill in any low spots. Subsoil should be cultivated after grading to avoid a hard pan base. A shallow layer of organic matter or humus such as well-rotted manure, compost and/or peat moss should come next, followed by a 15 cm (6 in) layer of topsoil. This should all be rototilled together before final soil preparation of raking, rock picking and finally compacting by use of a garden roller until the soil can be walked on without leaving indentations. The better the site is prepared, the better your lawn will be.

Lawns tie the garden together and provide a place for children to play.

SEEDING

The next thing is to choose the proper seed mixture for your location. If your lawn can be watered and is in a sunny location, you could use 25% Kentucky Bluegrass, 75% Creeping Red Fescue or, if the lawn is in a shady location, 100% Creeping Red Fescue. If no supplementary water will be available, then seed the following drought resistant mixture in the fall:

20% Creeping Red Fescue 10% Annual Rye
20% Tall Fescue 20% Crested Wheat (Fairway)
20% Kentucky Bluegrass 10% Perennial Rye

This mixture could be made up by grass seed suppliers in your area. Fall planting takes advantage of the melting snow in spring. The rate used is 0.5 kg per 18.5 m² (1 lb per 200 sq ft). If using a packaged mixture, seed according to the directions on the bag. Seed does not need to be covered, although a light raking followed by rolling helps to anchor the seed. In Alberta, June seems to be the best month for starting lawns if irrigation is available, although lawns have been planted anytime from May to September. In the hot summer months, irrigation is vital to help the seed germinate and establish itself. It must not be allowed to dry out until it is well on its way. This may take daily watering, or you may get a rest, depending on what comes out of the sky.

SODDING

Sodding provides an instant lawn, but for large areas it is usually impractical. If you are using sod, the same soil preparation is needed. Lay the sod like bricks so that all the joints do not fall in the same place. Butt the edges up tight and fill any gaps with soil or peat moss. It is advisable to roll the sod several times after laying it in place so that the roots make good contact with the soil. Water thoroughly and do not let it dry out until roots are well established and the grass needs mowing.

If you must lay sod on a steep slope, lay the long side across the slope and use wooden pegs to anchor it to prevent sagging.

LAWN CARE

The first thing to do after the snow melts in spring is to rake the lawn. This helps to aerate it and remove the old, dead grass, or "thatch." Your lawn will benefit from a spring fertilizing with 27-14-0 or 16-20-0 at the rate recommended on the package. Be sure it is spread evenly. This serves as a wake-up call. A rainy or snowy day in April is ideal. Applying fertilizer to a dry lawn risks burning it. You can repeat the process in early July. It is not advisable to fertilize late in the growing season. The lawn needs to become dormant for the winter season.

The moisture requirements of established lawns will depend on two factors: the soil in which the grass is growing, and the rate of moisture loss from the turf itself. If there is insufficient rain and you are going to water the lawn, be sure to give it 3–4 cm (1–1½ in) or more of moisture. Light waterings do more harm than good, as they encourage a shallow root system. The roots will stay near the surface waiting for the next handout.

A well-established and well-managed lawn is rarely subject to severe weed problems. It is better to try and build up the condition of the lawn than to apply herbicides.

Regular, frequent mowing is required to maintain a good turf. When maintained at a height of 4–5 cm (1½–2 in), lawn grasses will compete favourably with weeds.

The most devastating turf disease is snow mould, caused by a fungus that is active only during the winter. Areas where the snow is slow to melt are prone to snow mould. Removing snow from these areas to speed up melting helps to solve the problem.

Another disease common to lawns is fairy rings, which are caused by a mushroom fungus which if allowed to develop will cause circular or sometimes crescent-shaped patches of dead turf. The infected areas increase in size progressively from the centre and in the early stages show up as bright green rings. Sometimes the turf inside the rings becomes thin, turns yellow and eventually dies out. Recommended control measures involve punching holes 15 cm (6 in) deep through the turf of the fairy ring where the mushrooms are, and, with a watering can, soaking the ring with 5 mL of dishwashing liquid per 3.7 L of water (1 tbsp per gallon). This helps the water to penetrate the very dry fungus beneath the fairy ring. Now you should apply lawn fertilizer to the whole lawn to turn all the grass green, disguising the appearance of the fairy ring. Water the fertilized area heavily and keep it moist for at least a month. Fairy rings tend to appear and disappear with no rhyme or reason.

A healthy, well-kept lawn adds greatly to the beauty of a house and garden, and is actually not too hard to achieve.

Helpful Hints

✽ If you treat your lawn for dandelions, DO NOT use the clippings to mulch plants or trees. The chemical will kill or damage them. Do not put these clippings in the compost pile either, as the chemical persists. Do not use dandelion killer if you have a baby, small children, or pets, as they can become very ill from playing on treated lawns.

✽ Female dogs urinating on lawns can cause burn spots. To minimize damage, water the lawn thoroughly.

8

Wildflowers

Wildflowers in the Garden
by Janet MacKay

Some wildflowers do very well under cultivation, but so many of them become so rank they are almost like weeds.

I think the most successful flowers to transplant are shooting stars. If you have a damp place, they will grow up to twenty stems on a plant with sometimes as many as twenty blooms and buds on each. The stems are very thick and strong and the plants will last for years.

The blue violets are nice for about two years but then they have always died. I tried the white Canada violets one time but soon dug them out; they'd spread underground so fast that they soon got out of hand. There is one little patch of yellow violets on our land. I tried transplanting a few but they bloomed only that year and never came up again.

The tall lung wort is another plant that gets too big under cultivation. They look so pretty in the woods with their pink buds and blue bells. In the garden the leaves are so big that they overwhelm the flowers. Harebells also grow too many stems and flowers and they fall over.

I've tried to transplant the crocus but have never had them live. They have such a long tap root that transplanting is next to impossible.

I have had very good luck with two native junipers. The creeping juniper is very easy to start from a small piece. With the low juniper I

Shooting Star (Dodecatheon pulchellum).

think you need to get the whole plant. I've tried to transplant a small piece of it and couldn't get it to grow.

The native ferns are very successful. We don't have the big ones in this country that grow further north. I have some on the north side of my house that are really very beautiful. The fronds are huge and so strong that they never fall over. A small fern does grow in this district where there are rocks. I have a few plants on the north side of the house and they have done very well.

Generally I think it is best not to transplant wild plants. They are difficult to transplant and do not do well under cultivation for the most part. Why not stay with domesticated plants for your gardens and appreciate wildflowers in their natural environment where they look so much more at home.

Growing Wildflowers From Seed
By Anne Vale

Although it is ethically frowned upon to dig up wildflowers anywhere, and illegal in the Parks, it is all right to collect a few seeds and start them at home.

Collecting wildflower seed is harder than it sounds. First you have to identify them at flowering time and then mentally mark the spot

Brown Eyed Susan (Gaillardia aristata).

Fall leaves of Sticky Purple Geranium.

so that you can find them again when seed is ripe for collection. Seed will not ripen after picking, so to find the right time between ripening and the seed having scattered is difficult.

Take only a very few seeds from each location so that the survival of the patch of your chosen variety is not threatened. Change locations each time you collect more seed. The seed will be viable for many years in most cases.

Collect the seed in paper bags and store in a cool, dry, dark cupboard where there is no danger of mice finding them. Don't forget to mark the bags with the variety, date, and location. After a few weeks, when the seed pods are crisp and the seed sheds easily, they can be cleaned and stored in envelopes or film canisters in a cool, dark location such as the refrigerator.

Growing native flowers from seed is a little more difficult than just growing marigolds or pansies. In the wild the seed would be scattered when it is ripe, whether by wind, digestion by animals, or other methods.

If the seed were to germinate as soon as it hit the ground, the little seedlings would not survive the winter. Nature has provided them with a germination inhibitor that requires a lengthy cold period before the seed coat breaks down enough to allow germination to take place.

If you want to sow them right outdoors in the fall, this works just fine provided you can remember exactly what they were and where you sowed them, to avoid subsequent danger of accidently hoeing them out in the spring.

Better success can be achieved by starting the seeds indoors in January and giving them a cold damp period. This method is known as stratification. Choose a small container with drainage holes. Use a mix of peat moss and perlite, moisten the mix and let stand overnight. Adjust the moisture if necessary.

Sow the seed thinly and cover lightly with more of the same growing mix. The depth of the cover should be four times the diameter of the seed, but for the very small seed, hardly cover them at all. (Four times nothing is nothing!) Water very gently. Damp, not soggy, is the rule. Do not cover with plastic. They take so long to germinate that a cover builds unwanted heat and humidity in the sunlight and will cause the seeds to rot.

Indian Paintbrush (Castilleja miniata).

Place the seeds in full sunlight but in a cool place. The temperature can be just below freezing at night and just above freezing in the daytime. Check them routinely every day for moisture. What you are trying to do is replicate their natural conditions. After six to eight weeks of this treatment you have fooled them into thinking they have had a winter and you may move them to a warmer spot. Too hot too soon is too much of a shock; 10–15°C (50–59°F) is about right. Any warmer is too abrupt and does not occur in nature. Within three to five weeks of moving them to a warmer place, germination begins. Do not let them dry out in the germination stage. The embryo inside the seed is starting into life, and to let them dehydrate at this stage is certain death.

Transplant the seedlings when the second set of leaves appears and they are sufficiently robust to handle. Keep them cool and not too wet in full light and you will have sturdy little plants to set out in spring. This method also works well for hard-to-germinate perennials.

Bear in mind that wildflowers nearly always grow in colonies of the same variety and will come true from seed. Garden flowers are often side-by-side neighbours with another plant with compatible pollen and the bees may produce variable hybrid results.

Helpful Hints

❀ When seeds are cured and dry, use canisters from 35 mm film to save your seeds, as they are airtight. (Fresh seed contains too much moisture and might rot in an airtight container.)

9

Water Gardens

My Pool
By Joy Watkins

I decided I wanted a water garden. I had the space, the time, and hopefully the energy. Being well into my seventies, I wanted quick results, so something quite simple would do. I bought a couple of books and pamphlets full of helpful hints and advice. I decided on a ready-made plastic pool. All it needed was a hole in the ground and water. It was called a "patio pool." It was the largest I could afford and turned out to be very small indeed. My pool had the advantage of being self-supporting on the patio or being sunk into the ground. I chose the latter since I did not have to worry about toddlers falling into it. Another advantage of a plastic pool is you can always dig it up and take it with you if you move house. This I did a few years later.

I duly dug the hole and surrounded the pool with broken slabs of concrete paving, leaving small gaps to be filled by rock plants and to keep down the weeds. I filled the pool from the garden hose using my well water, as I intended to have fish, and chlorinated Calgary water does not agree with goldfish. A kind friend who owned a large lake allowed me to take a couple of gallons of lake water together with all the bugs, insects, snails and two tiny minnows to help "settle the water."

The most important plants are the oxygenators. I put in three kinds, two submerged types and one floater. It is a good plan to keep all your plants in pots, as different plants like different depths. You may have to anchor the pots with rocks or gravel. If you have tall plants, they must be very firmly anchored or have the pot near the edge of the pool so that you can tie the plant to a small stake stuck in the ground outside the pool. A strong wind can blow your plant flat.

At last I introduced my fish. I had three. They were very small and very cheap. I fed them daily. I kept an old, long-handled kitchen sieve near the pool to clear the surface daily of dead leaves and debris. Floating dead leaves are a no-no.

Since my pool was fairly shallow, I did not think the fish would survive the winter so I scooped them out and they enjoyed the luxury of a holiday in a tank in the house. I did my best to prevent the mass of fall leaves accumulating in the pool by stretching a piece of netting over the surface. This met with limited success.

The next spring, as soon as it was warm enough, I returned the fish

Ferns flourish near a shady waterfall.

to the pool. I discovered that I had two males and a female, judging by the way the two were bullying the third, chasing her madly in and out of the roots and under water plants. At the end of summer I was faced with a problem. Goldfish are cannibals and my tank was too small for the seven fish. I took the babies indoors and left the adults to survive if they could. They couldn't.

When I moved house I lost my well water supply, so keeping fish was out. My son-in-law took them away to an unknown destination. I have my suspicions.

Pond Plantings
By Deb Francis

There are numerous books available to the reader that contain excellent advice on the design and construction of a water feature. This section will focus on what grows and is effective in and around water features in the Chinook Zone.

Fortunate to have an existing low, boggy area, I persuaded my patient husband to enlarge and deepen the area so that it formed a large kidney-shaped pond. The approximate dimensions are 4.5 m (15 ft) wide and 17 m (55 ft) long. My husband's patience would have been extremely tested if he did not own a backhoe amongst his fleet of questionable acreage toys! As the pond has a summer source of water and very silty clay, the major aspects of pond construction were avoided. The pond can be partially viewed from the house and as the initial excavation quickly filled in I remember reflecting that it looked as though it had been there forever. Time spent looking at natural pools in the surrounding countryside led to a very natural design.

The existing boggy area leads into a shallow pool and then into the pond proper. Shelves and ledges were left in place for marginal plantings. A narrow expanse of 2 m (6 ft) will one day have a bridge; a rowboat will grace the deeper end; and perhaps eventually I'll have an array of tropical water lilies. The pond can turn the gardener into a dreamer and has proven a great diversion. This is one place you can actually sit

Natural-looking waterfall with mechanics well hidden.

beside and rest. Gardeners rarely rest. As soon as you sit, you spot a weed and then charge madly from one spot to another, forgetting of course that the original intention was to sit! Resting by the pond, you are diverted by nature and the water scenery. The water is fascinating and always interesting. Happily I sit and dream of recreating a Monet scene, but reality is watching the endless parade of nature's visitors and enjoying what can be grown. At the beginning of each season, clumps of artificial lilies attached to a weighted nylon fishing line create a shimmering illusion of that other garden.

Several years have passed since Project Pond commenced. This has proved a relaxed undertaking that can be planted and created as time permits. The tranquil water with a canopy of trees at the deeper end and the endless parade of wildlife are enough. There is not the stress of instant perfection. Watching and observing wildlife activity prompted the decision to maintain long native grasses on the distant side and to develop the bog and marginal plantings on the near side. A coyote willow (Salix exigua) planted close to the water's edge has evolved already into a small, attractive thicket that gives the illusion of bamboo.

Types of Water Plants

BOG PLANTS

These can simply be described as plants that will thrive in continually moist but not waterlogged soil. They should always be in full sun.

Some examples for our area:

Botanical	Common	Height	Spread
Aconitum napellus	Monkshood. Blue or bicolour blue/white.	1–1.5 m (3–5 ft)	38 cm (15 in)
Filipendula rubra.	'Venusta.' Queen of the Prairie. Frothy pink cotton candy flowers.	2–2.5 m (6–8 ft)	1 m (4 ft)
F. ulmaria	Meadowsweet. Creamy white flowers.	60–65 cm (24–36 in)	0.6 m (2 ft)
Iris sibirica	Siberian Iris. Blue, lilac, pink, yellow, white.	46 cm (18 in)	indefinite
Ligularia dentata.	'Othello.' Dark leaves and stems, orange daisy flowers in clusters.	1–1.5 m (3–5 ft)	1 m (3 ft)
L. stenocephala	'The Rocket.' Toothed green leaves,spikes of yellow flowers.	1.5 m (5 ft)	1 m (3 ft)
Peltandra virginica	Arrow Arum. Arrow-shaped leaves, white calla-like flower.	46 cm (18 in)	0.3 m (1 ft)
Petasites palmatus	Arrow-leaved Colts-foot. White flowers.	30 cm (12 in)	-
Phalaris arundinacea	Ribbon Grass.Varie-gated green-white grass	0.6–1.5 m (2–5 ft)	invasive
Phragmites australis	Spire Reed. Purple feathery heads.	1–3 m (3–9 ft)	indefinite
Primula chungensis	Whorls of orange flowers on tall stems. Very hardy.	30 cm (12 in)	-
P. florindae	Candelabra type. Tall yellow clusters of flowers. Very hardy.	46 cm (18 in)	-
P. rosea	Deep crimson red flowers on a short plant. Forms a wide patch. Very hardy.	10 cm (4 in)	-
P. sikkimensis	Tall yellow cowslip type. Very hardy.	46 cm (18 in)	-
Thalictrum aquilegifolium	Meadow Rue. Airy purple flowers.	1 m (3 ft)	0.6 m (2 ft)

MARGINAL PLANTS

"Marginal" is not a description of the merit of a particular plant, but refers to the correct depth of planting in water. Remember, margin means edge. This group of plants is planted on ledges surrounding the pond, with roots beneath the water. Plant groups can be further divided into shallow or deep water marginals.

Some examples for our area:

Botanical	Common	Height	Spacing
Calamagrostis canadensis	Marsh Reed Grass. Plant in 10 cm (4 in) of water.	0.6–1 m (2–4 ft)	indefinite
Calla palustris	Hardy Calla or Water Arum. Spikes of green and white flowers. Plant in 20 cm (8 in) of water.	15–25 cm (6–10 in)	0.3–0.6 m (1–2 ft)
Caltha palustris	Marsh Marigold. Single bright yellow flowers.	30 cm (12 in)	indefinite
C. palustris plena	Double bright yellow flowers.	30 cm (12 in)	30 cm (12 in)
Eleocharis palustris	Spike Rush. Spikes tipped with small brown egg-shaped heads.	30 cm (12 in)	clump forming
Iris pseudacorus	Yellow Flag Iris. Narrow leaves, yellow iris.	1 m (3–4 ft)	indefinite
Juncus effusus	'Unicorn.' Corkscrew Rush. A rush which is for summer only. Winter indoors with the water lilies.	46 cm (18 in)	leave in a pot
Pontederia cordata	Pickerel Weed. Blue flowers. Plant in 15–30 cm (6–12 in) of water.	46–91 cm (18–36 in)	61–91 cm (24–36 in)
Ranunculus flammula	Water Buttercup. Shallow-cupped bright yellow flowers. Plant in 10 cm (4 in) of water.	2.5 cm (1 in) above water	indefinite

Botanical	Common	Height	Spacing
Typha latifolia	Common Cattail. For large ponds plant in the mud, or containerized in smaller ponds.	to 2.5 m (8 ft)	very invasive

OXYGENATING PLANTS

These are submerged aquatic plants which float free in the water. They absorb carbon dioxide and release oxygen. This group of plants is essential for healthy plant and animal life. Oxygenators compete with algae and help to keep the water clear.

For a large pond, a few bales of barley straw in the deep part help control algae. (This was discovered by chance when a farmer accidentally lost a load of barley straw in his algae-covered dugout. From then on the water became clear.) For smaller pools, a swimming pool skimmer works well to skim off debris and algae (which makes good compost).

Botanical	Common	Description
Elodia canadensis	Canadian Pond Weed	Submerged plant, long trailing stems float free under water.
Myriophyllum proserpinacoides	Parrot's Feather	Submerged foliage plant. Not winter hardy.
Polygonum amphibium	Water Smartweed	Flowers are held 8 cm (3 in) above water. Cylindrical pink flowers. Native to Alberta.
Potamogeton crispus	Curled Pond Weed	Clump forming. Large leaved, long wiry stems.
Ranunculus aquatilis	Water Buttercup	Clump forming. Small white flowers 2 cm (1 in) above water.
Floaters		
Azolla caroliniana	Fairy Moss	A floating flat fern. Sometimes survives the winter but may have to be replaced in spring.
Eichornia crassipes	Water Hyacinth	Orchid-like bloom. Blue, lavender or yellow. Tender annual, but beautiful. Do not put in pond until mid June. Blooms are 30 cm (12 in) above water.

Botanical	Common	Description
Lemna minor	Duckweed	Carpet of tiny bright green leaves will cover the surface of the pond very quickly.
Pistia stratiotes	Water Lettuce	Succulent clusters of broad upright leaves float free on the water surface. Do not put in pond until mid June. Annual

WATER LILIES
(*Nymphaea*)

Beautiful aquatic lilies are the queen of the pond plantings. Water lilies are increasing in popularity and a wide selection is available. Although described as hardy, winter care is recommended in the Chinook Zone. Remember when purchasing water lilies to check that they are a hardy lily. The beautiful tropical lilies require a constant water temperature of 21°C (70°F) or they will not bloom.

Water lilies grow well in depths that range from 30–61 cm (12–24 in). A pond's margin or ledges are excellent for placing pots and baskets, and in smaller ponds or barrels, flat rocks can quickly be utilized to ensure the correct depth. Usually the lily is already in a container,

Water Lilies highlight this small pool.

but if it requires potting, place the non-growing end against the pot or basket edge, allowing the active rhizome to spread across the container. Water lilies must not be placed too deep underwater or they will not bloom. Start with the container 5–10 cm (2–4 in) underwater and when the foliage develops, gradually lower the plant a few inches at a time until the recommended depth is achieved. You can skip this step but plants will be far slower to bloom. Remember not to plant too early in this area; early June is recommended.

REQUIREMENTS

Full sun is a must for lilies to vigorously grow and bloom. Lilies also require regular fertilizer. Slow-release pond fertilizer tablets are available with directions for use. The advantage of fertilizer tablets is that they can be pushed firmly into the plant container and remain in situ until absorbed.

Good loamy soil is best with stones or gravel at the base of the container to prevent the pot floating away. Do not use perlite, vermiculite or peat moss, as they will float straight to the surface.

WINTER CARE

Conventional winter care requires removing the containers when nighttime temperatures consistently drop to freezing. Before ice forms on the water, lift containers and place them in a frost-free environment. Tubs, paddling pools, and all sorts of creative indoor containers can be used for this purpose. A cool location is best, such as a basement. Keep the rhizomes and crowns wet. In April, light levels should be increased and fertilizing started again, to give the plants a head start before returning to the pond.

The second method of winter protection is used in deeper ponds. At least 2 m (6 ft) of water is required for this method, and it is quite tricky. Sinking the pot in an upright position to the pond floor in fall is the first step. The second step of retrieval is interesting. I have been observed creeping into the house in an extremely wet and muddy condition, certain family members sniggering and asking how the water lilies are! Wiser ones pretend they haven't seen me.

If all else fails there are some beautiful artificial lilies! But chinook gardeners love a challenge, don't we?

Recommended Varieties of Water Lilies (Nymphaea):

Botanical	Description
Nymphaea alba	White; yellow stamens. Excellent for large ponds. Vigorous
N. 'Aurora'	Dwarf lily. Orange/red, golden stamens. Useful for mini-ponds or barrels.
N. 'Charles de Meurville'	Wine red; golden stamens. Large ponds. Vigorous
N. 'Conqueror'	Medium water lily. Crimson; yellow stamens.
N. 'Firecrest'	Small water lily. Pink with orange/red streaks.
N. laydekeri 'Fulgens'	Small water lily. Deep pink. Suitable for mini-pond or barrels.
N. laydekeri 'Lilacea'	Dwarf lily. Pale pink; yellow stamens. Fragrant.
N. marliacea 'Albida'	Medium water lily. Pure white; yellow stamens. Extremely popular.
N. pygmaea 'Helvola'	Tiny Dwarf lily. Pale yellow; golden stamens.
Nuphar advena and Nuphar lutea	Yellow Pond Lily (Spatterdock). Golden yellow flowers. Nuphars are not true water lilies but make a wonderful display and are hardy.

The combination of water and plants leads to a huge increase in flora and fauna. Dragonflies in blue and red constantly flit by. Hummingbirds and redwing blackbirds nest close by. Frogs, toads, and enormous salamanders spend a lazy summer. Geese have touched down but not stayed yet. We have a mother duck plus ducklings and of course the deer.

Many plants have been gathered from rural roadside ponds. Local garden centres also stock a wide variety of water plants. A pond of any size is a wonderful garden feature.

10

Artistic Gardening

Some Hints for Flower Arranging
by Patty Webb

When arranging flowers it is not necessary to rob the whole garden to make an arrangement. A few blooms can be made to go a long way, especially if the right containers and stem supports are used.

One of your first concerns when arranging fresh or dried flowers is what you are going to use for a container. The container need not be elaborate or expensive. In fact, you may find that some of your best containers are found in the kitchen cupboard. Old tea pots, earthy co-loured baking dishes, even wine glasses can be used. Driftwood and sea shells make unique containers for dried materials.

Flowers can be dropped into a vase or container and left alone, but they will not look as attractive as when they are arranged in such a way that any unique quality such as a lovely curve, vivid colour or just the beauty of each bloom is clearly seen.

In order to position the stems in a definite design, some means of support is necessary. Some supports that can be used are foam blocks (Oasis and Sahara blocks), pin holders and wire netting (chicken wire).

Foam blocks are the easiest support to use, because they hold the stems exactly in place. It is sold in blocks which can be cut easily

Summer flowers from the garden.

with a knife to whatever size is needed. The foam blocks called Oasis are used for fresh flowers because when the foam blocks are placed in water, they absorb it. Sahara is used for supporting dried materials.

Pin holders consist of a lead base in which sharp vertical pins are embedded; shapes and sizes vary. Pin holders are very useful in shallow containers and are secured with florist clay.

Wire netting is cut into a desired size, crumpled up and pushed into a container. This support is sometimes more difficult to work in, but I find that the flowers stay fresh longer, mainly because there is nothing interfering with the water going up the stem.

Mechanics is a term used by flower arrangers for all the equipment that holds plant material in position. Since most mechanics are not very attractive, they need to be hidden. This can easily be done with extra leaves or moss. Small pieces of driftwood, shells or stones are useful for concealment and they also add some interest.

After making your decisions about a container and supports, choose your flowers and foliage. Cut only a few flowers and foliage when you begin; otherwise you will end up with an overcrowded arrangement. In order to have flowers and foliage last for any length of time after being cut, you have to condition them properly. This takes some time and effort but it is worth it.

The best time to cut flowers or foliage is in early morning or late evening. Have a bucket of warm water and a sharp knife with you. Cut the stem of the flower on a slant, remove any unnecessary foliage, and place in the bucket of water. Stems which have not been put into water immediately should be recut to remove 5 cm (2 in) off the stem. Most flowers benefit from standing in deep water for a minimum of two hours. During this time it also helps if the bucket of water and flowers are put into a cool, dark place.

Stems vary in their structure, which may be soft, hard and woody, hollow, or milky. Each type requires a different preparation for conditioning so it can absorb as much water as possible to prevent wilting later.

Soft stems take in water easily and require no further preparation. However, cut down on the soaking period for spring, bulbous flowers because they tend to get soaked and floppy. Also they should be arranged in shallow water, e.g., tulips and daffodils.

Hard or woody stems have a thick protective covering which does not let water in easily. About 5 cm (2 in) of this covering should be peeled or scraped off. In addition to scraping, the ends should be smashed to expose more of the inner stem to the water, e.g., lilac, crabapple blossoms. An exception is the rose, on which the stem is cut on as long a slant as possible.

Hollow stems are upended and filled with water, and cotton batting is used to plug the end of the stem. The cotton acts as a wick. Filling of the stem prevents premature falling of the flowers, e.g., lupins, delphiniums.

A few stems contain a milky substance which, when cut, leaks out or bleeds. It then dries and forms a layer over the stem preventing it from taking up water. This can be prevented by holding the stem end in a flame until it stops sizzling and there is no sign of bleeding, e.g., poppies, dahlias, poinsettias.

Leaves also have to be conditioned. Since they can take in

Summer flowers from the garden.

water through their outside surface without damage, they can be completely submerged in warm water for two hours or more. Don't submerge grey foliage, however, as it will become water logged and will appear green. Just place stem ends in the water, e.g., Dusty Miller.

There are a few guidelines to follow when arranging your flowers. The height of an arrangement can be determined by making the arrangements one and a half times the height of a tall container, or one and a half times the width of a low one. The flowers at the top of your arrangement should be light in colour, with the darker ones closer to the container, to give a balanced effect. Place the tallest flower or branch in the centre and vary the heights of the other flowers or foliage around it. Try to create a triangle in the frame of your arrangement.

Drying and Preserving Flowers and Foliage
By Patty Webb

Of all the numerous ways to preserve flowers and foliage for decorative uses, there are three methods I prefer to use as they are simple and very effective. They are the hang dry method, the sand method, and the glycerine method. Before describing these, there are three important points to remember in gathering plants to be dried, no matter which method you use:

1. Select plants for drying at the best stage of development. Underdeveloped is preferable to overdeveloped.
2. Choose only fresh, perfect plants or flowers. Inferior quality will prove worthless.
3. Pick plants or flowers when their leaves, petals or other parts have the least amount of moisture content (i.e., at noon on a sunny day—never after watering or a rain shower).

HANG DRY METHOD

1. Gather plants, keeping in mind the three points mentioned above.
2. Remove excess foliage from plants. This reduces the bulk and speeds drying.
3. Group and bunch stems together and fasten bunches securely. Since stems shrink in drying, elastic ties are best.
4. Suspend bunches on a line or clothes hanger in a warm, dry area with good circulation of air.
5. Dry for seven to ten days. If stems snap easily, the plant is dry.
6. Remove dry plants. Do not dry longer than necessary. Store in a covered box until you want to use them.
7. Crushed material can sometimes be restored by steaming.

Examples of plants suitable for the hang dry method are grasses, grains, foliage (large leaves), everlastings, heathers, herbs, peonies, seed pods on stalks, goldenrod, and other similar plants.

SAND METHOD

Excellent results can be obtained with a much wider range of plants by using a little more complicated method. This requires burying the flowers or leaves in an absorbent substance which functions as a drying agent. This method not only draws out the moisture but keeps the original shape of the plant. There are a great many substances which can be used such as silica gel and borax mixtures, but I have found that clean, dry sand (not too coarse) works very well, plus it is far less expensive than the other substances.

1. Select a container of a suitable size to hold the flowers or leaves. It can be made of any material other than metal.
2. Sprinkle 1 cm (0.5 in) of sand on the bottom of the container.
3. Gather flowers or plants for drying, keeping in mind the three important points mentioned at the beginning of the section.

4. Remove unnecessary parts and foliage.
5. Place the flower on sand. It may be placed with head up or down, depending on its size and shape. A spike form may be laid lengthwise.
6. Sprinkle the sand in and around all parts of the flower. Make sure the flower is completely covered with sand.
7. Never cover the container during drying.
8. The time of drying depends on the size, texture, and thickness of the flower. A week to ten days should be adequate.
9. Flowers are dry when stiff to the touch.
10. Tilt the container to allow the sand to run from it and shake gently to remove sand.
11. Use an artist's camel hair brush to remove any sand particles left on the petals.
12. If any petals come loose, glue them back in place and store dried flowers or leaves in a box until needed.
13. Stems may be replaced with wire and taped with florist's tape.

This is an excellent method for the so-called tender flowers, such as roses, peonies, lilies, daffodils, tulips, and all types of leaves.

Some colours may change as the flowers dry. For example, red and purple turn darker; pink and blue remain fairly true to colour; white turns creamy-white. Scillas stay a true dark blue and mock orange stays a true white. Yellow holds its true colour.

GLYCERINE METHOD

The glycerine treatment method is a very easy way to preserve mature foliage. The results are supple and not brittle as with the other two drying methods. However, the natural colours are not retained as with drying.

1. Pour into a jar one part glycerine and two parts very hot water and stir well.
2. Cut foliage which is in good condition and is at a mature stage

but not old or beginning to dry. Young foliage does not take up moisture easily and usually wilts.

3. Place the stem ends in the glycerine and water mixture to cover about 5 cm (2 in) of the stem end. Placing the stems in the glycerine mixture while it is hot is helpful for rapid absorption.
4. Remove foliage when it has changed colour. As a rule, the tougher the leaf, the longer the time necessary.
5. Store preserved leaves in boxes in a dry place. Mildewing will occur if there is dampness present.
6. If glycerined foliage becomes dusty, it can be washed in warm, soapy water and then rinsed. After rinsing, shake off excess water and hang up until all water has evaporated.

Everlastings
By Betty Nelson

Everlastings are mostly grown for dried arrangements. These, the most common, all need starting indoors in April and planting out around the first of June.

- *Helichrysum* (Strawflower)—Comes in many colours. Gather the buds before they open, immediately cut the stem off flush with the back of the bud, and insert floral wire. If you wait until they dry, you won't be able to get the wire in. The bud opens when it dries; small buds make small flowers, larger buds larger flowers. If the flower is open when picked it will dry out of shape. This is the only everlasting that can be washed. Dunk quickly in soapy water and then clear water. The flower will go back to the bud stage when wet but will open when hung to dry.
- *Helipterum* (Sunray or Acroclimium)—Flowers are pink and white with a yellow centre. Pick in the bud or "just open" stage and hang to dry. These are rather delicate.

- *Limonium* (Statice or Sea Lavender)—Comes in many colours. Let the bloom come well out before picking, then hang to dry.
- *Xeranthemum* (Immortelle)—Colours are pink and purple. Pick in the bud or "just open" stage and hang to dry.
- *Lunaria* (Money plant or Honesty)—A biennial like sweet rocket, which blooms the second spring. The seed pods are silver membranes about 2.5 cm (1 in) across. These seed pods are used in dried arrangements; sometimes the outer covering of the membrane has to be flicked off.
- *Echinops* (Globe Thistle) and *Eryngium* (Sea Holly)—Both are perennials. You harvest the seed heads in the fall when they turn a metallic blue.

Other annuals worth trying are: *Amaranthus* (Love-lies-bleeding), *Nigella* (Love-in-a-mist) for its seed heads, and *Scabiosa* (Starflower) for its seed heads.

GRASSES

- *Briza* (Quaking)—and Lagurus ovatus (Hare's tail) are annuals. Pick before they get too ripe so they don't shatter.

Mixed packets of everlastings are usually annuals and produce some unusual plants. One, Ammobium alatum, is very nice. Pick the buds, hang to dry and they open into dainty little white stars.

Garden Décor—How to Personalize Your Garden
By Linda MacKay

Garden décor can be any object that a gardener wishes to place in the garden. There really are no rules unless you are entering your garden into a competition. There are design principles that can enhance your outcome, but the bottom line is that your garden is for you to enjoy. All you have to do is be aware of how you want to use your garden and then be willing to plan and create a garden that suits your tastes.

Art students and garden designers learn about colour, depth, texture, repetition, balance, space, harmony, shape, contrast, scale, and other design principles. They learn about the use of odd numbers to help balance and provide harmony and the use of even numbers for symmetry and formality. Repetition of colour, theme, or shape can help to unify a composition. Reds, oranges, and yellows are warm colours, while blues and greens create a cooling effect. Grayed colours appear further away than bright intense colours. These are the same elements that can help you to decorate your garden.

Design is simply organization. To create a design, you organize the decorative or functional components into an orderly composition. In other words, you just play with the pieces and arrange them. You can always move things later if they don't work or add to them to provide balance. Think of your garden as a work in progress and you will enjoy it more and be more willing to experiment.

An old grain tank brings memories.

A whimsical willow arbour in a woodland garden.

The use of garden décor is really just exterior decorating and can enhance your experience while outside and when viewed from inside the home. Sculptural elements with four-season appeal make sense in our climate, where much of the viewing time is from the indoors. You can create mood and direct the viewer with your choice of objects and their placement. Garden rooms or areas dedicated to different uses can be aesthetically enhanced with the infusion of your personality.

Aesthetic appeal does not depend on whether a particular decorative object is good to use or not, but rather on how that object relates to its surroundings. Décor works better if it is placed in context with surrounding plants and other decorative features. In the right setting, well-positioned "junk" can become charming. At the same time, a valuable sculpture can look silly if it isn't well-sited or doesn't fit the garden scheme. A fish or mermaid statue in the middle of the woods is not as effective as near a water feature. Rabbits and gnomes prefer a woodland motif. Willow structures present a casual country look. Rundle rock is more formal than sandstone. A sundial is most effective in an area where it gets enough sun to actually tell the time.

Garden décor can have a lot of power and in some cases can make or break a garden. Décor can make us stop and reflect, laugh, beckon us to sit, or help us to appreciate the plant material around it. Some ornaments are more subtle as they peek at us from behind a rock or foliage, while some are showstoppers in their magnificence or grand scale.

Try creating small areas of interest or vignettes throughout your garden. In general, it is best to keep to one theme in an area rather than randomly scattering your garden art. Otherwise, you risk having a cluttered look that will detract from your plantings. For example, I have created a woodland vignette with a squirrel statuary placed in context around moss-laden deadfall and stumps. This forms a whimsical backdrop for some creeping thyme in front, and causes the viewer to stop, sit, touch, and smell the thyme and surrounding plants.

Décor is your chance to introduce some personality into your garden. Don't be afraid to add a keepsake that has meaning only to you. I have a number of broken cups, plates, vases, and wine goblets that I

place into collections in the garden. Some are usefully placed to hold back the dirt or provide shade for clematis roots, but others are part of a crockery graveyard that delights me because I can reminisce about the history of the dishes and parties with family and friends. Invariably, some of the breakage is due to a gathering of some sort. Using the castoffs of beautiful but chipped or broken dishes in the garden prolongs their life in my world of aesthetics. This is the key to decorating your garden—do what delights you! Community hall luncheon plate castoffs became a useful upper "rail" to my planter. They hold back the bark mulch and provide a colourful display along the entire length of my front walkway. Broken pots can be assembled beside a seating area as part of a collection of objects.

Garden gnomes can be fun and hold special memories. I don't care if they are in vogue or not—they provide family memories for me, since my mother is such a fan of happy garden gnomes. Gnomes can work in a setting if they are not made to stand on their own decorative value. Rather they are placed into a larger grouping that diminishes their status but still allows them to be a part of the scene. Evergreen plantings and woodland surrounds are particularly effective for gnomes to feel at home.

It is often recommended that you do not ignore your house style in determining your garden décor. Although you can effectively create various "rooms" within a garden, incorporating different themes, you should at least consider that your house is the largest backdrop and garden ornament you have.

To help you establish and decorate the garden of your dreams, you could ask yourself some questions. Do you need a place to entertain, a place to relax and read, an area to barbecue, a place for games or for children to play? Do you have places to sit in the sun and in the shade? Once you have created the areas suited to you and your lifestyle, then you can utilize décor to enhance their functionality and add some fun, whimsy, formality, folly, or whatever it is that suits your personality.

Another point to consider is that you don't have to decorate "country" just because you live in the country, and you don't have to conform to your city neighbours' version of suitable décor either. Taste has nothing and everything to do with decorating your garden. The only taste that matters is yours—if you like it and you'll use it or admire it, then it is suitable for your garden, simple as that.

The great thing about garden décor is that it can change as your tastes change—very few decorative items are that expensive or time-consuming to make or buy that you can't change them within a few years if you want to. Also, as your garden fills out and transitions to a new level, your use and type of décor could change. At the very least, the placement of an ornament changes as the plant material around it grows and covers it.

You can also move certain pieces around for fun and/or function. For example, a rabbit collection gets to travel around the garden for sentimental reasons and also for function. A large hare can fill a temporary hole in the garden, draw the viewer to an eye-catching rose display, or serve as a backdrop for a bed of beautiful lettuce leaves. It delights in all seasons.

CREATING MOOD IN THE GARDEN

The material a garden ornament is made of can affect the mood around the object and in your garden. Stone, ceramic, wood, and metals have been used throughout the centuries and provide a sense of permanence to a garden feature. Some imitations such as concrete can also provide a similar feel. Resins and plastics often don't have the same allure but can be appropriate in a more whimsical or less formal garden—it usually depends on the quality of the item. The bottom line is that the use of different materials depends on personal taste. Just be aware that the materials you choose have an impact on how the garden feels. If you want to change that feel, you can do so by adapting your garden contents and materials to suit the mood you want to create.

- Wood usually provides a less formal feel to a garden and is more associated with country and whimsical moods. Painted wood can provide a more formal look than unpainted wood. The colour and gloss of the paint can also affect the impact of the object (whether

it is a gate, a fence, a wooden figure, birdhouses, or a major structure). Glossy paint is usually more formal or modern-looking than
a stain, but the entire setting also plays a role on how the wooden
object will affect the look.

An arrangement of birdhouses or objects on a railing with a garden beyond can be a useful tool to draw the viewer to a closeup view
with an awareness of a distant garden to explore beyond. It gives a feeling of depth to a garden.

The grouping of birdhouses (opposite) contributes to a country
mood because of the use of country fence posts as the poles for the
birdhouses, the setting amongst the grasses, and the use of stain rather
than paint. This grouping is also effective because it is a collection of
similar types of houses that repeat a colour scheme.

Tree stumps and deadfall can be collected and utilized in your
country garden to provide functional planters or backdrops for vignettes you might wish to create.

Willow, dogwood, and other twig structures are very prevalent in
the country garden. Willow has been used to make trellises, sculptures,
planters, arbours, chairs, wattle fences—just about anything you can
think of. My garden has incorporated a lifesize willow garden angel
which has been attached to a growing tree. The angel continues to grow
up and be airborne as the tree grows. It is fun to watch your sculptures
move and grow up on their own!

- Metals weather very well, which adds to their charm and sense
  of permanence in the garden. The patinas on copper and bronze
  can help to provide an aged feel or timeless elegance to a garden.
  Painted or treated metal usually provides a more formal mood and
  withstands the elements superbly.

The metal dress form (page 246) combines an interest in textile art
with a passion for gardening. It has functioned as a support for clematis and as a backdrop for other plants. Perched amongst some hardy

All Birds are Welcome

roses and monkshood, it also provides a surprise element as the viewer takes a closer look at the form behind the function. I have changed the theme in the area by adding combinations to the dress form. For example, one year I hung a moon on the fence post behind the dress form and titled the composition *Moon over Madonna*—a play on words since this was the year the singer Madonna performed wearing her conical metal torso. Again, have fun with your art pieces and title them if the mood suits you!

The function of the sculpture changes as the garden changes. It is impossible to maintain the same look in the garden as it grows up—be prepared to be flexible with the function and placement with certain

Metal dress form provides a surprise element.

items. The dress form demonstrates how it has had to adapt to different plants as vines die off and others grow up.

- Terra cotta pots and sculptures can work well in all types of settings, from the more formal or aged to a natural setting. They come in a variety of styles and can be painted or stenciled to customize the look. Some terra cotta breaks down unless protected. This characteristic can be part of its charm when assembled into a graveyard collection of broken pots and can provide a feeling of maturity when surrounded by beautifully overgrown plants in an area.

- Stoneware and pottery adds colour to a garden and isn't as fragile as terra cotta. Their firing at higher temperatures makes them more durable but they also do not acquire patina with age like the terra cotta pots. Glazed urns, pots, and jars can suit a variety of styles depending on the colour and decorative features. Quality glazed pots can be used outside in all seasons and can withstand a winter arrangement that has been watered and frozen into the pots.

- Rock is a popular choice for most gardens and is low maintenance. Rocks can be stacked to produce seating arrangements, contain elevated gardens, and be part of a water feature. They can be sculptures in themselves, be a base for a sculpture, and be made into containers. The sandstone and glacier-carried rocks in the foothills of Alberta are very suited to the country garden. A more formal look can be achieved with the use of rundle rock. This is partly due to its colour (medium-dark grey) and its strong, angular and flat structure, that allows for flatter stacking. Sandstone is usually light brown, softer and more rounded. Volcanic and porous tufa rock can provide drainage and moisture retention properties not available in other rocks. Marble is usually associated with a more formal, classical mood, but it is very lustrous, which might adapt to a contemporary feel in the right setting.

- Cast stone and concrete can give the feeling of real stone and comes in a variety of textures such as aggregate and smooth. Seating, fountains, and bird baths are often made of painted concrete and can suit many styles. However, they do break down over time unless they are protected from the winter moisture and freezing cycles. Even preformed concrete objects can be personalized. The troll on the fountain below wears a white collar—one way to incorporate my husband's occupation into the garden. Is there a favourite shirt of a loved one with a collar that can be recycled into one of your garden features?

- Fabric can be used in many ways but is primarily a seasonal or short-term treatment. Flags and banners of nylon can be sewn to personalize the content. Fabrics can be used to wrap around tenting, arbours,

gates, and balconies to provide a festive air for special gatherings. Colour unity is particularly important if you try this. Manmade fibres withstand the sun and other elements better than natural fibres if you plan on leaving the fabric outside for the summer.

- Plastic is light weight and usually inexpensive. Some high-quality plastic pots can be integrated into a timeless garden mood. But you should be aware that plastic usually does little for a garden since it tends to look lifeless and appears more prominent than it should. However, you may wish to have a more artificial or irreverent theme, or may simply want the more practical advantages of plastic. I have used dark green plastic planters inside a decorative container to avoid unwanted dripping.

The mood in your garden can also be affected by the country of origin which you may be trying to emulate. Garden décor along with the appropriate plants can help duplicate the feeling of being in a certain area of the world without ever leaving the garden. Some brief descriptions may give you an idea of directions you may wish to pursue further.

- Southwest gardens can contain cactus, dry river beds, skulls, tumbleweed, weathered wood structures, and bleached-out colours.

- Western motifs can incorporate some of the Southwest characteristics of skulls and tumbleweed, but also utilize barbed wire, weathered barn wood, rope, antlers, wagon wheels, wagons, milk cans, antiques, cowboy boots as planters, farm animal statuary, native plants and shrubs, and barnyard motifs such as horseshoes, straw bales, and cowboy hats.

- Country themes are similar to Western but can have a less western feel if specific western cowboy elements are excluded. The use of willow can be more prevalent, and antique or homesteading items

are often utilized. Scarecrows are a common feature and country mailboxes can be decorated to portray the ranch business and brand. The collection above features a huge metal rooster, washstand, metal basins, willow boxes, birdhouses and an antique watering can to create a country vignette. Nestling it among the native aspen forest helps to give it a more natural backdrop.

- Woodland gardens in the foothills often contain naturalized areas with wildflowers, evergreen and aspen trees, or woodland creatures such as squirrels and rabbits. If a European flavour is sought, gnomes are sometimes incorporated.

- English country gardens are informal, romantic, and softer. Usually you think of abundant, overflowing perennial and annual beds, roses, and décor which includes birdhouses, birdbaths, sundials, lead statuary, stone troughs, floral finials, etc.

- French Versailles-type gardens are very formal, rich, symmetrical, grand-scale gardens. They often contain bronze or marble statuary, fancy carved fountains, classical urns and, straight paths. The Provence style is less formal, with lavender and terra cotta being trademarks.

- Italian Renaissance includes marble columns and statuary, urns, classical motifs, and mosaics. This style is usually quite formal and often contains humorous and irreverent motifs in its statues and fountains.

- Japanese gardens are contemplative, tranquil, simple, natural gardens that excel in capturing nature within a small space. The use of rock groupings, stone lanterns, small ponds, and raked gravel or sand also creates the ambience of a Japanese garden. Because cranes have special significance, they are often the featured statuary. Asymmetrical groupings of rock and stepping stones contribute to this look, and hidden views and special viewpoints are also characteristic. Little flower colour is involved, and leaf and bark textures become more predominant.

- Chinese gardens are associated with carp ponds, animal figures such as lions and dragons, stoneware fish bowls, flowering trees, bonsai plants, and carved stone or strange rock forms.

- Tropical gardens evoke images of bamboo structures, tall fern-like plantings and tropical shrubs, grass-thatched roofs, and stone structures covered in mosses. An oasis on a protected deck is one way to achieve this look without shredding your plants in the wind.

Creating a garden room in a style inspired by another country can be effective and is a unique way to take a trip without leaving your patch of dirt. Your travel photos and books can lead you to create the ambience you wish to achieve. These foreign styles are usually most

effective if they are done in their own garden room and if consistency
to that style is maintained within that room.

The list of ideas to decorate your garden is endless but here are a
few low-cost ideas to get you started in your quest to personalize your
exterior spaces.

Make a scarecrow from old clothes. This does not have to be a "Wiz-
ard-of-Oz" type; it can be a cowboy, a musician playing an old guitar, a
housewife in apron wearing a bad hair day "do," someone wearing your
clothes doing your favourite hobby or occupation, or an alien being.

- Make a scarecrow with an accompanying scarehorse, scaredog or
  scarecow. You can stuff clothes or a wire form with straw, leaves,
  sawdust or baler twine. Have fun with this one!
- Paint or draw a face on a pot and grow various hair styles out of
  the pot—you could have a collection of bad hair days!
- Use your fence to hang your garden art objects and your fence
  posts to hold birdhouses.
- Make a birdfeeder or birdbath using an upside-down terra cotta
  pot with a large dish placed on top.
- Use concrete and large rhubarb leaves to fashion a birdbath or water trough.
- Place old or broken dishes in the garden and use as a backdrop,
  birdbath or focal point, or make into mosaic stepping-stones.
- Think of any object that will hold soil as a potential container for
  plants. Remember to add drainage holes. Some examples could be
  shoes, boots, pots and pans, hats, wastebaskets, wagons, suitcases,
  the trunk of a car…absolutely anything you can think of that will
  hold soil or can be made to hold soil.
- Elevate a garden object by placing it on a rock, bricks or tree
  stump—this can add height to help you enjoy the object more.
- Make garden seating or planters out of tree stumps, rocks or dis-
  carded picket fences. Recycle and reuse whenever possible. Rustic
  seating can also serve as a scratch pad for cats and keep them from
  destroying your trees.

- Create a dry river bed to suggest the presence of water.
- Make chimes out of pieces of glass or cutlery wired together.
- Use wire or willow to make sculptures such as insects, animals or other creatures. Try fashioning an obelisk, topiary frame, or vine support.
- Place a gift you received that doesn't suit your house décor into the garden. This is one way to enjoy the goodwill and friendship that came with the gift.
- Place quirky folk art or objects from your travels that are collecting dust in the closet out in your garden where you can enjoy them.
- A unique boulder or rock, interesting roots or bark can draw attention to an area or become part of a functional display.
- Paint up some popsicle sticks or stakes to use as garden markers. Or fashion some out of wire and copper plating.
- Make cement stepping stones decorated with children's handprints or add broken-up china, tiles, glass marbles, stones, shells, glass—whatever you can think of.
- Old furniture such as wood, wicker, willow or metal chairs might be used to contain a plant, place a statue, or provide support for other plants.
- Trees—alive and dead—can become the structure for climbing vines.
- Use wood cross-sections or flat rocks to build walkways, seating and walls. If embedded into cement, they are low maintenance.

In conclusion, there are many ways to personalize your garden with décor and with decorative structural elements. Some considerations for a well-used and -enjoyed garden can be summarized as follows:

- Have several seating areas to facilitate garden activities, entertaining, and to find sun or shade when it suits.
- Use décor to guide the visitor through the garden by providing a series of focal points.
- Decide on the mood or theme you wish to create and choose

materials that enhance that. Think of cohesive collections when assembling objects to create a mood or theme.

- Use décor to fill up spots where plants are small or non-existent. Move the ornaments around when the mood strikes or when surrounding plants obscure them too much.
- Take away ornaments when you outgrow them.
- You can completely change the look and mood of an area with your use of colour and décor.

Have fun and decorate. Share your personality and passion. Take a chance and play!

Flowers and Art
By Linda MacKay

Many flowers and leaves can be used to dye fabric. Some can be used in a boiled bath with your fabric and yarns, using different mordants to set the dye. Flower pounding has also become popular in recent years. Various flowers can be smashed onto a piece of fabric or paper to transfer the dye. Usually the fabric has to be soaked in alum and dried before pounding for the dye to be colourfast. There are several books available on natural dyes and dying and on flower pounding to give you the "how-to" directions. This section is meant to make you aware that these things exist and may be of interest as you look for ways to use and enjoy your flowers.

Of course, photography in the garden as you do your early morning walk-through is a must. I often walk through my morning duties in the garden with a camera in tow so I can capture those special moments with flora and fauna.

If you paint, you know what an abundance of subject matter you have. But you may also wish to record the leaves in your garden and their veining structure of the leaves for future reference. I have walked through my garden and recorded all of the leaves of annuals and

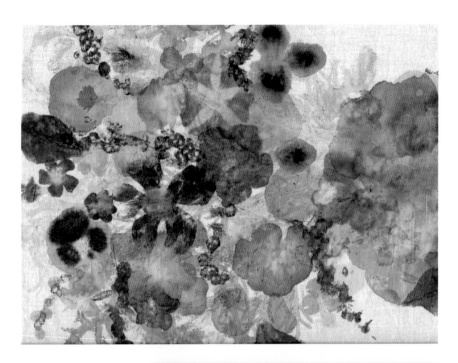

Flower pounding onto cotton.

Sunprinted leaves on fabric were further embellished with stitching and then quilted.

perennials by doing crayon rubbings of them. The detail comes through very clearly and is a useful tool for any artist or crafter. It is as simple as placing a leaf underneath your paper, holding it firmly in place, and using a crayon, pastel, soft pencil, or pencil crayon to rub over the leaf. The more delicate the leaf, the softer the utensil you use to rub with. I find that Crayola wax crayons work the best for me. For bark and log rubbings, I like to use carpenter pencils or crayons.

Impressions of leaves and bark can also be made onto a heated piece of special foam that can in turn be used as a stamp. The ideas are endless. I have used the materials in my garden for many different techniques and applications (including silk-screening, cyanotyping or blueprinting, sunprinting, flower pounding and flower dying). I have used flowers and leaves from the garden and purchased bouquets to dye an array of fabrics. Dyed silks, cottons, and wools resulted in a collection of bright yellow, golden, sage green, taupe, brown and other earth colours to be used in artwork.

Edible Flowers and Garden Parties
By Linda MacKay

There is something about decorating your salads, cakes, and meals with edible flowers that makes the occasion more festive. An everyday meal can become an event when the aesthetic beauty of flowers and their unique taste and aroma are included. More of your senses are utilized when you incorporate flowers into your cooking or presentation.

There are few rules to using flowers in your cooking, but they are important ones.

1. Make sure the flowers you use have not been sprayed with anything.
2. Wash your flowers to remove dust and bugs.
3. Remove stamens from flowers before eating, as the pollen can affect the taste.

4. Remove sepals from flowers before eating, except from pansies and violas, because they can also affect the taste.
5. Only eat edible flowers. *Not all flowers are edible and some can be toxic.*
6. If you have food allergies or asthma, avoid edible flowers or try in small quantities at your discretion. I have hay fever and asthma, but edible flowers are not a trigger or a problem for me.

If you grow your own flowers, you will know whether they have been sprayed, but be careful of flowers bought in stores and markets—make sure to check how they were raised. (Organically grown flowers are preferred, and definitely don't eat any flowers if pesticides have been used to keep bugs at bay or herbicides used to kill weeds.) Flowers picked from the side of the road could contain automobile emissions or have been soiled by animals.

Pick your flowers early in the day if possible or when the shade has helped to firm them up. At suppertime, I just look for the pansies and nasturtiums that have been shaded for a few hours and they are just fine. Wash flowers and leaves gently in cold water, pat dry, and use directly or refrigerate in a covered bowl or baggie with air in it. You don't want to crush the flowers in a tightly closed plastic bag—be somewhat careful with these delicacies!

The same flower grown in different parts of my garden tastes the same to me, but I have read that the soil type can affect the taste of the flower. So if you have a variety of growing conditions or soil types in your garden, you may find that the same flower may have a different taste. You can use this to your advantage, depending on your purpose. Do you want a sweeter or more savory, more herbal or more bitter taste added to the dish you are serving? In other words, you may wish to taste test your flowers before you add them to your dish.

Personally, I stay away from using non-edible flowers to decorate around food—how do your guests know what they are to eat? They are so busy trying to be good sports and eat the different flowers without fussing too much that it would really confuse matters if you were to include a non-edible flower in the mix. I know that certain chefs in fine restaurants do place non-edible flowers on foods, but I strongly encourage you not to.

You can add freshly chopped and dried edible flower petals to cream cheeses, butters, honeys, syrups, icings, vinegars, and margarines to infuse flavour and colour. Try to do this at least twelve hours in advance so the flavours have time to infuse themselves. Vinegars, honeys, and syrups usually take longer for the flower flavour to penetrate.

Candied flowers are also effective with cakes and desserts. They can be stored at room temperature for months if you live in a dry climate like Alberta or placed in the freezer to keep them longer. Violets, pansies, Johnny-jump-ups, rose petals, lilacs, and scented geraniums all candy well. Pick a few at a time, candy them, and then pick some more to keep the petals as fresh as possible.

To candy, beat 1 egg white to a froth and add 1–2 drops of vodka to help the flower dry more quickly. Gently paint the petals with the egg white mix, using a fine artist's brush. Gently sprinkle superfine granulated sugar on the flower, making sure to cover all surfaces. Place the flower face up on parchment paper on a wire rack. When completely dry, store in an airtight container at room temperature or in the freezer.

Because some flowers crush easily, you may wish to add them to a recipe when they will be damaged the least. For example, in a salad, you may wish to add most flowers after the dressing has been added. I find that adding violas with the lettuce and herbs is fine because they are small and don't really crush. But pansies, roses, and nasturtiums look best placed on top and throughout the salad just before serving and after the dressing has been added. The other option is to put your dressing on the side and have all of the flowers mixed throughout. This also works well.

The first year I went on a Millarville Horticultural Club garden tour in 1990, one of the stops was to Mary Dover's garden. This was not just a regular stop, however, as Mary greeted us in the garden with a linen tea service and my first garden party in the country. How special that

Menu for a Summer Garden Party
Hostess Linda Mackay
Tea Sandwiches
smoked salmon with dill butter
egg with parsley, tarragon, & chervil butter
cucumber with chive cream cheese & begonia butter
goat cheese & sun-dried tomato with toasted rosemary butter
English cheshire & port with walnut butter
watercress with nasturtium butter
Buttermilk Cream Scones with
citrus butter & strawberry rhubarb jam
rose petal & lavender jelly
Sweets & Pastries
turtle brownies
lavender shortbread
strawberry almond linzer bars
berry tartlets with bay laurel pastry cream
honey nougat with toasted hazelnuts & glaced fruit
chocolate peppermint brownies
chocolate raspberry truffles
lemon balm squares
Summer Fruits
August 15, 2002

Scribe: Vickie Newington

was! None of us knew about it, so we were dressed in shorts and summer gear while Mary wore a dress and hat waiting to properly dispense tea. I will never forget that and indeed it left a lasting impression when I later had my own garden parties. I have given several since then, with varying themes and activities. Food presentation has always been a large part of the experience, and edible flowers are a major part of the food presentation.

The photos showcase the colour and beauty of flower-laden dishes. A healthy dose of edible flowers in salads, on cakes, and surrounding the foods and tea cups goes a long way towards making a garden party an event. Occasionally, a more elaborate menu includes the use of flowers and herbs in several cooked and baked dishes. Lavender jelly and rose petal jelly for home made scones is a highlight and can also be bought at markets if you are not inclined to make your own.

I have my favourite edible flowers and so, undoubtedly, will you. Some are easier to grow than others and some are more suited to a sweet salad than to a savory one. Some flowers are great as an appetizer on their own and some suit cake decorating. Some can become containers for dips and jams. The best way to decide how to use these flowers is to taste them and decide which seasonings you think will complement them. Once I knew that snapdragons were edible, after attending an Olds College horticultural seminar, I made up my own recipe for an hors d'oeuvre based on their more savory taste. I stuffed the mouths of the snapdragons with cream cheese and cut slivers of carrot and red pepper to act as tongues for a fire-breathing-dragon ap-

petizer. This was quite time-consuming, so I had to limit guests to one dragon apiece, but it was fun to make my own edible creation. I think that playing with food from the garden stems from when I was a child, creating lettuce rollups to "sell" to the neighbourhood kids from my storefront, the milk chute!

Edible flowers I have grown and used from my Millarville garden include the following:

- *Nasturtiums*—The flowers and leaves have a nice, peppery taste which works well in salads. The bright yellow, orange, and red colours also provide a great contrast to the greens in a salad. Nasturtiums are also effective for decorating plates of other foods, and the leaves can be used in place of lettuce in tea sandwiches.
- *Pansies*— These are my all-time favourite because I can use them in salads, to decorate cakes and desserts, and to decorate plates. They look nice for an entire party and I don't have to worry about wilted flowers as my party progresses. Pansies can be candied effectively

and they have a milder taste so they don't intimidate first-time flower eaters. (Women don't seem to have trouble eating flowers; some men and children need to be convinced.)

- *Violas or Johnny-jump-ups*—These have a similar taste to pansies and are also a favourite for salads and desserts because they add a lot of colour and beauty and the size is easy to incorporate on top of a small, delicate dessert or cake. They are fairly benign—they do not have a strong flavour to turn people off. Violas are great for candying as well.
- *Daylily buds and flowers*—If I had more daylilies in my garden, I'd use the buds in a stir-fry. I don't have a lot because the voles and squirrels keep eating my bulbs (planted before I knew about the wire-basket trick). But every so often I sacrifice a "flower-to-be" by picking the bud and eating it raw. It has a wonderful savory taste to it—hard to describe—you'll just have to try it. Daylily buds can also be dipped in batter and fried. The flowers could be used as a container for dips and the petals can be put into salads. Remember to remove the pistil and stamens.
- *Chives*—The flowers can be used along with the leaves in sauces, meats, and salads. The flowers have a mild onion flavour to them and add a pretty pink- or mauve-coloured garnish to salads, potatoes, and egg dishes such as omelettes.
- *Thyme*—The flowers can also be added to salads and soups.
- *Chamomile*—The flowers are great fresh or dried and made into a tea simply by pouring boiling water over them. My nieces enjoy eating the fresh flowers after they've been boiled.
- *Roses*—The petals can be used in salads and to decorate cakes and frostings. Rose petals can also be crushed and chopped and used to bake into cakes and breads, to make jellies, and to flavour butters. Candied rose petals are also very nice.
- *Marigolds*—Remove the petals and sprinkle into a salad—one flower goes a long way in adding little yellow specks of colour to your salad. I've used the petals fresh and dried.

- *Dandelions*—Other than for making wine, dandelion flowers and leaves can be added to soups and salads. I find this is a more acquired taste since they can be bitter, so use them sparingly until you decide if you like the taste. Younger flowers and leaves are not quite as bitter. Also be careful no-one has used dandelion controls or herbicides!
- *Geraniums*—The flowers and leaves are edible but the leaves are somewhat of an acquired taste and you may wish to limit their use until you have acquired an appreciation for them. There are many types of geraniums, with various scents (including special varieties bred to have unique aromas such as the rose-scented and lemon-scented types). You will need to sample them to decide how you want to use them.
- *Hollyhock*—The flowers and petals can be added to salads, and the flowers can be used as containers for dips or jams.
- *Daisies and painted daisy petals*—These can be separated and sprinkled into salads.
- *Violets*—Great in icings and confectionery and they add sweetness to salads. They can be used raw or dried and are great candied.
- *Dianthus (Pinks)*—The flowers add pungency and spice to a salad but can also be candied and used to decorate a cake. They would also be suitable in vinegars and sauces.
- *Gladiolus*—The flowers and petals can be added to salads. Try using them as a flower cup or container for jellies or fruit dips.
- *Snapdragons*—The flowers can be put into salads, or try my invention of stuffing them with cream cheese and serving them as an appetizer of dragon heads.
- *Lavender*—The flowers are great in jellies and as an infusion for butters and honeys. I only managed to grow lavender for two years as a perennial but it is growing in other Millarville gardens in special microclimates.

Additional flowers that I have not tried but are said to be edible:

- *Chrysanthemums*—The petals are popular in oriental cuisine and can be added to salads. Some say to blanch the petals first and then add to salads.
- *Primroses*—The petals can be added to salads.
- *Sunflowers*—In addition to the seeds, the petals can be eaten raw or cooked in salads and cereals.
- *Borage*—The flowers can be candied and used in salads. The leaves are used as an herb.
- *Common Lilacs*—The flowers can be candied and used in dishes. Apparently their flavour varies a lot between shrubs, so it is best to sample first.

So, enjoy looking at the flowers in your garden and try using the edible ones in some of your salads, cakes, and cooking. As with any new food you introduce into your diet, start out with limited quantities, and if you like the taste and have no allergic reactions, enjoy them in your food groups. Now, go have a party!

11

Birds and Butterflies

Birds—Nature's Bug Catchers
Essay and Drawings by Janet MacKay

Among the most rewarding and useful things you can raise in your garden are young birds. They're fascinating to watch, delightful to listen to and, useful in keeping down insects. There are many ways to attract the different kinds to one's yard.

In the wintertime a strategically placed feeder will bring in chickadees by the dozens. The mixed bird seed sold in stores isn't the best thing to put in it, though. They won't eat the millet and other seeds like that. They just throw them aside to get at the sunflower seeds and the peanuts that are in these mixtures. I put oatmeal in mine and they really like that. They love sunflower seeds too, but my birds just get those for a treat each day. With so many birds around, a feeder-full won't last long. I find if they get a seed that is a bit tough they drop it and get a new one. I have a storm window that has ventilation holes in its base, so I just slide pill bottles in there with the seeds in them. When the seeds are gone the birds will rap on a pill bottle to let me know they would like some more. They likely know I'm pretty soft-hearted.

You might wonder what good the birds are doing in the garden if they have a steady handout. But they spread out from the feeder and are busy all day coming and going. In my yard there are a lot of big spruce

trees and they are full of chickadees all day. A great many
bugs, including aphids, lay their eggs on the branches in
the fall. Every branch and twig on the trees is exam-
ined hundreds of times by the birds during the long
winter, and I'm sure they don't miss much.

I also hang fat in an onion bag for the chickadees and woodpeckers. There are two kinds of
woodpeckers—the hairy, which is black and white,
with the male having a red spot on the back of his
head; and the downy, which is the same colour but
about half the size. They also search the trees for grubs,
etc. under the bark and in dead wood. The only woodpecker that does any damage, and this is in the summer, is the sapsucker. They make rows of holes in the
trees, then come back and lick up the sap and insects at-

Downy Woodpecker

tracted to it. To prevent further damage, spray or paint the
affected area on the tree with pine tar just as though it were a pruning
scar. The sapsuckers don't winter here.

You can have many hours of pleasure watching the chickadees and
woodpeckers, particularly if your feeder is close to your window. Also,
if your feeder is by a window you can scare away the English sparrows
when they come. They are most unwelcome around here because they
steal nests and chase away the good birds such as bluebirds and tree
swallows. To discourage these sparrows from nesting, cover the holes
on your nest boxes until the bluebirds return.

There are many other winter birds to be seen if you are always
aware of a strange sound or shape. Occasionally both kinds of nut-
hatches, the white breasted and the red breasted, will come. They run
down the tree trunks upside down peering in every nook and cranny
for eggs and hibernating larvae. I have never had one at the feeder, but
I know people in the district who have.

Sometimes a big flock of evening grosbeaks will come. They love
sunflower seeds, and at today's prices they can cost a lot to feed. They

are wanderers and will disappear as quickly as they came. One of their favourite foods are seeds of the Manitoba maple and the green ash.

I have occasionally had a small flock of white winged crossbills eating the seeds out of the spruce cones. The grosbeaks and crossbills probably don't do a great deal to benefit the garden, but it is so nice to see such colourful birds on a cold winter day. The males of the crossbills are a beautiful pink colour and the evening grosbeaks have quite a bit of bright yellow on them.

The bohemian waxwings travel in flocks in the wintertime. Mountain ash berries are their favourite food. They also like the fruit from hawthorn, saskatoon, honeysuckle and cotoneaster. They occasionally eat the highbush cranberries. Those berries must be a bit too acid for the birds to make a feast on. I've seen the chickadees take one berry and eat some of it. Some of the highbush cranberries hang on for most of the winter without the birds bothering them.

We have another waxwing in the summer, the cedar waxwing. They are smaller and slimmer with a bit longer tail. The two birds are much the same with slight differences in their markings. Both birds have that lovely smooth look to them. They have a top knot and a black mask over their eyes.

Redpolls travel in large flocks in the winter and descend en masse on any patch of weeds or grass. They especially love the seeds of the pigweed. Quite often, large flocks of snowbirds are seen. They too eat grass and weed seeds. Tree sparrows are another winter bird that travels in flocks eating seeds. They are one of the few birds that sing in the winter. They have a lovely canary-like song, and to hear a flock of them singing on a cold winter day is something to remember.

The chickadees have a spring song; to me it always sounds like "spring's here" but I have heard them sing it in the dead of winter. It's very different from their familiar "see-dee-dee" call.

Chickadee

Our summer birds are too numerous to mention. In general, they are tremendous insect eaters. Even the many different kinds of sparrows, which are seed eaters, feed their young on insects. I have seen eleven different kinds of sparrows in my yard in the spring. At this time I put mixed wild bird seed in the feeder, and as well as eating at the feeder, they are constantly eating on the ground. This is especially true when we get our April and May snowstorms. There are hardly any chickweed plants in the garden and I'm sure it must be because of these beneficial seed eaters. Some of the little sparrows nest in the trees in the yard. I have found that as my spruce, pine, and other trees and shrubs get larger, the bird population increases each year.

Regarding late snowstorms, which are peculiar to the foothills, birds migrate by the calendar, not by the weather, and thus they can be devastated by these storms. To help them out, clear the snow from an area for birds such as robins which feed on grubs and worms and will not eat from feeders.

The robin truly is the harbinger of spring. Always digging for worms in the lawn and garden, robins make our spring evenings that much more pleasant by their cheerful songs.

Robin

In the spring there are many kinds of birds migrating. The warblers are beautiful little creatures. You need a good pair of binoculars, lots of patience, and an ear for any strange songs to identify them. They nearly always stay around the yard for a day or two. If you keep watching, quite often you are rewarded with a good look and then you can identify the bird. That is the advantage of knowing the different calls. If you hear something strange, you know it is a new bird for your list. Quite a few of the warblers go on through and nest further north, but some do stay around the Millarville district. Perhaps the best known one is the little yellow warbler. Some people call them the wild canary. I have heard the goldfinch called a canary as well. The goldfinch has the black wings and tail, and a spot on top of the head. The rest is bright yellow. They belong to the finch family, the same one that the sparrows belong to.

Warblers have slim beaks and are strictly in-sect eaters. They generally nest in more wooded areas than they find around houses. During mi-gration in the fall you see hundreds around the garden. At that time of year they are all rather drab in colour. The yellow rumped warbler is the one that we see so many of at this time of the

Yellow Warbler

year. They seem to be everywhere, and for some reason you will see a mixed flock of bluebirds and warblers migrating together.

We have five different varieties of swallows and all of them prac-tically live on mosquitoes. The cliff swallows, the ones that build the gourd-shaped mud nests, are discouraged from nesting on the house here, because a whole colony will move in. I just knock the nests down as soon as they start to build. That gives them lots of time to go to the barns and build under the eaves over there. The barn swallows also have a rust-coloured breast and a long, forked tail. They aren't as social as the cliff swallows—just one pair nests by themselves—so I always let them build their cup-shaped mud house where they want. I love to watch them dipping and diving around the house and through the trees catching insects on the wing. Then we have the little tree swal-lows nesting in the bird houses. They are the ones that nest in a lot of the bird houses along the roads. They have a dark blue back (it looks black) and a white breast.

There are also the various species of birds belonging to the fly-catcher family that do their bit catching insects. The kingbird, phoe-be, wood pewee and different species of flycatchers belong to this group. Sometimes they nest close to the buildings but they don't nest in birdhouses.

We can't forget the saucy little house wren, which consumes a great many insects. They like a nest box with a hole about the size of a quarter. Nothing else can get into it then. I have a nest box quite close to one window and it's surprising how many insects those little birds

Hermit Thrush

bring while they are feeding the young. And the little male sings constantly while the female is so busy. It's such a nice little bubbly song.

Of course one of our most beautiful summer birds is the mountain bluebird. They have made a nice comeback since the disastrous snowstorm in June of 1951. The young were in the nests and the older birds got so cold and wet that they were dying, so naturally the young ones died too. For years after that you were lucky if you even saw one bluebird in a summer. Many people blame DDT and the starlings, but it wasn't those, it was the snowstorm. They were completely wiped out in this district in two or three days.

The bluebirds eat a great many cutworms. People are more aware of the birds now and they put up nest boxes, which has helped the bluebirds make a comeback. I always have a family of bluebirds in a nest box. If the hole is no larger than 4 cm (1½ in) across, the starlings can't get in. As I am quick to discourage any English sparrows, there aren't any problems with them killing the young bluebirds and stealing the nest boxes.

When I started watching birds, you didn't tell people you were a birdwatcher for they thought you were a bit odd. Now, many people do it. You will never be sorry if you encourage all the different birds to come around. Cats are the birds' worst enemy, although some cats are worse than others. I have barn cats, which you almost have to have to catch mice, but these ones don't seem to bother the birds much. Of course, I feed the cats, which helps.

HOW TO ATTRACT BIRDS

- The more trees and shrubs, the more birds. Plant any kind of tree or shrub that produces fruit, berries, hips, haws, seeds or cones, such as mountain ash, cotoneaster, chokecherry, fruiting crabapple, saskatoon, currants, high bush cranberry, Amur cherry,

Nanking cherry, honeysuckle, Canada buffaloberry, mayday, hawthorn, dogwood, all roses, Manitoba maple, green ash, junipers,
spruce and pine. As well, plant sunflowers, leaving the plants in
the fall for the birds to eat the seeds.

- Evergreens provide not only food, but winter shelter and year-
round refuge from predators. For this reason an ideal location for
a bird bath or a feeder is near an evergreen tree.
- Water is essential if you are attempting to attract birds. Put water
in pans or basins if you are going to put up bird houses. It's best to
elevate bird baths so the birds can see their enemies. A 25–30 cm
(10–12 in) disc off an old farm implement makes a good stand.
This can be welded to a 2 m (6–7 ft) foot piece of pipe or it can
be fitted on top of a post. You then place a pan or basin on top of
the disc with some rocks in it so the birds have something to stand
on as the water level goes down in the basin. Always place a piece
of wood in your rain barrels and water troughs, as birds have often
drowned in these containers.
- To discourage cats from climbing up poles or trees which hold
nest boxes, wrap a 30 cm (12 in) width of tin around the base of
the trees or poles at a height of about 2 m (6 ft).
- Upon adding a flock of bantam chickens to eat the slugs, one of
our members discovered an increase in types and numbers of wild
birds in his garden.
- For those people who suffer from allergic reactions to wasp stings,
it is worth noting that guinea fowl will eat great quantities of
wasps.

WHAT TO FEED BIRDS

- Place oatmeal, peanuts, sunflower seeds, and commercial seed mix
for wild birds in your feeders.
- Hang fat in an onion bag from a branch.
- Mix a bit of vegetable oil with equal parts of smooth peanut butter, ground suet, and cracked wheat and spread over a 25 cm (10
in) long log suspended from a branch. You may drill 1 cm (½ in)

holes in the log in which to put food, although the natural indentations in the bark will hold the mixture nicely. It's a good idea to
drill small holes in the log and insert sticks for the birds to perch
on while they eat.

- Place feeders under some sort of cover, such as 5 cm (2 in) chicken
wire, to keep the magpies away.
- Fill a half-empty coconut shell with leftover fat drippings mixed
with rolled oats from the feed store.
- Hang up half a coconut, with the white meat still in it, with strings.
Using a darning needle, you can thread peanuts in the shell on the
strings.
- Moistened dog kibble is a less expensive food which birds enjoy.

Helpful Hints

❋ To attract birds, cover pine cones with hardened bacon grease or other
types of fat. Roll in bird seed and hang from a tree branch or tuck into
bushes.

❋ Grow currants next to raspberries. The birds prefer currants and will
leave your raspberries alone.

Birdhouse Construction
By Alex Lyall

Wood is the best material to use for the construction of birdhouses. Softwoods such as cedar and white pine are the best. Hardwoods are rather difficult to drive nails into. You should use 1.3 cm (½ in) or 1.9 cm (¾ in) lumber.

There are several species of birds which will nest in bird houses. Some variations in the size of nest boxes are required for different birds.

HOUSES FOR BLUEBIRDS

Dimensions
12.7 x 15.2 cm (5 x 6 in) inside
20.3 cm (8 in) deep from peak of roof
15.2 cm (6 in) from bottom of floor
3.8 cm (1½ in) entrance hole

HOUSES FOR WRENS AND OTHER SMALL BIRDS

Dimensions
10.2 x 10.2 cm (4 x 4 in) inside
15.2 cm (6 in) deep from peak of roof
10.2 cm (4 in) from bottom of floor
2.5 cm (1 in) entrance hole

A swing-out bottom can be fitted with a nail on each side and a screw nail in front. When the screw nail is removed, the bottom will swing down for cleaning. Use non-rusting nails and screws.

Leftover shingles are good to use for roofing. Put some sticky caulking compound under the shingle and nail down. This will keep the shingles from blowing off.

Bird houses should be ventilated. Drill some 0.6 cm (¼ in) holes in the sides up near the roof and on the ends. Extend the roof on the front 3.8 cm (1½ in) over the entrance hole. The rough side of the lumber should be put inside the house for the birds.

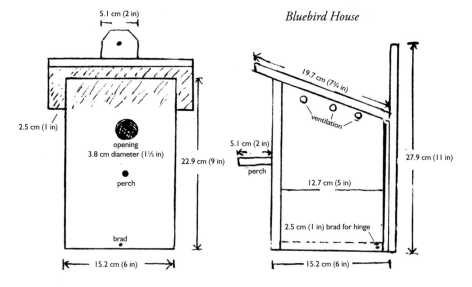

Bluebird House

5.1 cm (2 in)

19.7 cm (7¾ in)

ventilation

2.5 cm (1 in)

opening
3.8 cm diameter (1½ in)

5.1 cm (2 in)

22.9 cm (9 in)

perch

27.9 cm (11 in)

perch

12.7 cm (5 in)

2.5 cm (1 in) brad for hinge

brad

15.2 cm (6 in)

15.2 cm (6 in)

Dimensions and location:
• floor of cavity: 12.7 x 15.2 cm (5 x 6 in)   • entrance above floor: 15.2 cm (6 in)
• depth of cavity: 20.3 cm (8 in)   • diameter of entrance: 3.8 cm (1½ in)

Bluebird house should be placed in an open, sunlit area approximately 1.5–3 m (5–10 ft) above ground on a post or in a tree.

Hummingbirds
By Deb Francis

A year is marked with important events—holidays, birthdays, anniversaries, etc.—but gardeners are a race apart: we have additional highlights. A gardener's year starts with the seed and plant catalogues and continues merrily along until late fall, when the garden is put to bed. Around mid-April the hummingbird feeders are filled and placed strategically outside the house. Great anticipation awaits the spotting of the first tiny visitor.

Hummingbirds are often heard before they are seen. The little "hummers" will arrive any time from the third week of April. The sight and sound of these birds have a tendency to make everyone stop,

watch, and wonder at these exquisite birds. This fascination continues all summer long until the departure of our tiny visitors in early
September.

Varieties common to the area include the rufous hummingbird,
calliope, and ruby-throated hummingbird. Attracting hummingbirds
depends not on good gardening skills, but on having the right requirements. This ensures that birds will visit all summer long. Hummingbirds have retentive memories and will return each year if their needs
are met.

Natural nectar is likely the best energy source for the little birds,
but many birdatchers enjoy setting up extra feeding stations around
their homes. Each year, red feeders may be placed in strategic positions
by April 15. The feeders are red but the solution does not contain dye.
The "recipe" is as follows:

- April 15 until June 15: A mix of 250 mL (1 c) sugar to 500 mL
  (2 c) water. Change mixture every 7–10 days.
- June 15 until August 21: A mix of 250 mL (1 c) sugar to 1 L (4 c)
  water. Change mixture every week during the hottest days. The solution is weakened during the period of maximum flower bloom.
- August 21: A mix of 250 mL (1 c) sugar to 500 mL (2 c) water.
  This ensures that the birds are in optimum physical shape prior
  to their long journey south. To encourage the hummingbirds to
  set out for their winter homes at the proper time, some people
  prefer to take down their feeders before mid-
  September.

It is important to replenish the feeders regularly,
as the birds come to rely on this source of food. If
you are going to be away for a few days, have a neighbour
refill them for you.

If ants become bothersome by crawling
into the feeders, try applying Vaseline to the
string or wire holding the container. This will deter ants,

but at the same time ensure the ants can't use tree or shrub branches as a highway to the feeder. Trees and shrubs can be pruned if necessary.

Hummingbirds devour aphids, spiders, and mosquitoes. Next they prefer the tubular or trumpet-shaped flowers that their long bills fit into. Certain plants can be pollinated only by hummingbirds. Although attracted to vibrant reds and oranges, hummingbirds will visit other favourite plants. Scent is not a factor but shape is.

Plants favoured by hummingbirds:

Perennials   *Annuals*
Anthemis   Four O'clocks
Asiatic Lilies   Fuchsias
Bee Balm   Geraniums
Bellflowers   Nasturtiums
Columbine   Petunias
Daylilies   Snapdragons
Delphiniums
Lupin
Maltese Cross (Lychnis)
Penstemon
Phlox
Salvias

Vines
Honeysuckle (Dropmore Scarlet, Mandarin)

Butterfly Gardens
By Ida Wegelin

To offer an invitation to butterflies to come into your garden, all you need is a sunny, sheltered location with carefully selected, easy-to-grow plants. As well as forming part of your regular garden, successful butterfly gardens have been planted in window boxes and hanging baskets on terraces and balconies. Butterflies are sun worshipers. Since butterflies cannot drink from open water (e.g., ponds or fountains) you must provide in or near your garden an area that is constantly damp.

Butterflies require two types of plants: Nectar-providing plants for the adults and host plants where eggs can be laid. These plants will later provide food for the emerging caterpillars. Since butterflies are known to be able to identify colour, the preferred nectar plants are usually pink, purple, yellow, or white and should be planted in groups or masses for best results. Some examples of flowers are bee balm, marigold, lobelia, delphinium, zinnia, sweet pea, and many common herbs. Popular bushes are elderberry, gooseberry, honeysuckle, and lilac. Be sure to plan for continuous blooming throughout the growing season.

The host plant area may not be the most beautiful part of your garden. Those of you who live near a woodland may be the lucky ones. Examples of good host plants are milkweed, nettle, members of the carrot family (carrot, dill, fennel, Queen Anne's lace), rue, aspen, willow, alder, lilac, sweet clover, alfalfa, and cottonwood. Since some butterflies have specific choices of host plants, if you wish to attract a particular species you may have to do some research in the library or on the web.

In your fall cleanup, do not destroy or cut your host plants, as you may be eliminating eggs, larvae or hibernating adults.

Have fun.

Waxwing

12

Greenhouses

Your Own Greenhouse
By Anne Vale

To have your own greenhouse is the ambition of every serious gardener. When British Columbia gardeners are rejoicing in their springtime and enticing us with news of daffodils and forsythia in bloom, those thumbs start to itch to begin growing. When you dig your way out to the greenhouse on a snowy March morning, there is nothing like the smell of the green freshness of growing things that greets you when you open the door on your own patch of spring.

It doesn't have to be a very expensive or elaborate greenhouse. A simple structure of old storm windows with a fibreglass roof, or rigid sheets of double walled acrylic or Coroplast screwed to a wooden frame, will grow plants which are just as good as those grown in a glass and aluminum greenhouse with all the gadgets. Even without extra heat it is possible to extend the growing season a month at either end and attempt the growing of vegetables not normally possible because they cannot tolerate our cold nights.

You will be able to start your own bedding plants and vegetable transplants, and also grow an amazing quantity of tomatoes, cucumbers, squashes, etc. Usually it gets too cold and dark by the end of October

A small, basic greenhouse ripens tomatoes and peppers.

to ripen tomatoes successfully, but there are always pet plants looking for a cool winter home and others which can be grown in a cool greenhouse at 12–15°C (55–60°F) all winter. Fuchsia, primula, azaleas, spring bulbs, and lots more ornamentals will grow and bloom happily at these temperatures.

The greenhouse should be located with sunlight in mind. If you are going to start seeds and grow tomatoes and cucumbers or operate it year round, you are going to need every minute of available sunlight in winter and early spring. We are so far north that our winter hours of darkness severely reduce the growth of plants until after the spring equinox. If your greenhouse is shaded for even part of the day in winter or early spring, you will only be able to grow plants with a low light requirement. It is much easier to shade the greenhouse from too much light later in summer than to create extra light when you really need it.

When considering the size of your greenhouse, remember that the smaller the bubble of air you have captured, the quicker it will change temperature every time the sun goes behind a cloud. If you cannot be there all the time to open and shut windows and doors, it is a good investment to purchase some automatic ventilating equipment to take care of temperature extremes for you.

In an attached lean-to greenhouse on the south side of a building, obviously there is a solid north wall insulated by the warmth of the attached building. This is a great help to your fuel bills. In a free-standing greenhouse it is better to orient it from north to south so that the sun travels around and shines on it from each side. The north wall can then be fully insulated, as well as the sides up to bench height and down a foot into the ground. Use Styrofoam insulation, which will not absorb moisture. This too goes a long way to help with your fuel economy. Remember also that the winds can play havoc with anything not securely anchored and create a wind chill factor which can mean severe heat loss. Fences and hedges far enough away to provide shelter without shading can be of great benefit.

Heather Driedger grows a great tomato crop in a basic, small, homemade greenhouse.

A lot of work is being done on solar greenhouses, but they have a long way to go before they are an economic proposition. Actually, all greenhouses are solar greenhouses to some extent in that they trap and increase the heat of the sun's rays. One hundred seventy litre (forty-five gallon) drums, filled with water and painted black on the side facing the sun, white on the greenhouse side, and placed on the sunny side of the greenhouse under the bench, will absorb the sun's heat during the day and store the heat in the water to be radiated into the greenhouse at night. The soil and the plants themselves absorb the heat from the sun and radiate it out again at night, and condensation on the inside of the greenhouse's covering reflects the infrared rays back down to the plants again.

Infrared heaters are the coming thing in greenhouse heating. Other alternatives are natural gas or propane heaters, either of which should be vented to the outside. Conventional electric heaters are too expensive and not capable of producing sufficient reserve BTUs to cope with a sudden plunge in the outdoor temperature.

Even if you only run your greenhouse from the first of March to mid-October, this will be time enough to grow some of the longer season annuals like pansies, lobelia, and snapdragons and to have them blooming by the beginning of July. You can then follow the spring seedlings with a respectable crop of tomatoes and cucumbers.

Reference: See chapter five for annuals and starting seeds.

COLD FRAMES AND CLOCHES

Basically a cold frame is a large box that sits on the ground. They are usually made out of lumber, although they can be made of fibreglass or concrete blocks. Cold frames are covered with either plastic or glass and slope down from the back to the front for the purpose of shedding moisture and receiving more sun. An average cold frame is about 2.5 m (8 ft) long by 1.2 m (4 ft) wide, 0.9 m (3 ft) high at the back and 46 cm (18 in) high at the front. Some gardeners insulate their cold frames with 2.5 cm (1 in) thick styrofoam, for example. Most people build their cold frames next to their house or garage. A southern exposure is best, but shade from the hot afternoon sun will be required.

Old storm windows make good cold frame lids as do lids made from double-walled acrylic or Coroplast fixed to a wooden frame. Lids should be adjustable to allow for good ventilation. During

Mini-greenhouse acts as a cloche to protect seedlings on a deck.

the day the soil in the cold frame is heated by the sun. The heat retained in the soil is given off at night, which keeps flats of seedlings warm. If, however, a bad storm is due or a drop in temperature is predicted, you should cover your cold frame with blankets and canvas. Some gardeners install a portable heater or a light bulb to provide extra heat to prevent frost from penetrating the frame. Soil-heating cables may also be used.

Plants which have been started indoors are placed in cold frames to adjust to outdoor conditions and therefore toughen up before being transplanted directly into the garden. This process is called "hardening off." Sometimes tender, frost-sensitive plants such as squash, cucumbers and tomatoes are grown right inside a cold frame so that on cool nights they can be protected and therefore have a much better chance of reaching maturity.

One of our members uses cloches to protect young plants seeded directly in the garden. They are described as follows: "Each cloche is made from two panels made of 2.5 x 5 cm (1 x 2 in) wood hinged together. They are 2.5 m (8 ft) long, 46 cm (18 in) high and their corners are strengthened with plywood gussets. Use double-walled acrylic or Coroplast as a cover. They can be folded up flat or opened to form an inverted V. They are used to protect young plants from early spring frosts. Place them over your plant rows in an inverted V fashion, end to end. At night, block the ends to stop the frost from coming in. Open the ends and leave in place during the day. They act as miniature greenhouses. I cover dahlias, corn, potatoes, glads, beans and celery with cloches. They certainly give plants a head start in the spring."

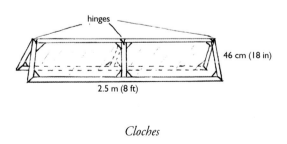

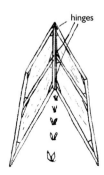

Cloches

Tomato Cold Frame
By Catherine Laycraft

The frost conditions in some parts of Millarville certainly do not lend themselves to growing tomatoes out in the garden. We have a small cold frame shelter to protect the plants during cold nights. It is a permanent wooden structure built to fit on a side hill. The peaked roof is four doors that lift up and are clear fibreglass. The west side and south end are also fibreglass. The north end butts up against the house, and on the east side the roof slopes right down to the ground.

Each of the doors is fitted with upright two by fours and nails for locking them at a certain height so that the wind cannot whip them about. When up they provide the plants with ventilation and pure sunlight. This shelter contains no other heat than what it receives and traps from the sun during the day. The plants, of course, must be watered by a sprinkler, as the roof prevents rain from entering. Primarily the project is for the protection of tomatoes, which cannot be left uncovered at night. A simple lowering of the lids is all it takes.

The tomato plants are usually set out about the first of June. However, the cold frame is operational before that. We have planted leaf lettuce, radishes and onions in one section of it and were eating them in May. We have harvested tomatoes as late as October.

As part of the review of this publication, I was asked as a contributing author to look at my article (I was pleased to find it still very relevant) and add this footnote. Although the original cold frame is long gone, the basic premise for one in the Millarville and foothills area remains the same—most sites are too cold for regular garden production of tomatoes. Catherine Laycraft, 2005.

13

The Country Garden
by Dr. Mary J. Dover, O.B.E., C.M., LL.D.

The other day I unearthed a book of newspaper drawings: "Barron's Calgary Cartoons," vol. 1, 106 cartoons from *The Albertan*, price $1.00. No date, but probably 1966. Across the top of most of the drawings an aeroplane is to be seen pulling an advertising banner bearing the legend "Aren't the mountains pretty today?" A lovely idea—perhaps we all like yielding to its enchantment.

So we move into the country, building on acreages of assorted sizes. Some buy a couple of horses, a dog, and perhaps a cat, and then all of a sudden it's spring—what about a garden?

Mine began with levelling the piles of earth thrown up from the basement, and after a short discomfort with mud, the quick laying of sod.

Since then, nearly twenty-two years have passed, and there has been a great deal of planting. In the ditches beside the highways I found spruce and pine which I dug up and replanted. Today they are fine trees. Junipers found in pots at various garden centres and planted either beyond a stretch of lawn, outside a window, or within the plans where there has been clearing are now large, graceful, and a joy to waxwings and grosbeaks.

Fruit trees, shrubs, and herbaceous plants have followed, as has clearing to make space for others. But over the years I must confess to studying and learning and a quest for greater knowledge about the treasures of the earth and riches of the soil. The legacy which I found is a hilly spot, rich in native grass and wildflowers. There are woods, deep in their growth, where throughout time animals have had the same pathways and where now I have the privilege of wandering.

After all the excitement of purchase, building the house and having a lawn right around it, there follows a surprising question. Where do we go from here? We buy books and magazines, join horticulture clubs, go to shows, and end up wondering what it is all about. The biggest thing which comes our way is a huge mass of advice, all free and often embarrassing, or perhaps I mean conflicting.

I have come to a few conclusions over the years, so for what they are worth I shall write down a short list.

The first is, "Aren't the mountains pretty today." Here is the year-round inspiration by which I live and also show off to my visitors. Some of it is the view from my window.

One of my books has been of great interest and assistance. In *The Creative Art of Garden Design*, published by Country Life, Percy Graves, architect and landscape gardener, writes of glades. There are garden

glades and woodland glades, also including borders, shrub selections for continuity of interest—all of which can be made into vistas. There is one lovely sentence: "There is a distinct difference between grandeur and beauty, and just as grandeur comes of wide spaces and long distance and height in proportion, beauty belongs to more sophisticated scenes and can be created in smaller spaces."

My second conclusion arises from the wonderful fertility of the soil. The bunch grass, deep rooted and forever growing, fed the buffalo throughout the hills from time immemorial and if cut early makes a splendid lawn. There are wildflowers of such abundance and colour that they never cease to make one marvel. Early explorers usually had botanists along in the expeditions. Hector was with Palliser, 1857–1860, and before that, David Douglas (who found and named the fir which bears his name) sent an astonishing number and variety of seeds home which were successfully introduced into the gardens of Scotland and Britain. Douglas went just to what is now Oregon and Washington, returning to Edinburgh, going up the Columbia to Jasper and thence to York Factory in 1827. For the gardener here what a thrill. The Douglas fir prospers, so does the birch. Often unknowing we buy many of these plants.

There are other names—Centennial Crab, Hopa, Rudolph, Aurora, Spectabilis and Strathmore—all coloured, and the lovely whites Rescue and Dolgo and the pink budded "Johnny Appleseed." This last is not the true name—it is the wild fruit which Johnny carried on his back, handing the seeds to early settlers. One tree here is so beautiful. I searched for more, finding them in Dauphin—I wanted them to grow along a new path, so there are John, William, Tony, Andrew, Neil, Matthew and Gordon all to be seen from the windows.

Near the kitchen are two spruce. On their wedding eve Connie and her handsome John planted a blue, so a green joined it later.

The peony row came from Brooks but there have been additions by the careful green thumbs of Bob and Stanley, who delighted in weeding them.

All the above names and plantings are illustrative of the fun gardening can be. It is another conclusion—that gardening is a year-round occupation, especially to occupy mind and time during the frosty months heading to the winter solstice and through the lengthening days when birds call their sounds and scillas and daffodils force up their green spears.

Somehow there is a conclusion with which I am unable to cope. I should like to have a collection of our wild roses. They are tall, medium and dwarf—crimson, pink, striped, and white. They grow in unbelievable profusion and fill June and July with the delicate scent of summer. The silly thing is that, having them all about me, I have left them in their natural state and not brought them together.

All of this, it is hoped, will show that Oksi Hill is not a garden of an expert. It is a place of peace and frustration, of hope and wonderful thankfulness. Someday the first steps may be finished—but that is probably one hundred years hence.

Mary Dover's garden, Oksi Hill, is one of thirty-five gardens from all of Canada chosen to be in the award-winning book In a Canadian Garden, *by Nicole Eaton and Hilary Weston, published in 1989.*

Oksi Hill Gardens Today
by David Dover

Mary Julia Dover died on 8 June 1994. The legacy she left us was her fierce pride of being a Canadian, a person with an extensive military background and of course her unique living space called Oksi Hill Gardens. The historical development of how she developed this garden is contained in the original edition. Today Oksi Hill Gardens is the home to her son, David and his wife, Frances Jackson Dover.

Mary Dover's house was removed and presently finds its home on the north side of Turner Valley. Noted Calgary Architect Jack Long designed the current house at Oksi Hill. The house blends into the existing landscape in colour and form. This home is a true "Environmentally Green House" as it is constructed entirely out of concrete and glass with elaborate vistas of the gardens and the mountains.

The gardens are maintained in the same condition as Mary Dover left them. The paths and walking areas have been expanded to accommodate golf carts to make the furthest reaches of the garden accessible. The peony collection has grown to over 125 plants and is now located with deer resistant plants in four areas of the gardens. The evergreens have grown into large and majestic trees.

We have permanent wild game including deer, moose, coyotes and skunks, with seasonal visits by bear, cougar and lynxes us from time to time.

We welcome interested people to visit our gardens to experience a beautiful part of foothills history.

14

Vegetables, Herbs, and Fruit

Raised-bed Gardening
By Pam Berrigan

The uniqueness of our climate and the location of our acreage provided many challenges to our gardening experience. With gophers, mice, moles, extreme wind, and the occasional July snowstorm, we knew a conventional summer garden was not for us.

We built two raised beds 10 m (32 ft) long x 1 m (3 ft) wide x 81 cm (32 in) high that we could cover to extend our growing season. The boxes were constructed out of 5 cm x 20 cm x 5 m (2 in x 8 in x 16 ft) rough sawn planks and reinforced every 1 m (3 ft) with a two-by-four support frame. We filled our boxes with screened loam and peat moss. We water the boxes with soaker hoses that sit on top of the soil. This allows us to adjust the hoses when needed and keeps the water below the leaves to conserve water. We attached 2.5 cm (1 in) PVC pipe over the boxes every 1 m (3 ft) to form an arch support for the plastic cover (we used 6 mil vapour barrier). We extended the plastic 1 m (4 ft) on each end so we could form a strong seal on the ends of the boxes. The plastic was secured along one side of the box with ribbon ties underneath to tie back the plastic when not needed. We used grosgrain ribbon, as it was the only thing we could untie when it got wet.

We plant our garden around May 15, including our tomato plants, which I start from seed in February. I plant the tomatoes about 15 cm (6 in) deep to help combat the wind. We plant the rows close together to reduce weeds and conserve heat and moisture. We then water it well and cover it until the end of June. We open the ends to let air pass through on warm days but always close them again at night until the cover comes off.

This gardening technique has served us well. Although we are continually making adjustments, we can successfully grow large pumpkins, corn, peppers, and tomatoes as well as celery, peas, parsnips, beans, and the usual garden delights. On average our yields are about 27 kg (60 lb) of tomatoes, 27 kg (60 lb) of potatoes, 7 kg (15 lb) of peas, 27 kg (60 lb) of carrots, 6–10 pumpkins, and generous amounts of the other vegetables.

Pam Berrigan's raised bed, bursting with tender vegetables despite the mountain view.

Al Wells's Vegetable Garden

Al grows a huge vegetable garden back in the foothills where frost-free days are few. It is sheltered by stands of aspen at quite a high elevation. He rototills it with a tractor. He designs and makes his own labour-saving tools which keep his garden free of weeds and his back free of aches. Al delights in sharing the produce of his garden with family and neighbours. He says he spends very little time maintaining his garden, but there is not a weed in sight.

Many people hesitate to have a vegetable garden because the labour seems so excessive. This problem can be minimized by selecting proper tools and adopting good gardening methods. First-time gardeners should start with a small garden that has fertile soil with good water and air drainage. Frost and cold air travel to lower areas. Avoid areas where wind causes excessive drying and chilling of tender plants. Select an area which will give maximum sunshine. If there is a shallow amount of loam, more can be added. Don't try to plant every kind of vegetable available. Select early maturing plants suitable for your climatic zone.

Till the soil as early in the spring as possible, thus allowing the soil to warm up. This also kills freshly germinated weeds as well as roots from perennials. It is much easier to kill weed seedlings before planting your garden.

Garden seeders are available which can save a lot of work. However, some people find it difficult

Al Wells with one of his special tools.

to justify the expense of many elaborate garden tools. Sometimes the cost of such tools can be reduced by sharing ownership with others.

I have found it an advantage not to plant everything at the same time. Planting some of each kind at different stages avoids loss from early frosts. Some vegetables such as lettuce, radishes, spinach, and green onions mature and go to seed in a short time. Spreading out planting times gives a harvest when vegetables are at their best.

If you have a large area for a garden and have access to power garden implements, you could summer fallow half the area each year, and thus reduce weed-killing work.

VEGETABLES

Ideally your vegetable garden should be located in a sheltered area where there is the most available sunlight and good drainage. A deep, rich soil that is neither too light nor too heavy is best for most vegetables. Well-rotted barnyard manure applied in the fall not only replenishes soil nutrients but improves soil texture as well. It can also be applied in the spring along with compost and should be worked into your garden either by digging with a spade or rototilling. Most gardeners in our area rototill two or three times in the spring and then rake the soil evenly in preparation for planting.

Squaring off your vegetable garden gives it a neat, tidy appearance and adds to the overall effect of your home gardens. To mark off your vegetable rows, use a garden line, which can easily be made by tying an appropriate length of strong twine to two stakes. Insert a stake at one end of your row, then run the twine the length of your row and insert your second stake at the other end, keeping the twine taut. Using the twine as your guide, hoe-in your trench. Some gardeners recommend soaking each trench before planting your seed, as this may aid in faster germination. If possible, run your rows in a north/south direction, planting your shortest plants (i.e., carrots, radishes) on the east side of the garden. By arranging your garden in this manner, you will ensure the plants receive full sun

Serious deer fencing.

on three sides. If your garden is on a north or south slope, rows should run from east to west to retain moisture and prevent soil erosion.

It is a good idea to make a gardening notebook for yourself in which you can make annual notations about the types and varieties of vegetables you grew, the success you had, when and how you planted them, and so forth. Keeping a record of what you planted in each row of your garden (best done by numbering the rows) will assist you in crop rotation. This process involves moving your root, top, and leaf crops to a different location in the garden every year, which greatly helps in disease prevention.

Your garden soil needs to warm up before you plant most of your vegetable seeds. Cold soil can retard germination and growth. If you plan to mulch your garden to retain moisture and keep down weeds, wait until early July when the soil has had a chance to get warm. For mulch you can use peat moss, compost, lawn clippings, sawdust, hay, well-rotted barnyard manure, or clean straw. To be effective it should

Vegetable garden in a quilt pattern makes a change from hoeing long, straight rows.

be put on in a layer several inches thick. In the fall it is simply dug into the soil. Black plastic has also been used as a mulch by some gardeners. It not only conserves moisture and keeps down weeds, but helps retain heat as well. Not everyone uses a mulch. It is something each gardener can experiment with to see if it is of advantage or not.

If you don't use one of the above mulches, hoe and rake after each rain or watering as soon as the soil is dry on top. This is known as dust mulching, which is just plain good farming. It will keep down the weeds and conserve moisture.

In most cases it is best to water your vegetable garden in the morning before the sun gets too hot. Try to avoid watering in the evening. A long, deep soaking is much better for your garden than frequent sprinklings, and if at all possible, try to water with warmish water. Ponds and dugouts are a good source of water. Their water is usually warmer than well water and contains many organic nutrients. It is also naturally soft water, which is better for your plants. If soil and slope conditions permit, we recommend trickle irrigation as the best method of watering.

Barrels to catch rain water from roofs are a must. This is the best water for your plants, inside or out. Water conservation should be the main concern of every gardener. Surface watering rather than overhead sprinkling should be practised where possible. The water table is having more holes drilled into it every day, and the supply below ground is not inexhaustible.

When it comes time to thin your vegetable rows (when seedlings are about 5 cm (2 in) high), try to do so when the soil is damp. Be sure to firm your soil down well after thinning.

RECOMMENDED VEGETABLES AND VARIETIES

Even though we live in an area where late and early frosts are a frustrating reality, a number of vegetables are grown successfully. These are listed below. All the varieties mentioned in this chapter have been tried and proven successful. However, bear in mind that new and improved hybrids are being developed all the time so you should refer to your Alberta Horticultural Guide each year.

- *Asparagus*
  This perennial vegetable takes four years from seed to be edible. Otherwise, transplant two-year-old plants purchased from a nursery. Needs deep, rich well-prepared soil. Fertilize in April with a high nitrogen fertilizer before the plant starts to grow. Needs lots of water. Harvest spears until the middle of June. Female plants bear berries, so dig up and discard them, as they don't produce as well as male plants. *Storage*: Best to eat fresh. Asparagus enthusiasts have the water boiling before they even go out and cut it.
- *Beans: Bush Type (Green)—Blue Lake, Tendergreen, Dwarf Stringless; Bush Type (Yellow)—Golden Wax*
  If the soil is warm you can sow beans in mid-May. Cover on cold nights. Very susceptible to frost. Don't cultivate or disturb beans when wet. In low-lying areas near the mountains it is difficult to grow beans, due to frost. Harvest when beans break easily when snapped. In fall, after frost, cut off tops, leaving roots in the ground, as they provide nitrogen. *Storage*: Blanch and freeze; can.

- *Broad Beans: Broad Windsor*
Plant early, as they are slow growing. Quite hardy—will withstand spring frost. Pinch out growing top when plants are about 76 cm (30 in) high or when they have four or five sprays of flowers. *Storage*: pick when young and tender to blanch and freeze.
- *Pole Beans: Scarlet Runner*
Sensitive to frost—must be grown with protection either against a wall or fence. Attract hummingbirds. *Storage*: blanch and freeze.
- *Beets: Tendersweet, Detroit Dark Red, Formanova, Early Wonder*
When harvesting beets, twist tops off rather than cutting, to prevent bleeding. Beet greens are very high in vitamins. They can be harvested when young and cooked like spinach. *Storage*: Pickle; cook and freeze.
- *Broccoli: Green Comet, Green Duke, Di Cicco, Cleopatra*
Start indoors under lights or in the greenhouse in mid-April. Harden off in cold frame as early as possible. After transplanting in garden put a tin can from which both ends have been removed around seedling and push down in soil about 5 cm (2 in). Remove before plant gets too big. This protects plant from wind and cutworms. Likes manure and well-watered rich soil. Harvest centre head first when still hard and green. Take 8–10 cm (3–4 in) of stem with flower head to produce high yield on side shoots. *Storage*: blanch and freeze.
- *Brussels Sprouts: Jade Cross Hybrid F1, Half Dwarf*
Same procedure as for broccoli. To hasten development, remove growing point when first sprouts are firm and remove lower leaves as sprouts form. Pick lower sprouts first. Require long, cool growing season. Harvest in late September. *Storage*: blanch and freeze.
- *Cabbage: Red—Red Head, Savoy—Chief Tan Drumhead.*
Early cabbage: Golden Acre or Early Marvel have a small, firm, round head which matures in early July. Mid-season varieties such as Bonanza are a general purpose cabbage which can be used for coleslaw, etc. For storage purposes, you should grow a late season cabbage such as Danish Ballhead or Ultragreen. Red

Cabbage is grown for salads and pickling as well as for its ornamental effect. *Storage*: Blanch and freeze; store in cold room; pickle; make sauerkraut.

- *Carrots: Amsterdam, Nantes Strong Top, Early Cross Hybrid F1, Imperator, Touchon, Chantenay Types*
  Gourmet Carrots—Parisienne (harvest when young) like a sandy soil. Sow in garden in May. Water regularly—too much or too little water causes problems. To prevent green shoulders, keep roots covered with soil. Plant in rows the width of your hoe and sprinkle seed randomly down the trench. This helps carrots to come up, and although not much more space is used than if you planted a thin row, your yield is much greater. Harvest before heavy frost. Thin by using young carrots early in the season. Carrots for fall harvest must have room to grow. *Storage*: Cut 1 cm (½ in) down from the crown to prevent growth and store in sand in cold room or in plastic bags in fridge; blanch and freeze; dry; pickle.

- *Cauliflower: Self-blanching (this variety doesn't need to be tied up), Super Snowball, Early Snowball, Igloo*
  Same procedure as for broccoli. As soon as head becomes visible, tie the leaves loosely up around the plant to prevent yellowing. Cauliflower requires a great deal of water, so keep soil moist. Cold nights after planting out causes blind heads (no head at all). Plant out later than broccoli and cabbage. *Storage*: Blanch and freeze at their prime; dry.

- *Celery: Utah Green, Golden Crisp, Self-blanching*
  Start indoors under lights or in the greenhouse in mid-March. Plant in garden after danger of frost is past in 25 cm (10 in) deep trench which is filled in as celery grows. Needs lots of water and likes rich soil. Cold nights can cause bolting. Utah Green tolerates cold weather. *Storage*: Blanch and freeze in unsalted water; dry.

- *Corn: Amazing Early Alberta, Alberta Gold, Spancross, Polar Vee, Earlivee*
  Likes lots of sun and rich, light loam. Must be sheltered from the wind. Needs constant water at silk stage. Plant three or four rows

together with a distance of 1 m (3 ft) between rows for pollination. Most sweet corn will not germinate at soil temperatures under 10°C (50°F), so it cannot be sown in your garden until your soil has warmed sufficiently, which may mean early June. Cover on cold nights after growing point comes up, for it is very sensitive to frost. Pick corn when silk on cobs is brown and dry and kernels are well formed. Corn seldom ripens here; the growing season is too short. *Storage*: Blanch and freeze on or off the cob; dry.

- *Horseradish*
  This perennial vegetable spreads rapidly, so you should plant in a separate bed. Can harvest roots two years after planting. Harvest roots early. *Storage*: Make into sauce.
- *Kohlrabi: Early Purple, Early White*
  Start indoors or sow seed directly in garden. Freezes well. *Storage*: Blanch and freeze.
- *Leeks: Large American Flag, Titan*
  Start the same way as onions and hill them as they grow. *Storage*: Blanch and freeze.
- *Lettuce: Head—Iceberg, Great Lakes, New York, Tom Thumb Butterhead—Buttercrunch; Cos—Cosmo; Leaf—Grand Rapids, Ruby Red*
  Sow seed thinly in early May. When 5 cm (2 in) tall, thin to 30 cm (12 in) apart. Thinnings may be transplanted. Water with trickle irrigation. Doesn't like hot weather. Can make successive plantings for continuous crop. Slugs can be a problem.
- *Onions: Autumn Spice, Sweet Spanish Utah Strain, Yellow Globe Danvers, Canada Maple, Fiesta; Pickling Onions—White Port Silverskins*
  Start indoors or in the greenhouse—the later you plant them the hotter the flavour. As they grow, add more soil and feed instead of pricking out. Near the end of May, immerse flat in water so that seedlings can be easily pulled apart. Plant 10

cm (4 in) apart in a trench 8 cm (3 in) deep. In August, remove soil from the top half of the onion and bend the tops over—this assists in the ripening process. At the first sign of frost, remove onions from the garden. Set out in sunny location every day to dry on a screen for air circulation. When tops shrivel up, they are dry. Hang in a dry place in old nylon stockings or net bags. *Storage*: Dry; braid and hang in dry place; freeze (no need to blanch).

- *Parsnips: Improved Hollow Crown*
Slow to germinate, so sow radish seed with it to mark the row. Deep soil preparation is a must. Light frost improves the flavour. Leave some in the ground all winter and dig as soon as the soil thaws in the spring. Thin to give growing space. *Storage*: Blanch and freeze; dry.

- *Peas: Little Marvel, Homesteader, Laxton's Progress, Freezer 69, Green Arrow; Edible Pod Peas—Sugar Snap.*
As soon as your vegetable garden is dry enough to work, plant at least one row of peas. Plant varieties with different maturing dates for a continuous supply of fresh, young peas all summer. Often, peas are planted two rows at a time, the rows being 15–20 cm (6–8 in) apart. In the space between the rows put in support posts every 1 m (3 ft) and stretch 2.5 cm (1 in) chicken wire between them. Your peas will climb on and be supported by this wire and harvesting will be much easier. Peas like moist, rich earth, so do not let your soil dry out. To avoid powdery mildew, remove old, unproductive plants by pruning at ground level. If your plants are attacked by powdery mildew, be sure to remove and burn all the infected plants—don't put them in the compost heap. Leave roots of plants in the ground, as they are full of nitrogen. *Storage*: Blanch and freeze; dry.

- *Potatoes: Kennebec, Norland, Netted Gem, Pontiac, Yukon Gold, All Blue*
Potatoes help to clean the soil of weeds by competition, and they

break up the soil. Potatoes use a lot of soil nutrients, which must be replenished the following year. Potatoes like a well-drained loam. Avoid letting the ground dry out or get too wet. Plant potatoes in rows 1 m (3 ft) apart with plants 46 cm (18 in) apart in the row. When they break through the soil, build the earth up around them. As they grow, continue to do this to support the stems and keep the sun off the tubers. This process is called "hilling." It is best to harvest potatoes on an overcast day. Spread them on a dry, flat surface to dry out, leaving some dirt on them. As soon as they are dry (a few hours) put in a humid, cool spot that is completely dark, for exposure to light causes their surface to turn green and poisonous. Potatoes keep well in bushel baskets in the cold room. *Storage*: As above.

- *Pumpkin: Spirit, Neon*
  Grow the same as squash—needs lots of space and lots of heat. *Storage*: On a shelf in cold room or root cellar.
- *Radishes: Early Scarlet Globe, Cherry Belle, French Breakfast, White Icicle*
  May be planted every ten days for continuous supply from early May on. Mix with rows of lettuce and carrots, which assists in their germination. Otherwise, plant in blocks 0.6–1 m (2–3 ft) square. Flea beetles can destroy radishes—to repel beetles, plant mint with your radishes or spray them with catnip tea. Maggots can be controlled by spreading crushed egg shells over the soil surface around the plants. Grow best in cool weather, so plant in spring. *Storage*: Winter radish can be stored in cold room or root cellar.
- *Rhubarb*
  A perennial vegetable that prefers rich, well-drained, deeply worked soil and a sunny location. Plant roots just below the soil surface in May and allow to grow for two years before harvesting stalks. When seed stalks form, cut them off near the ground. To force a rhubarb plant for early eating, encircle with a bucket from which the bottom has been removed or else with several rubber tires. Remove later in the season. For jelly recipes calling for lemon

juice, use rhubarb juice. *Storage*: Jam; jelly; freeze; make juice, relish or chutneys; wine; dry; use in pies and other desserts.

- *Rutabaga: (Swede Turnip), Altasweet, Laurentian*
These are grown for winter storage. Sow outdoors at the end of May. Must be thinned to 25 cm (10 in) apart. Water and cultivate regularly. Root maggots and flea beetles are a problem. In the fall when harvested, paint with a thin layer of melted paraffin wax after removing all maggot holes, then store in the cold room, or put in plastic bags, leaving the tops open, and store in the cold room. *Storage*: As above. Also can blanch and freeze or cook, mash and freeze; dry.

- *Spinach: King of Denmark, Hybrid #7 Fl, Leaf Beet Perpetual Spinach, Long Standing Bloomsdale*
Sow seed in garden in early May. Water frequently. Likes well-rotted manure and rich soil. Keep cut so it keeps producing and doesn't bolt. Leaf Beet Perpetual Spinach will not bolt. *Storage*: Blanch and freeze. Cook in larger quantities and freeze in family-size servings, undrained.

- *Squash: Zucchini Summer Squash—Zucchini Select, Gold Rush*
Start indoors in peat pots and transplant to warm, protected spot that has lots of sun, or start outdoors under hot caps. Likes well-rotted manure or manure tea. When fruit starts to develop, pick flower off end of fruit and discard. Young fruit is generally best. Very susceptible to frost. Zucchini is the fastest growing squash. *Storage:* Pickle; dry; freeze; grate and freeze for later use in baking. *Use:* Bread & butter pickles and dills; can be used instead of cucumbers.

- *Summer Scallop Squash: St. Pat.* Grow as above.
- *Vegetable Spaghetti Squash:* Grow in cold frame.
- *Buttercup Squash: Sweet Mama.* Grow in cold frame.
- *Swiss Chard: Silver Giant, Ruby Red, Fort Hope Giant*
Plant end of May. Water frequently. Both stem and leaves are edible. *Storage*: Blanch and freeze; dill; make relish.

- *Tomatoes: Brandywine, Early Girl, Manitoba, Starfire, Sweet Million, Tumbler (hanging baskets)*

Should be started indoors. Like rich well-drained soil. Fertilize with manure tea or Tomato Food. Epsom salts are good to acidify the soil. Prune a number of the shoots from the axils of the leaves and in mid-summer pinch off any blossoms, as there is not time for them to produce fruit. You want to concentrate the plant's energy on developing and maturing existing fruit. Must be grown in a warm, sheltered spot or in a cold frame. The plastic device called "Wall Of Water" is good to protect young plants. To prevent blossom-end rot, an even supply of water is essential. Tomatoes are pollinated by the wind, not bees. When planted in greenhouse, shake plant at mid-day to assure pollination and proper fruit formation. Variety maturity days mentioned in catalogues refer to the number of days from setting of blossom to the ripening of the fruit. Don't grow anything with a longer maturity than 56 days, unless you have a greenhouse. *Storage*: Blanch, peel, stew and freeze; puree raw in blender, put in containers (e.g., empty yogurt cups) and freeze; can; make juice; dry.

- *Turnip: Purple Top White Globe*
  Not a storage turnip. Same growing directions as rutabaga.

Helpful Hints

※ Spinach can be sown in August, as the small plants will live over winter and you will have greens in May.

※ Peas can be sown in fall. They will come up in spring before the garden is ready to work. Cold nights don't hurt seedlings.

※ When onion seedlings started inside reach 15 cm (6 in) in height, cut back to 8 cm (3 in). When transplanting to garden, trim both roots and tops.

STORING CARROTS OVER WINTER

- Cut off enough of the carrot to remove growing part so they won't sprout and grow in storage.
- Store in layers separated by newspaper in styrofoam coolers with lid closed.
- Store in cardboard boxes with lid closed.
- Store in pails covered with plastic bags.
- Store in moist sand or peat moss. Do not allow the mix to become too dry.

When planting out cabbage family plants and onions, prune leaves back halfway, especially if the temperature is high. It cuts down on evaporation, prevents wilting and plant shock and gives roots time to get established.

Throw in a few radish seeds when you plant slow-germinating seeds like parsnips, parsley, carrots, and asparagus seed. It helps you find the rows when doing your first weeding.

When staking tomato plants, tie the stalks to support stakes with panty hose. This will not cut into the stems.

Herbs
By Patty Webb

Since I have started growing herbs I have found it a fascinating and rewarding part of gardening. Herbs can be grown along with your vegetables and flowers or you can plant them in a special spot of their own. Some of them can also be potted up and kept indoors to use during the winter. Most herbs grow well in a protected area in full sun. I would like to share with you some of the experiences I have had growing and using herbs.

Pick leaves and flowers when flower buds are about half open— they have the most flavour and aroma at this stage. Also pick before noon, as soon as the sun has dried off the dew. Try not to crush them, as they will lose their fragrance, and do not gather more herbs than you

Herbs and vegetables on the deck, handy to the kitchen.

can deal with quickly. It is, of course, better to use fresh herbs when possible, but this is not always practical, so we have to preserve them in some manner for future use.

AIR DRYING

Method 1
- all herbs should be dried in an airy, dry, darkened place
- cut herbs with a sharp knife
- tie into bunches and hang upside down
- should be dry in 1–2 weeks
- ready when brittle to touch

Method 2
- faster method
- spread wet herbs on newspaper, cotton, cheesecloth or non-metal-

lic mesh and arrange so air can circulate around them
- drying area should be warm and dry (can use food dryer)
- check herbs after about 12 hours—if they are brittle to touch, they are ready to be stored

STORING
- strip leaves from stems
- do not crumble too much or they lose their flavour
- for best flavour and aroma, crumble or pulverize just before using
- put into clean, airtight containers
- label and date containers (after a year discard old herbs)
- keep jars in dark part of the kitchen

FREEZING
- herbs are quickly and easily frozen
- gather herbs, wash and shake off any water
- put into plastic bags, label, date, and freeze

Note: Flavour in dried herbs is more concentrated than in fresh or frozen, so you need a smaller amount. Usually ⅓ to ½ the amount you would use of fresh or frozen herbs.

Basil (Ocimum basilicum) annual (frost tender)
- use fresh or dried
- wonderful flavour when used with all tomato dishes, eggs, bland vegetables, meat, chicken, fish, and pasta dishes
- use fresh leaves in salads and oil and vinegar dressings
- add to butter sauces for fish

Balm or Lemon Balm (Melissa officinalis) annual
- use fresh or dried
- refreshing lemon flavour and aroma
- use fresh in fruit or vegetable salads
- season sauces, egg dishes, chicken, and fish

- makes excellent tea
- use in potpourri
- use in herb baths

Borage (Borago officinalis) annual

- use fresh for the cucumber-like flavour
- use young leaves in salads and cold drinks
- beautiful blue flowers can be used as a garnish in punches, iced drinks, and salads
- flowers can be sugared or candied to decorate cakes and other confections

Chamomile (Matricaria chamomile) annual

- self seeds
- makes a soothing tea for stress and digestion
- add fragrant flowers to potpourri

Chervil (Anthriscus cerefolium) annual

- delicate parsley-like flavour with a hint of anise
- use fresh in soups or egg dishes
- sprinkle generously over chicken, pork, fish, and shellfish
- add chopped leaves to butter sauces for vegetables
- especially delicious on carrots, peas, and tomato dishes
- use to garnish and add to salads
- flavour does not withstand long cooking

Chives (Allium schoenoprasum) perennial

- use fresh, frozen, or dried
- mild onion flavour
- use as a seasoning in salads, baked potatoes, omelets, and sauces
- the lavender flowers are also flavourful and can be added as a garnish

Garlic Chives (Allium tuberosum) perennial

- not as hardy as regular chives
- use fresh
- use like regular chives where you want to enhance with garlic flavour
- can replace garlic in sauces and salads

Dill *(Anethum graveolens)* annual
- use fresh or dried
- dill's pungent flavour is present in both seed heads and leaves (dill weed)
- the stronger dill flavour is more pronounced in the mature seed heads than the fine leaves
- use both leaves and seeds to flavour vinegar, cream cheese, dips, sauces, salads, salad dressing, eggs, poultry, and especially fish
- dill weed makes an attractive garnish
- chewing dill seeds will freshen your breath

Garlic *(Allium sativum)* annual
- use fresh or dried
- when garlic blooms, cut off the scapes before they set seed so all the energy goes to making bulbs.
- harvest garlic in fall when foliage is yellow about halfway down
- replant garlic cloves in fall when planting tulips. Mulch if soil is very dry.
- store like onions
- for drying, peel and chop garlic bulbs and dry. Put dried pieces into blender and grind into powder.
- garlic flavour is enjoyed in a variety of main dishes, dips, and appetizers

Hyssop *(Hyssopus officinalis)* perennial
- can be toxic in large quantities
- use fresh or dried
- leaves have a slightly bitter and light minty combination of flavours
- the unusual tang of flavour goes well in salads, soups, and meats (especially lamb and stews)
- a little hyssop can be added to fruit and drinks
- hot hyssop tea is reported to help coughs

Marjoram *(Majorana hortensis)* annual
- use fresh or dried

- strong sage-like flavour
- used to season meats (make duck, goose and pork, seem less heavy)
- sprinkle over vegetables and legumes
- fresh, finely chopped leaves added to salads and salad dressings
- use sparingly, as it is a dominant herb

Mints (Mentha species) aggressive perennial plant
- use fresh or dried
- use when cooking lamb
- makes excellent jelly and sauce
- use fresh leaves in salads, with early spring vegetables or in cool fruit drinks
- makes a refreshing tea (helps with digestion)
- plant in a contained area to curb its aggressive habit (e.g., plant in a bottomless pail or bucket)

Nasturtium (Tropaeolum majus) annual
- use fresh leaves and flowers
- peppery flavour similar to watercress
- good in salads and for garnishes
- add finely chopped leaves in cream cheese and whipped butter for unique spreads on sandwiches and canapes
- unripe seed pods can be pickled and used as a substitute for capers

Oregano (Oregano heracleoticum) tender perennial*
- use fresh or dried
- sharper and spicier flavour than marjoram
- common ingredient in Spanish, Mexican, and Italian dishes
- can be used in same dishes as marjoram

Parsley (Petroslinum sativum) annual
- use fresh or dried
- there is practically no main dish it will not improve
- parsley accentuates the flavour of food without being dominant
- when used as a garnish it makes any dish look more tempting

* Tender perennials will not winter reliably outdoors in this area.

- makes a good tea
- combines well with other herbs
- tones down the odour of strong vegetables like onions and garlic
- chew fresh leaves to freshen breath

Rosemary (Rosmarinus officinalis) tender perennial*
- keep over the winter as a houseplant in a sunny location
- use fresh or dried
- pungent savory taste
- pick young, tender leaves as soon as their aroma develops
- do not wash
- excellent in flavouring meats, fish, and chicken dishes (especially good with lamb)
- use sparingly because the flavour can be dominating
- use in potpourri

Sage (Salvia officinalis) tender perennial*
- use fresh or dried
- pungent aromatic flavour when dried
- fresh leaves are more delicate in flavour
- do not wash leaves
- good with all rich fatty meats, poultry, and fish (e.g., pork, goose, duck, mackerel)
- an important ingredient in stuffings
- makes a good spring tonic tea
- a strong herb; use with care; tends to get bitter with long cooking

Summer Savory (Satureja hortensis) annual
Winter Savory (Satureja montana) tender perennial*
- both savorys have a robust flavour, though winter savory is stronger
- use dried or fresh (use fresh in season; it dries well)
- do not wash leaves
- very strong flavour; use sparingly
- good with all rich fatty meats, and poultry
- best known for their use with all types of beans

* Tender perennials will not winter reliably outdoors in this area.

- savorys not only give flavour but cut down on gas produced by beans
- put 2–3 fresh leaves in cooking water to eliminate the strong odours in cabbage and turnips
- a few sprigs in wine vinegar makes a tasty vinegar to use in French dressing

French Tarragon (Artemisia dracunculus sativa) tender perennial*
- use fresh (can be preserved by holding in vinegar until needed)
- distinctive flavour
- important herb in French cooking
- make tarragon vinegar by steeping the fresh herb in white wine vinegar; use to make French dressing.
- add to roast meats, poultry dishes, and fish
- blend into light, buttery sauces and serve with mild-flavoured vegetables
- will only grow from cuttings, not from seed. Even the seed reverts to the common Russian type, which is a hardy perennial but has no taste.

Thyme (Thymus vulgaris) perennial*
- use fresh or dried, do not wash
- has a very strong, pungent flavour, so use sparingly
- another important herb in French cooking
- used in meats, poultry, fish, stuffings, egg, and cheese dishes. Also good in salads, vegetables, soups, and stews.
- helps in digestion of fatty foods
- use for tea
- use in potpourri
- use in bath for tired, aching muscles

* Tender perennials will not winter reliably outdoors in this area.

HERB TEA

Whatever your taste buds desire in flavour will determine what herb or combination of herbs you will use for your herb tea. Just about every herb can be used for tea. All teas are made in the normal way. Just warm the pot, put in the herbs, pour in boiling water and allow to steep for 5–10 minutes. Use 5 mL (1 tsp) of dried herbs for each 250 mL (1 c) and one for the pot, or, if you use fresh herbs, use 15 mL (3 tsp) per 250 mL (1 c).

HERBS IN THE BATH

Herbs added to a bath are refreshing and fragrant. Just add fresh leaves or flowers to the bath water or you can put them into a bag and hang under the hot water tap. You may also make a strong herb tea and add it to the bath water. The following herbs can be used: thyme, mint, lemon balm, or dandelion.

HERB POTPOURRI

The sweet fresh scent of summer can be captured all year round in potpourri. It is easy to make and makes a nice gift. It is used to scent drawers and cupboards and it helps keep moths away.

The following herbs can be used in a potpourri:

borage	oregano
chamomile	rosemary
hyssop	sage
lemon balm	savory
marjoram	tarragon
mint	thyme

Flower heads can be added for colour, fragrance, and bulk. Orris root is the dried root of the Florentine iris and is added to the potpourri and acts as a fixative. Orris has no scent but has the unique qualities of enhancing and holding the fragrances of the other ingredients. Use it in chipped form, not powder, for longer effectiveness.

Make sure all leaves and flowers are dried well before making potpourri. Extra scent can be added by mixing in spices such as cloves, allspice, nutmeg and cinnamon. Mix thoroughly and put into a suitable container or make into sachets for drawers or closets.

Fruit—Apples
By Theresa Patterson

Growing apples in this region is definitely a challenge! However, when you harvest the first pail of apples off your own trees you will decide it was really worth the effort.

There are a few tricks to achieving success with your orchard. The first is to choose varieties that are hardy enough to withstand our climate. The second is to plant them where they get some shelter from prevailing winds. A good snow cover is a help in keeping the roots frozen. Mulching with leaves and clippings after freeze-up helps, too. Be sure they are well watered-in late in the fall.

Now, what varieties can we grow? Crabapples are the hardiest. There are lovely flowering ones, such as Hopa and Royalty, grown mainly for their blooms; their apples are small and hard. The birds love them, though. Others such as Dolgo produce bigger apples that are good for jelly making.

Then there are applecrabs, which are a cross between crabs and regular apples. Rescue is one of the best, a vigorous grower that produces when quite young.

If you want to try real apples, here are a few:

Early
- Heyer 12—good cooking green apple, does not keep long
- Norland—a new one in 1981. Keeps better than Heyer 12

Mid-season
- Battleford—worth a try
- Patterson—worth a try
- Sunnybrook (new in 1982)—worth a try

Currants
By Theresa Patterson

No garden is complete without a few currant bushes—red, white, black, or all three. The black ones have a strong, pungent flavour, delicious in jam or jelly. Old-time remedies for colds recommend black currant juice in hot water; also good on a cold winter night even if you don't have a cold. Red and white currants make superb jelly. Their seediness does not make nice jam. Added to other fruits such as raspberries, gooseberries, or crabapples, they make jellies of excellent flavour.

It is best to provide your currant bushes with a permanent home where you can keep them free of weeds and grass. They will produce for many years. Whatever kind of soil you have, it should be dug deeply and enriched with manure before planting. You can buy two-year-old plants or get some from neighbours by layering the lower branches or by taking cuttings.

Red and white currants are very susceptible to aphids and spider mites, which will denude your bushes of leaves if not treated. The crop will suffer as a result. Black currants do not seem to be affected as badly, perhaps because of their pungent odour.

It is important to prune currants to get a good crop of berries.

Raspberries
By Theresa Patterson

Raspberries are a prolific fruit crop, well worth the little extra care they require to be successful in this chinook area. Since they bear fruit only on new canes from the previous year, the problem is how to bring those canes through the winter. Location also has a bearing on how well they will survive. An ideal location is an east-west row on the north side of a row of poplar trees. Leave at least 6 m (20 ft) of space between the trees and the raspberries to allow for cultivation. Also, the trees will steal moisture from the raspberries. Avoid full sun and lack of protection.

Raspberries do well in black soil or in lighter soil if well manured and mulched with straw or hay. The mulch conserves moisture and keeps out weeds and grass. Do not cultivate too close to the row or it will encourage excessive suckering. Keep the row to no more than two plants in width. Remove extra suckers. It takes three or four years to establish a row that produces heavily.

Raspberries require ample amounts of water from flowering season right through fruiting. A plastic pipe with holes drilled every 13–15 cm (5–6 in) attached to a garden hose works well. Run the pipe down the middle of the row and leave it there all summer. Soak thoroughly as needed.

In late October or just before freeze-up, bend the canes in a curve, using a light pole, until the tips touch the ground. Then place a board on the tips and shovel enough soil on it to hold the tips securely down. Be careful not to break them where they leave the ground. The snow will drift over them and protect them from the drying effect of the chinook winds. They do not require covering with straw or hay.

In the spring, when the trees are beginning to leaf out, it is time to let the raspberries up. Uncover the tips and shake off the dirt. Now is the time to thin out the old canes that bore fruit last year. They will not have any new leaves coming. They look dry and lighter in colour than the new canes. Also thin out some of the new canes, leaving no more than four or five to a plant. The tops should also be cut back to no more than shoulder height. This encourages side shoots that produce fruit. Canes that grow 2 m (6–7 ft) tall are hard to pick; they dry out and fall over. The canes need tying up now, too. Posts located every 3–4.5 m (10–15 ft) down the row lend support. Strong baler twine run from post to post on each side of the row gives good support if cross ties are put in to separate the canes. Time spent in careful tying pays off at picking time.

Find a variety that thrives in your neighbourhood from a local source rather than ordering from elsewhere. Success is assured!

Everbearing Strawberries
By Norma Lyall

I have tried six kinds of strawberries in the last eight years and find the everbearing is the best variety for our climate and soil. This variety does well in almost any kind of soil, the berries are red all the way through, and you will have two crops of berries a year, in July and September, depending on the weather.

When planting strawberries you should have a place worked up the year before planting. You could work in natural fertilizer and old straw if you have clay soil. Try to kill all the weeds. If you don't have a place worked up the first year, try your luck anyway and start another patch the next year from the runners that grew from this year's plants. Once you have a few strawberry plants, you will always have them, for I don't think they would all winterkill.

As I have lots of garden space, I set my plants 60–75 cm (24–30 in) apart in the row and between the rows I leave 1.2 m (4 ft). For those who haven't got much space, put plants 35 cm (14 in) apart in the row and 91 cm (3 ft) between rows. I like to plant my strawberries like the diagram below so I can just leave two runners of each plant in between the mother plant. This saves transplanting. Once runners start, you should go out every few days and place them where you want them to

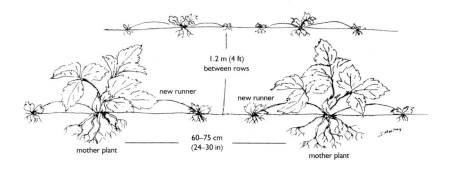

grow and cut off the ones you don't want. You should only let about four to six runners grow from the mother plant each year. I let them bear fruit the first year, as it is so much work to keep the flowers cut off. Remember not to hoe deeply around the plants, because the roots spread out and are just below the surface. You should plant some new plants each year and remove three- or four-year-old plants that are not doing very well.

Strawberries do best if there is a nice warm rain once a week and the weather is hot. Everything likes this kind of weather. Because of their shallow roots they should be kept moist, but don't allow standing water.

As strawberries catch all the weed seeds that blow around such as dandelions and thistles, which thrive around the plants, they are very hard to manage. At times, looking after runners and weeds keeps one busy all summer, but the berries are worth the work you put into them. Also, when you have visitors, all you need to do is take them out to the garden to the strawberry patch and tell them to eat as many as they like, then invite them in for tea. Sure handy when you haven't any cookies baked.

We have another problem in this part of the world, which is winterkill. This occurs when we have a mild winter and not much snow. One fall, before freeze-up, we covered the plants with old straw in which weed seeds had sprouted and died. I left it to rot between the rows, which kept the moisture in and the weeds down and also helped to keep the dirt off the berries. When the trees start to bud, you should take this straw off the plants a little each day and let the heat from the sun warm the plants. It might be late April or May when you uncover, as no two years are the same. Although this old straw did prevent winterkill, the dear little mice got into it and subsequently ate some of the strawberry plants off at the roots. Since then we have used old sawdust or old shavings as a winter cover, which has worked well. We uncover them the same way and leave the old shavings between the plants and the rows.

Strawberries must be planted with the crown of the plant level with the surface of the soil. If the crown is buried, the plant will have difficulty growing; if the crown is above the surface, the roots will dry out.

Recommended strawberry varieties:

- *Everbearing*—Produces a limited quantity over a long period—great for picking and eating fresh from the garden, or enough to make a dessert throughout the summer. 'Fort Laramie'
- *June Bearing*—Produces huge crop of big berries late June to early July. This is the one if you want to make jam. 'Kent'
- *Day Neutral*—These strawberries are affected by day length and will not bloom until the days start to shorten. Their fruit will extend your strawberry season right into September. 'Tristar'

Helpful Hints

❋ Grow currants next to raspberries. The birds prefer currants and will leave your raspberries alone.

15

Millarville Horticultural Club

Club History
by Heather Driedger

Who would ever have thought that local Foothills Continuing Education gardening classes would lead to the publishing of a best-selling gardening book? An enthusiastic group of gardeners attending continuing education classes loved learning about gardening so much they decided to form a gardening club. On 21 April 1976 a meeting was called to form the Millarville Horticultural Club, with Grace Bull as the club's first president, Linda Bull as vice-president, and Judy Williams as secretary-treasurer.

Residents of the foothills area live among breathtaking scenery, but this also means they are located in a unique Chinook Zone, which poses challenges when it comes to gardening. The keen group of gardeners soon found themselves wanting to share ideas and information about how to garden successfully in the foothills. Many new residents were living among the hills and they were anxious to learn the secrets. Monthly speakers have brought a wealth of information to the members. These monthly meetings continue today as members learn from expert gardeners and authors such as Sara Williams, David Tarrant, and Lois Hole. They also value the local gardeners who share their wisdom of gardening. Topics have ranged from growing vegetables, flowers and houseplants, building raised beds, and attracting birds to your garden, to identifying and eradicating weeds and learning pruning techniques.

At the December 1980 executive meeting of the Horticultural Club, Sandy Gregg suggested that a project for the club for the 1981 season would be to write a gardening book. Her suggestion was met with enthusiasm and she was asked to go ahead and get it done. She formed a committee that requested articles from club gardeners who specialized in certain aspects of gardening. As well as editing these submissions, many of the members of the committee wrote articles as well. After two years of hard work, 2,500 copies of *Gardening Under the Arch* were published. The book has since been reprinted five times, with sales totaling 27,500.

This homespun book was quickly a success and it became a bestseller. Not only have readers beyond our local community enjoyed this valuable resource, but the sales of the book have given the club a chance to give back to the community.

Since 1983, a portion of the proceeds from book sales has been used for a scholarship fund for students attending a post-secondary institution to pursue studies in horticulture or agriculture. As the income from book sales increased, the amount of scholarship monies available has increased. The Millarville Horticultural Club continues this fund and is proud to be able to promote and support those youth who choose to pursue their education in the area of horticulture.

Another way the proceeds from book sales have benefited the community is through Creative Landscaping Grants. These grants were created for non-profit organizations operating within the Municipal District of Foothills No. 31, west of the fifth meridian and north of Highway 540. The grants were designed to enhance the appearance of the grounds of the applicants. Numerous organizations have received funding over the years to enhance their facilities.

Not only have the membership contributed financially to the community, they have been able to share their expertise with landscaping projects and maintenance of the grounds at Christ Church Millarville. Since the monthly meetings have always been held there, the membership has always been active in horticulture related projects on the grounds. Landscaping of the grounds of the historic log church at Millarville can serve to inspire other communities looking to beautify a local site. Begun in 1975, the project has been a success due to well-organized volunteers working under the guidance of a master plan and drawing upon the horticultural expertise within the community. The project had to be done in stages over several years, and improvements have been made to reduce the amount of labour needed to maintain the grounds. In 1981 the crucifixion statue with a native garden was built. In 1996, one hundred peonies were planted in a special garden to celebrate the centennial of the church. All of these projects have shown that the members of the local community, church, and horticultural club have successfully created a sense of beauty and spirit in the community.

Decorating the church grounds with outdoor planters for the Christ Church Annual Flower Festival gives club members a chance to share their love of gardening with the hundreds of visitors who attend the festival.

As the members gather monthly for their meetings, families especially look forward to the spring potluck supper, when the junior members are anxious to learn about gardening through special projects. Each year brings new ideas, including building terrariums and flower presses, and making flower or herb planters. Some projects include having a fun competition at the fall potluck supper meeting. Usually the prizes are gardening tools or more plant projects to take home to do over the winter in preparation for spring. Thanks to the junior program, generations of gardeners have been inspired to get their hands dirty and their thumbs a little greener.

Being a member of the Millarville Horticultural Club goes beyond monthly speakers and meetings. For years the members have explored gardens and horticultural sites throughout southern Alberta. Travelling as a club gives the members the opportunity to learn new concepts in horticulture and enjoy fellowship.

Gardening in the Chinook Country of the foothills poses an

Junior Club members (2004) display the results of their potato growing project.

abundance of challenges, and members of the club share their successes each year on the annual local garden tour. Carpooling around the back roads of the foothills and finding a picnic spot for lunch, members learn the secrets of how to beat the challenges of deer, frost, and bugs, and how to have success with their hobby of gardening.

The Millarville Horticultural Club has been going strong ever since its inception, with membership ranging from sixty-five to over one hundred adult and junior members. This ambitious and dedicated group hosted the 39th Annual Alberta Horticultural Association convention. The delegates were treated to traditional foothills hospitality and acquired a wealth of local gardening knowledge.

In addition to publishing a best-seller, sponsoring scholarships, providing landscape grants, and hosting a convention over the last twenty-five years, the members have also contributed to the community through volunteer labour and resources. Along the way, members have not only gained knowledge but also fellowship and love of gardening.

Christ Church Millarville
by Sandy Gregg

Christ Church Millarville officially opened its doors on 6 May 1896. Built of upright spruce logs, it is a beautiful little structure with an artfully curved east wall and high, open-beamed ceilings. Its natural setting in the foothills enhances its peaceful, serene atmosphere. Christ Church has been a cherished part of our community for over one hundred years.

In 1930 the church bell was installed in the belfry. It rang for the first time on 2 June 1930 in celebration of the wedding of Dessa Jameson of Millarville and Hugh Macklin of Midnapore. Dessa was a member of the original book committee and contributed an article on her beloved begonias. Many of us treasure plants that came from her garden.

The parish hall of this wee Anglican church is known as "The Church House" and is actively used by the community. It is where the Millarville Horticultural Club holds its meetings. Helping with planning and planting the gardens of the church grounds has been a continuing project of the club.

Christ Church Millarville.

Graves at Millarville decorated for the Flower Festival.

An annual event at the church, which draws visitors from far and wide, is the Flower Festival. At this time the church and the cemetery are filled with flowers from the gardens of members of the community. All the colours, fragrances, and beauty of the many varieties of flowers displayed at the festival demonstrate that although gardening under the arch does come with many challenges, it also provides bountiful rewards.

The Crucifixion
By Ross Weaver

In 1981 during a tour of Stan Perrott's gardens in Bragg Creek, some of my sculpture was seen by Nancy Laskin and other members of the Millarville Horticultural Club. Unbeknownst to me or my family, Nancy took it upon herself to have a piece of my work commissioned for the new native garden proposed for the grounds of Christ Church Millarville. The funding would be raised by the Millarville Ladies Junior Guild through its art market.

Once the decision was made to go ahead with the commission, I was approached by Nancy to come up with an appropriate sculpture design for the native garden and then present that to the commissioning parties. All of my work up until then was of an abstract nature, and I struggled with a number of designs, none of which felt right for the area it would be displayed in. I met a couple times with Reverend Waverly Gant and after discussion with him I decided to produce a more literal piece, *The Crucifixion*.

For the next year I heated, hammered and welded the metal into what is seen today, Christ with his head held high, looking out over the Millarville landscape rising up into those ever-present mountains. The sculpture has taken on a patina quite unlike the day it was dedicated and which occurs only through the passing of many seasons. I wish to thank Bill Jackson, who was involved in its placing; David Enns, who did all the log work; and all who have continued over all these years to maintain the beautiful native garden that surrounds the sculpture.

The Crucifixion in the native plant garden.

Native Plant Garden
by Theresa Patterson

The native plant garden faces Highway 549 between the Church House and Christ Church. It surrounds the spectacular crucifixion statue sculpted of metal by Ross Weaver in 1981.

The garden was developed to set off the sculpture, and also to demonstrate how native plants can be incorporated into a landscape design. The garden comprises three beds; two raised ones bordering the statue and a third, lower one to the east of the statue. The two raised beds were constructed using large logs and some very large rocks, which give the illusion of mountains and foothills. The lower bed

Wildflowers in profusion after a wet summer (August 2005).

represents the prairie region. Log seats were built into the structure and a walkway of paving stones wanders around the statue. Native junipers soften the base and forget-me-nots grow in the cracks between the stones. The beds are surrounded by mown grass.

Delightful as they are, these beds have presented some problems. The intention was to plant wildflowers and let them reseed themselves. For this purpose, we restricted the use of landscape fabric. Unfortunately, seeds of invasive weeds are much more prolific than those of desirable flowers. Knowledgeable rather than merely enthusiastic labour is needed to sort out the weeds from the flowers. Lovely as some weeds are, they can completely take over an area and choke out many of their more delicate brethren. The decision-making as to what should stay and what should go is best when limited to one or two people of like mind.

The selection of shrubs and plants presents a challenge. Native potentillas are pretty but tend to get woody and less attractive as they age. Goldenrod is also pretty, and hardy, but very invasive. More successful choices have been dogwoods, with their attractive bark in winter; saskatoons, with beautiful fall colour; tall, graceful birch; native junipers, which retain their needle-like leaves year round; silvery-grey wolf willow; and pussy toes, which grow into a neat grey mat.

A big problem has been thistles and couch grass. Spraying an herbicide was not selective enough among plants we wanted to save. One solution we developed was to put on a cotton glove over a plastic glove (the "gloves of death!"). The gloved hand was then dipped in a pail of a solution of a systemic herbicide such as Roundup, and then stroked up the stems of tall thistles. Roundup kills anything green that it touches. Applied to the green part of the plant, it will travel through the roots and kill the whole plant but will not hurt the soil. This was found to be most effective just as the thistles were coming into bloom. Later, we went back and pulled up the ailing thistles. We found that this method set them back a lot, although the procedure might have to be repeated for the next crop. Couch grass needed similarly careful treatment. Annual weeds such as stinkweed and shepherd's purse were successfully hand-pulled.

Running a water line underground to several taps strategically placed around the garden solved the problem of keeping the beds watered. The use of perforated hoses threaded throughout the beds made it easy for a volunteer to go there, turn on the water and then go do something else such as weeding (or even shopping, for the time-stressed or less dedicated). Thus, watering was not a problem, even during hot, dry spells.

Dogwoods are among the plants that have proven successful. In the high areas, limber pines are slow-growing but quite beautiful. Native junipers require little care and spread nicely. Sage and wolf willow complement some attractive grey rocks on the south and west sides of the statue, and pussy toes at the base make a grey mat with either white or pink flowers. In the north bed we have some rare double pink roses, which were found growing wild years ago. Wild strawberries are pretty but need to be planted in an enclosed space, as they tend to spread rapidly. Jacob's ladder and forget-me-nots make lovely patches of blue, and the waxy-flowered buttercups add a splash of yellow.

There are an increasing number of commercial growers who specialize in native plants for the home gardener. Sometimes workshops are offered to assist in choosing and growing plants from the wild.

The Peony Bed
By Theresa Patterson

In 1996 Christ Church Millarville celebrated its centennial. To mark this occasion, the congregation decided to construct a raised peony bed. A large kidney-shaped area was staked out between the church and the church house. A four-by-four frame with a mowing edge was installed and the area enclosed was filled with good black loam. About one hundred peonies were collected. Some we bought and some were donated from neighbouring gardens. Landscape fabric was put in place and then holes in the fabric were cut. The roots were planted with bone meal, with compost added to the soil. Then the whole bed was covered with herculite (an extruded baked clay product), for a mulch.

The peonies were planted in the spring of 1996. They increase in beauty each year and require very little maintenance. The fabric and mulch retain the moisture well and weeds are not a problem. Peony cages are left in place to support the heavy blooms.

This bed is truly a spectacular sight in July when it is in full bloom.

The Peony Bed at the church.

Our Landscaping Project
by Theresa Patterson

When the Millarville Horticultural Club first formed in 1976 with an enthusiastic group of gardeners, the members were anxious to tackle a project. The club's home base was at the church house adjacent to Christ Church, with its extensive grounds. The cemetery beside the church had some spruce trees, some tall poplars, and some native willows in behind. Here was an ideal place to practise our gardening skills and some new techniques.

We discovered that some commercial landscape designers were using 6 mil black plastic and a mulch of some sort to simplify the care of shrubs and trees. They had found that three years growth could be achieved in two years because moisture conditions were constant and weed control was excellent. We decided to adopt this technique.

It was determined to plant a variety of shrubs on the west side of the cemetery, a section at a time, as money, energy, and time allowed. The mulch chosen was herculite, an extruded, baked clay product in

Landscaping workbee, 1975.

a brown colour. It has proven to be very effective, as it does not break down and does not provide a seed bed for weeds and grasses as unwashed gravel does. Wood chips and bark can also be used, but they don't last as long as herculite or 2 cm (¾ in) washed gravel. After thirty years the herculite is still doing its job and looking good without needing to be replenished.

The beds of shrubs were enclosed with a treated four-by-four mowing edge, installed flush with the surrounding lawns, which also served to hold the mulch in place.

Later, landscape fabric was introduced in place of plastic, as it allows rain to soak in while still preventing the growth of weeds. Plastic requires holes to be punched all over the place to let water penetrate. When using fabric or plastic, however, care must be taken to cut slits well back from each plant to allow expansion of the root system, especially with plants like peonies and most shrubs.

In the mid-1990s, an acre of land was added to the cemetery to the north of the church. This presented the huge challenge of landscaping three sides of this piece of ground. We never imagined one acre was so big!

Some generous members donated a number of spruce trees. We purchased a variety of shrubs and bushes in a fall sale at Golden Acre Garden Sentres. They kindly donated seven quite large exotic spruce as well. With some trepidation we over-wintered the potted shrubs in pots on the north side of a row of willows, since it was too late for planting. It was hoped that the willows would provide some protection and also catch snow to help keep the potted plants dormant. Our ploy was successful and the advent of spring saw a major work bee to plant our resilient shrubs in well tilled land, covered with fabric and mulch and well watered-in.

The project has served as a showplace. The grounds are a beautiful place where people can come to learn how the techniques work and apply the ideas to their own gardens.

Grant Recipients

STUDENT GRANTS

We are delighted that two of our student grant recipients have contributed articles to this book: Catherine Laycraft—Tomato Cold Frames , and Joleen Francis—Encounters With Wildlife.

LANDSCAPING GRANTS

Red Deer Lake United Church
One of the many landscaping grant recipients
By Irene Smith

Red Deer Lake United Church has a beautiful and very unique feature—an inspirational memorial garden that was established in 1998.

Overlooking the mountains to the west, the Memorial Garden is envisioned as a special place where the ashes or cremated remains of a loved one may be buried. It is also a quiet place just to sit, remember, and meditate.

Many people have contributed their talents to the planning, design, and construction of this garden, and we are most appreciative of the grants from the Millarville Horticultural Society. Their financial assistance, along with that of other contributors, enabled us to purchase the red shale, gravel, and border blocks to create the winding pathway of the garden. We encourage everyone in the community to enjoy this garden.

16

Contributors

Pam Berringan: *Raised Beds*
A natural green thumb, Pam knows how to get things
to grow but not why they do. She loves to be outside
gardening after a day teaching preschoolers and is determined to make this climate work for her.

Grace Bull: *Gardening without a Garden*
Grace was our first president when the Millarville Horticultural Club
was formed in 1976. She is no longer with us but we are forever grate-
ful for her sound leadership at the beginning. Her lovely garden was
way out in the country and a great example to us all.

Tom Davenport: *Sweet Peas*
Tom Davenport was universally known as the Sweet Pea
King. He won many prizes for his wonderful sweet peas
and also his vegetables, which were always beautifully
displayed on the show bench. After retiring from his
farm, he moved into Turner Valley and carried right on
gardening.

Heather Driedger: *Millarville Horticultural Club History*
Heather Driedger has been a member of the Millarville Horticultural Club for most of her life. The Driedger family was one of the first to get involved in the club and Heather tried various gardening projects as a junior member. Now her own children are junior members and love the challenge of growing their projects. The Driedger family continues to enjoy the experiences the club has to offer throughout the year.

Jerrid Driedger: *Weed Control*
Jerrid Driedger, at the age of 15, is the third generation to be a member of the Millarville Horticultural Club and has been participating in the junior program for many years. Jerrid enjoys the challenge of gardening and entering various vegetables in the Priddis and Millarville Fair.

In 2004 Jerrid entered a "Noxious Weeds of Alberta" display in the fair and won an Award of Excellence. He was a guest speaker for the Millarville Horticultural Club, giving a PowerPoint presentation entitled "Weeds—Friend or Foe?" He also wrote an article about weeds for the revised edition of *Gardening Under the Arch*. Who would have guessed that a fair entry would provide so many rewarding learning opportunities?

Mary Dover: *A Country Garden*
When Mary Dover retired from being a Calgary city alderman, she had to find a new focus for her energy. She poured it passionately into her sixty-acre foothills garden. Her friend Chief David Crowchild named it "Oksi Hill," meaning "a good place."

She was a remarkable lady with a talent for inspiring other people to achieve more than they thought possible. In spite of very painful arthritis in later life she walked a full circuit of her sixty acres every day with two canes to help her along and Bip, her black standard poodle, for company.

She shared the beauty of her garden with many visitors, including our club. Her garden was included in the book *In a Canadian Garden* by Nicole Eaton and Hilary Weston. She was born on Alberta's birthday, 1 July 1905.

Deb Francis: *Hardy Ornamental Grasses; Hummingbirds; Pond Plantings; Roses*

Deb grew up in Kent—the garden of England—the child of passionate gardeners who tirelessly spent all their free time viewing the great gardens of Britain. Deb cheerfully says she had absolutely no interest in gardening, but dutifully accompanied her parents, armed with a good book.

After spending her first winter in Canada and observing the frigid ground, she recalls being fascinated that anything could grow in such a climate. After her first cold winter she rushed out to plant her first garden. Deb says her gardening knowledge has been gained from the Millarville Horticultural Club. She potters in an extensive zoo of a garden and has a large rose collection. She is happy to have imparted a love of gardening to her four children. Deb is a certified Canadian Rose Judge.

Joleen Francis: *Encounters with Wildlife;* Millarville Horticultural Club Scholarship Recipient 2000

Joleen Francis grew up with the Millarville Horticultural Club. With the help of the club (and her dear mother), she cultivated a love of the outdoors and a passion for growing plants. She has always enjoyed the potluck suppers, fairs, speaker nights, and the hot afternoons picking raspberries in the Native Garden.

In 2001, Joleen graduated from the Northern Alberta Institute of Technology's forest technology program. From 2001 to 2003 she worked seasonally as a fire guardian for Alberta Sustainable Resource Development (formerly the Alberta Forest Service). She worked in the southern Rockies and continued to volunteer with the Millarville Horticultural Club.

In 2003, Joleen accepted a permanent position as a forest officer in Fort McMurray. In January of 2005 she took on the role of specialized wildfire investigator. Her goal is to eventually work in southern Alberta so she can be a part of the group again.

Sandy Gregg: *Foreword; History of Christ Church Millarville*
When Sandy moved to the foothills thirty years ago, she soon discovered the challenges of gardening in the chinook belt. Learning so much from the Millarville Horticultural Club, she suggested a gardening book be written to preserve and share the members' knowledge. To her great delight, that thought became a reality.

Sandy cares deeply about protective stewardship of the earth, and suggests that when working with the land the best words to guide us are "do no harm."

Dorothy Jackson: *Food Drying; Sprouts*
Dorothy and her husband, Bill, were founding members of the club and are Lifetime Members. They have been volunteers for many projects, and their daughter, Heather Driedger, and grandchildren, Jerrid and Breanna, carry the connection with the Jackson family into the third generation.

Catherine Laycraft: *Tomato Coldframe;* Scholarship Recipient
Encouraged by her mother, Pearl Laycraft, and her grandmothers, Veryl Laycraft and Barbara Cowling, Catherine has been a lifelong gardener. She designed and built her tomato cold frame as a high school biology project. She was still in high school and a Junior member of the Millarville Horticultural Club when she was asked to contribute to *Gardening Under the Arch* in 1980. After high school Catherine went on to get her diploma in horticulture—greenhouse production and a bachelor of science degree.

Norma and Alec Lyall: *Bird House Construction; Geraniums; Storing Trees & Shrubs; Strawberries*
What a pair these two were—ambitious, hard-working, kind and generous to a fault. Norma was a great gardener, both inside the house and out. She raised hundreds of house plants of many kinds which she donated to various causes. A major project was a booth at the farmer's market, where she sold plants every week all summer, donating many hundreds of dollars to STARS Air Ambulance.

Both Norma and Alec worked tirelessly for the Millarville Horticultural Club, digging trees from the wild to sell at the plant sale or helping at the church with ongoing landscaping activities. Alec was a real handyman, building birdhouses which were donated as door prizes at Horticultural Club meetings or sold at the farmer's market along with Norma's plants.

Janet Mackay: *Birds; Wildflowers in the Garden*
Janet was an artist, gardener, photographer and birder. She could tell all the birds by their song. I remember her standing in my yard and saying, "Listen! A least flycatcher!" She always illustrated the cover of our club's annual program with a bird or a wildflower. The cover photograph of the original edition of *Gardening Under the Arch* was Janet's and she did many of the line drawings which still illustrate the book.

Linda MacKay: *Art in the Garden; Edible Flowers; Garden Décor*

Linda J. MacKay is an economist, artist, and avid gardener who has always lived in the foothills of Alberta. She has a textile art certificate from England, reads a lot, and experiments continuously with her art and the garden. Linda likes to host garden parties utilizing edible flowers and herbs, and she delights in garden surprises such as her lilac bushes that bloom twice a year. Linda is shown harvesting her apples, sunflowers, and lilacs all at the same time in September. Her husband, Tom, has

been a major factor in her ability to grow in a special microclimate that is primarily a frost-free environment from mid-May through October. They live on a foothill, and their solid fencing shields the wind, collects the snow, and keeps the deer out. A major rainwater collection system means they rarely have to use their well to water the garden.

Dessa Macklin: *Begonias*
Dessa grew up in the Millarville area on the farm called Ballyhamage, named after her father's ancestral home in Ireland. She dearly loved her flower garden and houseplants. When she married Hugh Macklin, Dessa brought to her new home a pink rosebush from her mother's garden. Because it sends up suckers, many friends have been able to have a piece of "Dessa's Rose." It is hardy, vigorous, and quite beautiful.

Dessa enjoyed her association with the Millarville Horticultural Club and was named a Lifetime Member years ago. The bell at Christ Church rang for the first time at her wedding.

Betty Nelson: *Dahlias; Everlastings; Fertilizer; Lilies*
Betty and her husband, Leonard, were avid gardeners in the Millarville area. Betty's forte was lilies. She had many varieties which thrived in their hillside garden. Leonard's favourites were dahlias. He built a tiered rockery in front of their house, where the dahlias abounded in all their various colours and types.

For a number of years Betty convened the Flower Festival in the church. Her stepmother planted the idea from a trip to England, where she saw such a festival in a small country church. Betty was very adept at arranging flowers, using her lovely lilies and dahlias to decorate the old organ.

Art Patterson: *Chinook Poem; Shelter Belts*
Art Patterson, colourful local old-time musician, storyteller, farmer, inventor and native son, was born in 1913 and lived all his life at the Patterson Homestead, NE ¼ 33 21 2 W5, which is about halfway between Turner Valley and Calgary as the crow flies.

Scratch the surface of Art and you will get a Robert Service poem, a Depression tale, a dissertation on threshing machines and harnessing horses, or a history of the Ballyhamage School, the Mutual Telephone, or the Priddis and Millarville Fair. Because of his history, Art is proud to have been named the Southern Alberta Pioneer Son for 1998.

Art and his wife, Theresa, have been founding and contributing members of many community endeavours, including the Fair and Races, Christ Church Millarville, the hospital board, and in the early days, the inception of primary utilities into the area—power, telephone, gas, road building, and even the Co-op movement in Calgary.

In these poems, Art shares his homespun insights on life throughout most of the twentieth century and into the twenty-first.

Theresa Patterson: *Chinook Zone; Church Landscaping; Currants; Native Garden; Peonies; Peony Bed at Christ Church; Raspberries; Vines*

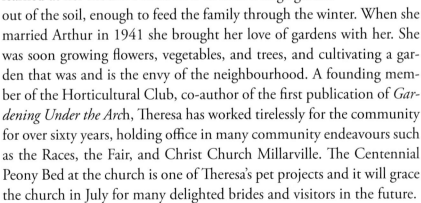

Theresa grew up in a large family on the prairie, where water was scarce, and the days were hot and long. She learned at her mother's knee how to coax a huge garden out of the soil, enough to feed the family through the winter. When she married Arthur in 1941 she brought her love of gardens with her. She was soon growing flowers, vegetables, and trees, and cultivating a garden that was and is the envy of the neighbourhood. A founding member of the Horticultural Club, co-author of the first publication of *Gardening Under the Arc*h, Theresa has worked tirelessly for the community for over sixty years, holding office in many community endeavours such as the Races, the Fair, and Christ Church Millarville. The Centennial Peony Bed at the church is one of Theresa's pet projects and it will grace the church in July for many delighted brides and visitors in the future.

Mary Poffenroth: *Gladioli*

Mary Poffenroth started her teaching career in the community in 1943 and has lived here ever since. Her association with the Red Deer Lake School has continued since her retirement and she still provides some

of the flowers for the school's graduation evening each June.

Mary has also been a member of the Millarville Horticultural Club since its inception. She was privileged to have helped with the first edition of *Gardening Under the Arch* and trusts that this edition will be equally successful. Mary still enjoys gardening and wishes everyone good luck in their effort.

David Teskey: *Containers*

David was born and raised in this area. He is the owner/ operator of Clay West Nurseries, where he grows ultrahardy bedding plants and geraniums for the local market and other clients. He has many strings to his bow, being a pianist, artist, teacher, and photographer. David's ebullient, cheerful personality is a great asset to the club.

Anne Vale: *Annuals; Chemicals; Fuchsias; Greenhouse; Growing Wildflowers from Seed; Hardy Bulbs; Perennials; Rockeries; Roses; Soils; Trees and Shrubs; Vines*

Anne Vale grew up in England in a family of rabid gardeners. From an early age, her strongest memories of everywhere she has lived have been of the gardens. She came to Canada in 1961. She has owned and operated a successful greenhouse business in Black Diamond, Alberta, since 1975, and has now retired to enjoy her own garden and the beauty of southern Alberta. She plans on doing some travelling to see the rest of Canada.

Joy Watkins: *My Pool*

Joy spent the first part of her life in England and came to Canada after her husband died so that she could be near her daughter and grandchildren. Then in her 60s she enthusiastically learned to garden in the foothills.

Her garden, right up against the forest reserve fence, was wonderful. In an area of great beauty but very few frost-free days, she created an oasis that was an inspiration to us all.

Patty Webb: *Drying and Preserving; Flower Arranging; Herbs; Winter Arrangements*

Born and raised in the area, Patty is a natural green thumb and has a wonderful garden. She is a talented florist, cook and gardener. Her children went through the Millarville Horticultural Club Juniors program and now her grandchildren love to help in the garden.

Ida Wegelin: *Butterflies; Companion Planting*

Ida Wegelin was born and brought up on the family farm just south of Black Diamond. Although, as an adult, she worked away from the area from September to June, most of her summers were spent at the farm helping her mother in their large vegetable garden. From her, Ida learned the joy of experimenting with new species and varieties of plants—trying to find plants that would survive and do well in our challenging chinook area. Most of her gardening experience has been by trial and error. She even tried growing a few things in Coppermine, NWT, when she worked there. Twenty-four hours of sunlight does wonders for plants.

Al Wells: *My Vegetable Garden*

Al grew up on a farm in east Saskatchewan in the Dirty Thirties. The kids' job was to plant and harvest the potatoes, enough to feed the family for a year. The garden meant a lot to them before the days of supermarkets and refrigeration. He takes great pride in his huge vegetable garden in the Millarville foothills, where he has lived for the past thirty years.

Beryl West: *Native Grasses in the Landscape*
Despite being born and raised in downtown Toronto, Beryl is quickly becoming the native grass guru of southern Alberta. She is currently managing a large private garden out in the middle of the bald prairie, where native grasses are used extensively. A sought-after speaker on the topic of gardening in dry areas of the prairies, Beryl has become a valued member of the horticultural community.

Pam and Ken Wright: *Propagation by Cuttings; Seed Propagation of Woody Perennials*
Pam and Ken operate Bow Point Nursery on the outskirts of Calgary, where they grow native trees and shrubs. They are passionate about the beauty, hardiness, and suitability of these plants for our area. Their nursery is an oasis in the satellite community west of Calgary.

Index

Malva, 127
Manchurian Elm, 72
Manitoba Maple. *See* Maple, Manitoba.
Manure, 33, 57, 70, 93, 94, 97, 191, 294, 316
Manure tea, 33, 42, 304
Maple: Amur, 65; Manitoba, 47, 72
Marigold, 194
Marjoram, 309
May Day Tree, 68
Meadow Rue, 130
Meadow Sweet, 122
Mealy bugs, 42
Methyl hydrate, 42
Metric conversion. *See* Conversion table, metric.
Mice, 41, 57, 318
Microclimate, 17
Mildew, 96, 301
Millarville Horticultural Club: grants, 333;
    history of, 321–324; Junior Club, *324*;
    landscaping project, *331*, 332; native plant
    garden, 327
Mint, 310
Mites, 42, 95
Mock Orange 'Waterton,' 62
Moles, 41
Monarda, 127
Monkshood, 119
Moose, 50
Morning Glory, 108
Mosquitoes, 41
Moss, 46; peat, 73, 94, 172, 192, 205; sphagnum,
    192, 200
Mothballs, 41
Mountain Ash. *See* Ash, Mountain.
Mountain Bluet, 120
Mugho Pine. *See* Pine, Mugho.
Mulch, 24, 43, 45, 57, 70, 118, 295, 296, 314,
    316
Myosotis, 133

Nanking Cherry. *See* Cherry, Nanking.
Nasturtium, 108, 310
Native grasses, 139–146
Nitrogen, 33, 397
Noxious Weeds. *See* Weeds, classes of under Weed
    Control Act (Alberta).
Nuisance Weeds. *See* Weeds, classes of under
    Weed Control Act (Alberta).

Oak: Bur, 68
Oksi Hill Gardens, 289, 290
Onions, 300–304
Oregano, 310

Oriental Poppy, *127*, 128
Ornamental grasses, 134–138
Oxygenator water plants. *See* Water gardens,
    oxygenator plants for.

Painted Daisy, 120
Pansy, 71, 72, *174*
Papaver, 127
Parsley, 310
Parsnips, 301
Parthenocissus quinquefolia. See Vines, Virginia
    Creeper.
Parthenocissus tricuspidata. See Vines, Boston Ivy.
Pasqueflower, *152*, 153
Pear, Ussurian, 68
Peas, 301, 304
Peat moss, 73, 94, 172, 205
Peony, 114, 118, *161*, *163*, 330
Perennials, 17, *25*; bed or border, 111; culture,
    114; division, 114; propagation, 72, 113;
    staking, 115; winter care, 115
Periwinkle, 109
Perlite, 172, 191, 205
Persicaria, 158
Pest control, 37, 38
Pesticides, 43
Pests, 39–42
Petunia, *176*, 193, 194, 199; Purple Wave, *198*;
    Wave, 199
pH, 30–32
Philadelphus lewisii. See Mock Orange 'Waterton.'
Phlox, 128, 153, 158, 159
Phosphorous, 33
Picea glauca. See Spruce, White.
Picea pungens. See Spruce, Colorado.
Pincushion Flower, 129
Pine: Bristlecone, 66; Mugho, 58, 62; Scotch, 66
Pinks, 111, 120, 157
Pinus aristata. See Pine, Bristlecone.
Pinus mugo. See Pine, Mugho.
Pinus sylvestris. See Pine, Scotch.
Planning a garden. *See* Garden, planning.
Plantain Lily, 124
Planters, 191, *192*; choosing materials for, 201;
    soil requirements for, 191; winter, 200, *201*,
    203
Planting dates, 179, 182
Planting out bedding plants, 182
Plants: for bogs, *see* Water gardens, bog plants for;
    for dry places, full sun, moist places, semi-
    shade, 177, 178; for shade, 177, 178, 199; for
    shelter, 199; for water, *see variously at* Water
    gardens.